JUL 2009

Charlie Chaplin at Keystone and Essanay

Charlie Chaplin at Keystone and Essanay

✦

Dawn of the Tramp

Ted Okuda and David Maska

iUniverse, Inc.
New York Lincoln Shanghai

Charlie Chaplin at Keystone and Essanay
Dawn of the Tramp

iUniverse books may be ordered through booksellers or by contacting:

iUniverse
2021 Pine Lake Road, Suite 100
Lincoln, NE 68512
www.iuniverse.com
1-800-Authors (1-800-288-4677)

ISBN-13: 978-0-595-36598-2 (pbk)
ISBN-13: 978-0-595-81027-7 (ebk)
ISBN-10: 0-595-36598-1 (pbk)
ISBN-10: 0-595-81027-6 (ebk)

Printed in the United States of America

To Scott MacGillivray and James L. Neibaur,
For their unstinting friendship, unprecedented generosity, and unlim-
ited encouragement…and for handing me a million laughs
—Ted Okuda

To my late father Norbert, who, with the patience of a saint and the love
only a father could give, encouraged my enthusiasm for these movies…
And to the love and support of my mother Shirley and my sister Kim, for
living with the results
—David Maska

And, of course, to Charles Chaplin

Contents

ACKNOWLEDGMENTS

We are greatly indebted to the following individuals: our research associate Scott MacGillivray, for his editorial supervision and contributions (especially regarding the entries for *Chase Me Charlie*, *The Charlie Chaplin Comedy Theatre*, *Laughing Till It Hurt*, and the home-movie market); Jamie Brotherton, for generously furnishing photographs from her collection; Ryan Reynolds, for his technical expertise (which included designing the book cover); and film scholars David J. Hogan and Mark A. Miller, for their valued feedback. We are also grateful for the assistance we received from James L. Neibaur, Mark Yurkiw, Bruce Ingram, Sam Mastromauro, Pam White, Leonard "Bela" Kohl, Jan MacGillivray, Steve Randisi, John Lazar, and Jim Mueller.

For their encouragement and support, we would like to thank Matt Berkowitz, Marlena Bielski, Vici Bielski, Jackie Brandstein, Ofelia Castillo, Robin Castro, John Cavallo, Mark Clark, Mary and Steve Cooper, Kimberly Cormier, Dennis Corpus, the Culbertsons (Bruce, Tammy, Damen, Caroline and Simon), Jason Dummeldinger, Jennifer Epley, Len Grodoski, Dustin Hambly, Karen Hand, David Harnack, Dennis Hayes, Ken Jernberg, the Johnsons (Don, Julie, Katie and Carrie), Jerry King, Joe Konrath, Rich Koz, Kim Kozak, Tony Lossano, Kim and Ed Magruder, Angie Maraccini, Dan Martini, Shirley Maska, Jesse Montanez, Christine Moran, Jack and Elaine Mulqueen, Frank and Mary Ann Nicolella, the Okudas (Sakiko, Belinda, Cheryl and Christopher), Susan Pierce, Eve Pool, Jim Rohrlack, the Rothsteins (Victor, Maureen, Joe and Jack), Ralph Schiller, Joe Sedelmaier, Linda Spence, Jennifer Taepke, Tori Tinkles, "The Woo," and Mr. Show Biz himself, Bill Zehme.

Additional thanks to the helpful and courteous staff at the Harold Washington Library in Chicago.

Last, but certainly not least, a tip of the Chaplin derby to all the sources quoted in our *Other Views and Reviews* entries. Their opinions regarding Chaplin's work will hopefully provide a welcome counterpoint to our humble evaluations.

FOREWORDS

Foreword by Ted Okuda

As a youngster, I was never a fan of Charlie Chaplin. This is an odd confession for the co-author of a Chaplin book to make, so allow me to elaborate.

During the 1910s, '20s and '30s, Chaplin was an international idol. By the '40s, however, he fell into disfavor in many circles due to his political leanings (he was unfairly branded a "Communist") and personal conduct (a much-publicized paternity suit had a ruinous effect on his public image). In the era of "witch hunts" and the House Un-American Activities Committee (HUAC), Chaplin went from being revered to being reviled.

In 1952 Chaplin sailed from the U. S. to England to promote his latest film, **Limelight**. En route, he was notified that he would not be permitted a re-entry visa. He chose not to apply for one; Chaplin and his family settled in Switzerland, where he resided for the rest of his life.

Chaplin had retained ownership of most of his finest work, and the exile meant that these films were no longer available for U. S. distribution—not that any American exhibitors were clamoring for these formerly hot properties. By the late '50s, the idea of sponsoring a nationwide Chaplin retrospective was unthinkable. His fall from grace had been *that* thorough.

My appreciation of movie comedians began in the early 1960s. Comedies with Laurel & Hardy, Abbott & Costello, and The Bowery Boys were a staple of local TV programming. Buster Keaton, The Three Stooges (with two of the original members), Jerry Lewis, and Bob Hope were still active in films and on television. But Chaplin was seriously underrepresented. With classic efforts such as **The Circus** (1928), **City Lights** (1931), and **Modern Times** (1936) in limbo, my exposure to Chaplin was limited to excerpted bits in anthologies like **When Comedy Was King** (1960) or the little 8mm abridgements sold on the collector's market. Many of these clips were taken from his early Keystone and Essanay films. Chaplin had no legal claim to these titles—in fact, no one did. Copyright laws no longer protected them, so filmmakers and distributors had open access to the material. Watching this footage, I was unimpressed. Chaplin was obviously adept at physical comedy, but a certifiable comic *genius*? What was up with that?

I had no idea I was looking at work from Chaplin's embryonic period, his development years—that they were important from a historical standpoint, even if their entertainment value was rather dubious. It wasn't until a few years later, when I saw complete prints of Chaplin's wonderful Mutual comedies from 1916-17 (*Easy Street*, *The Immigrant*, *The Cure*, etc.), that I discovered he truly was deserving of all the accolades heaped upon him.

Initially, I had no knowledge of Chaplin's controversial past, so I couldn't comprehend the hostility that erupted at the mere mention of his name. And when I finally learned the details, I couldn't have cared less. Charlie was a versatile, supremely funny man, and that's all that really mattered to me.

Chaplin struck a distribution deal in 1971, sparking a worldwide revival in his work. So, for the very first time, I attended theatrical screenings of some of his greatest accomplishments, and I roared with laughter along with the large crowds in attendance. This revived interest in his work coincided with Chaplin returning to America in 1972 to appear at the Film Society of Lincoln Center in New York and accept an honorary Academy Award in Los Angeles.

In 1973 a memorabilia dealer happened to mention that Chaplin still enjoyed hearing from fans. Despite my skepticism—Charlie already knows he's great, so why does he need to hear it from me?—and after much procrastination, I wrote a fan letter and sent it off to "Mr. Charles Chaplin, Vevey, Switzerland." I didn't save a copy of my letter, but in retrospect, I'm sure it was every bit as gushing and semi-literate as I remember it to be. A few weeks later, to my astonishment, I received an autographed photo of the famous Little Tramp character inscribed, "*Hello! Charlie Chaplin.*" His signature was extremely shaky due to his frail condition, but the fact that he responded to my letter is something that continues to amaze me.

I have difficulty writing about people and topics that don't interest me. Perhaps it's because I like to think of most of the books I've been involved with as extended "Thank You" notes to those whose work I've either admired or been intrigued by. I never really thanked Chaplin properly for his thoughtfulness, so I consider this book to be a long-overdue expression of gratitude.

At this point I must admit, for matters of full disclosure, that Buster Keaton is my all-time favorite comedian. But Keaton and every other cinema laughmaker owes a tremendous debt to Chaplin, who paved the way for everyone who followed. Even Keaton referred to Chaplin as "the greatest comedian that ever lived."

No matter who your favorite comedian is, there's no denying that Charlie Chaplin made an impact on the art of motion pictures that few have come close to rivaling.

Thank you, Mr. Chaplin.

Foreword by David Maska

I was never a huge Chaplin fan as a kid. Like many a boy of my generation, I grew up with televised reruns of The Three Stooges, Abbott & Costello, and Laurel & Hardy comedies. Chaplin was still alive when I was in my youth but I had no idea who he was; he had long since stopped making movies, and silent films didn't receive a lot of television exposure. My interest in the Stooges piqued my curiosity to find out more about them. I looked through the film books at my local library and started reading about the comedy pioneers: Chaplin, Harold Lloyd, and my favorite silent comedian, Buster Keaton (sorry, Charlie).

In 2005, home entertainment is commonplace, but in the '70s it was still a novelty. One of the only ways to see a silent movie was if you were lucky enough to have an 8mm projector, which was normally used to view home movies. Blackhawk Films was one of several companies that offered silent films to the home-movie market, and my library had some of them for rent. My father would take me there every Monday, and while I may have been the only one checking these titles out, I left there every week feeling like I was transporting a shipment of gold back to our house. There was a six-film limit per library card and in the tradition of "working the system," I eventually started to use my Dad's card to rent twice as many titles. They had a limited selection, but I didn't care; I rented what I could as often as I could.

This is how I was introduced to the Little Tramp. I was very lucky to be initiated by viewing films like ***One A. M.***, ***Easy Street***, and ***The Immigrant*** (not to mention some of the classic silent films of Laurel & Hardy and Buster Keaton). These, I came to learn over time, were part of Chaplin's "Golden Dozen" that he made for the Mutual Film Company between 1916 and 1917. Mutual agreed to pay him $10,000 a week along with a $150,000 signing bonus before a single frame of film was shot.

Chaplin was the original and those who followed took a cue from him. Imagine rock and roll without Elvis and you'll have an idea of Chaplin's importance to motion picture history. Chaplin defined and redefined comedy. He proved that it was possible to mix humanity with humor and that a comedian could elicit emotions other than laughter. Chaplin made people stand up and take a look at comedy, a category of the performing arts that many still believe to be the lowest form of theatre. His movements were choreographed like a ballet dancer—a term that W. C. Fields would use very unflatteringly when referring to Chaplin. When I watch some of the comedians of the past 25 years, I can see the influence of Chaplin directly or indirectly in the work of performers like John Ritter and Sean Hayes.

Chaplin made a total of 81 movies (the first in 1914, the last in 1967) and it's amazing to realize that the Keystones and Essanays comprise more than *half* of his overall output. As he gained more control over his work, Chaplin spent more time making each film. When he reached his artistically mature period, there were gaps of two to three years between releases, whereas his contemporaries (Keaton and Lloyd) released several films a year. Chaplin became the only major filmmaker to date who controlled his product from cradle to grave. Every penny came out of his pocket and he had nobody to answer to but himself. The public clamored for more Chaplin, even if he was taking more and more time to deliver new films. To meet this demand, many of the early films we cover in this book were re-released several times well into the 1940s. This was a blessing and a curse. Imagine working on a masterpiece like **The Gold Rush** or **The Circus** only to have something from your past like **Tango Tangles** come back to haunt you. While these reissues were for purely financial reasons, this practice did preserve many films that may have been otherwise lost to the ravages of time.

The Chaplin Essanays have been restored by David Shepard, but most of the Chaplin Keystones we see today are from prints that have been recopied so often that they are both artistically and visually difficult to sit through. Rumors circulate in Internet chat rooms that a restoration is underway for the Keystones, yet the shelves remain bare as of this writing.

In researching this book, I saw many of these films for the first (and, in several instances, for the *last*) time. I've tried hard to comprehend what made these films so funny in their day and I can't say that I have arrived at an answer after sitting through them. Perhaps I'm spoiled because I know **City Lights** and **Modern Times** do exist in the Chaplin canon and can't look at these early outings with an unbiased point of view. However, these primitive efforts are often as fascinating as they are painful to watch, and I could see the birth of ideas and themes that would follow Chaplin through the last of his major cinema works. While Chaplin's later films are without question more accomplished, there is a hint of pretension in offerings like **Monsieur Verdoux** and **Limelight** that reflects the personal troubles and public hatred heaped upon him at the time. The later image of a put-upon, reviled Chaplin would have been hard to fathom to his loyal audience of 1914-16. (Imagine your reaction if someone told you in 1983 that Michael

Jackson, the reigning "King of Pop," would one day be facing a possible jail sentence.) The films reviewed in this book are years away from any of that and represent Chaplin—and the industry he helped to pioneer—when things were more innocent and uncomplicated.

Revisiting a film is like hearing from an old friend whose company you really enjoy yet you've lost touch with. They never let you down, and in the case of Charlie Chaplin, his best films still hold the power to make me laugh and cry. I just want to thank you for that, old friend.

INTRODUCTION

o o o o o o o o o o o o o o o o o o o o o o o o o o o o o o o o

"There was a time when Chaplin was hailed as the greatest popular artist of the twentieth century, and his films were known to everyone. Today, how many people watch them? Are they shown in schools? I think not. On TV? Not very often. Silent film, the medium that gave Chaplin his canvas, has now robbed him of his mass audience. His films will live forever, but only for those who seek them out."

—Roger Ebert, The Great Movies (2002).

Charlie Chaplin holds a curious place in contemporary popular culture. The image of his celebrated Tramp character is immediately recognizable, his position as a motion picture pioneer is widely acknowledged, and his legacy as a comic genius is beyond question. And yet few have actually seen the majority of his movies, and fewer still are aware of his evolution as a performer and filmmaker.

We know this to be true because, as Chaplin fans, we've tended to collectively dismiss his early works, making little effort to place them in the proper context of his overall career. We've usually considered them a chore to sit through—and we're not alone. Millions have enjoyed **The Gold Rush** and **Modern Times**, but how many have bothered to check out **His New Profession** and **The Property Man**?

The idea for this book was conceived after we attended a screening of **City Lights** sponsored by the Chicago Symphony Orchestra. The event served as a reminder that for all the times we've seen this classic film, there were other Chaplin titles we completely ignored—particularly among his Keystone and Essanay efforts.

Researching this book marked the first time either of us had viewed these early films *chronologically*. In several instances, it also marked the first time we had even *seen* a particular title. As fans of Chaplin—and movie comedies in general—we don't have a valid reason for not watching them prior to this volume, especially when DVD copies are readily available in mass quantities at retail outlets, pharmacies, and even grocery stores. Many of these collections mix Chaplin's embry-onic Keystone and Essanay pictures with his later, more polished productions. An unsuspecting consumer has every right to wonder how Chaplin could be so hilar-ious in **Easy Street** (Mutual, 1917) yet so unfunny in **The Fatal Mallet** (Key-stone, 1914), since the liner notes often regard one as highly as the other. We hope this book will help to clarify such matters.

With the advent of home video, thousands of long-unseen movies have gotten a new lease on life, initially with videocassettes and now with the DVD format. Many obscure titles seemed to spring up out of nowhere, as did a number of enterprising independent distributors (not affiliated with the major studios) who specialized in merchandising films that had fallen into the "public domain." In other words, the copyrights had lapsed, so these companies were free to duplicate and sell them to consumers. As a result, you can find budget-priced DVDs prac-tically everywhere.

While most of the titles are unknown to all but the staunchest film buffs, a good number of them showcase appearances by well-known personalities. Cun-ningly, these movies are packaged for mass-market consumption, with graphics designed to mislead the consumer. For instance, **Hometown Story** (1951), a long-forgotten "B" movie, featured a pre-stardom Marilyn Monroe in a minor supporting role. In the hands of independent distributors, however, a later glam-our portrait of MM graces DVD covers and the film is routinely merchandised as a starring vehicle for Monroe.

Even when the actors shown on the cover art actually *do* star in the film, there's no guarantee that what you see on the outside is going to match the movie on the inside. **Utopia** (1951), Laurel & Hardy's final film, is one of the most notorious examples of this deceptive practice. Countless distributors have offered this title with ad art utilizing a younger '30s portrait of the team. L&H afficiona-dos are painfully aware that the boys were older and not in the best of health, with Stan Laurel in particular looking frail and sickly. So imagine the dismay of consumers who, guided only by the packaging, settle back to enjoy what they believe is going to be vintage Laurel & Hardy antics, and instead witness two enfeebled performers who barely resemble their former selves.

Similarly, numerous budget-priced Three Stooges collections invariably have the popular Curly Howard pictured prominently. These collections contain only one Curly short (the omnipresent **Disorder in the Court**), while the remaining titles feature the underrated Shemp Howard, who seldom gets a cover shot. (In some extreme cases, the running time is padded out with mid-'60s cartoons with later Stooge Joe DeRita.)

The same pitfalls are evident in the way Charlie Chaplin films have been marketed. Those with a general interest in Chaplin may be familiar with acclaimed efforts like ***The Gold Rush***, ***The Kid***, and ***Shoulder Arms***, but only a serious student of Chaplin's work will recognize ***A Film Johnnie***, ***His Favorite Pastime***, and ***Twenty Minutes of Love***. And yet an untold number of DVD collections have grouped these films together, as if Chaplin's appearance alone makes them worthy of classic status.

Putting a photo of Chaplin as his beloved Tramp character on the packaging only adds to the confusion. Uninitiated viewers who are in the mood for more Chaplin after watching ***City Lights*** or ***Modern Times*** will be dumbfounded by ***Making a Living***, ***Tango Tangles***, and ***Cruel, Cruel Love***, three early films in which Chaplin doesn't play the Little Tramp. Like many great artists, Chaplin underwent a formative period before producing his finest achievements. So if you were not aware of the back history and circumstances behind a specific entry, it would be logical for you to surmise that all of his work is of a similarly high quality.

For the uninitiated who've heard nothing but praise from those familiar with Chaplin's entire body of work, these bargain offerings do an injustice to the comedian's legacy. A neophyte Chaplin fan may decide to take the more financially expedient route and purchase some of the cheaper DVD collections for less than ten dollars per disc. Watching them, however, can be a bewildering experience, and will undoubtedly make one wonder what all the fuss is about—something even we would be hard-pressed to defend. We'd hate to think that anyone's interest in Chaplin would be curtailed because of this. It really is worth the effort to spend the extra cash. With the recent deal struck between Warners and French distributor MK2, DVDs of Chaplin classics like ***The Circus***, ***City Lights***, and ***Modern Times*** can be had for approximately $25 apiece.

Charlie Chaplin developed his screen persona and cinematic craft during his years at the Keystone Film Company (1914) and the Essanay Film Company (1915-16). These comedies were cranked out at a breathless rate, and the results prove beyond a doubt that historical value does not equal entertainment value. Which is not to say they're completely without interest. Viewing them in chronological order, you can see a bigger picture emerging, much like putting together a jigsaw puzzle piece by piece until a beautiful image materializes. And, where Chaplin is concerned, there are some rewarding revelations along the way.

This book is intended to serve as a guide to Chaplin's Keystone and Essanay output. Our primary goal is to call them as we see them, keeping in mind that personal opinion is ultimately subjective and that the final judgment rests with you. So if we praise **The Bank** and you don't find any merit to the film, it doesn't mean that we're right and you're wrong. Everyone's entitled to their own opinion, which is one of the reasons why we've included a section for each entry called *Other Views and Reviews*.

We briefly toyed with the idea of evaluating these early films solely from the perspective of the era during which they were made. While there's merit in that approach, we concluded it would be pointless if not impossible to do so. The later Chaplin films are too firmly ingrained in our consciousness for us to successfully divorce ourselves from our memories of them. When we watch an early picture like **Mabel's Strange Predicament**, we do so with the knowledge that **The Pawnshop** and **The Immigrant** are just around the bend.

Additionally, we don't subscribe to the time-honored notion that visual comedy died with the advent of "talking" pictures. Many silent screen historians sincerely advocate this sentiment, but it simply doesn't ring true. Laurel & Hardy were able to bridge the gap between silent and sound comedy, with their voices adding an extra dimension to their humor. The films of The Three Stooges, Abbott & Costello, The Marx Brothers, W. C. Fields, Jerry Lewis, Jacques Tati, Bob Hope, The Bowery Boys, Red Skelton, Norman Wisdom, Peter Sellers, Woody Allen, Mel Brooks, Albert Brooks, the "Carry On" gang, and the Monty Python troupe are loaded with sight gags every bit as funny and inventive as those found in silent-era comedies. Animator-turned-director Frank Tashlin made movies that were more like live-action cartoons. Lucille Ball, Ernie Kovacs, Benny Hill, and Rowan Atkinson (*Mr. Bean*) successfully brought silent-style visual humor to television. (It's worth noting that Chaplin enjoyed watching the Stooges, Abbott & Costello, Lewis, Wisdom, Hill, and other comedians most of his fervent admirers denounce.) More recently, the influence of silent screen comedy can be found in Asian cinema: Jackie Chan's physical clowning evokes the spirit of the old masters, and Stephen Chow's **Kung Fu Hustle** skillfully blends traditional sight-gag sensibilities with state-of-the-art computer-enhanced wizardry.

Contrary to popular belief, visual comedy didn't die with the coming of sound. What died was the uniquely silent universe that allowed certain visual artists to thrive. With the arrival of talkies, comedians were expected to *say* funny things as well as *do* funny things. Though Buster Keaton, Harold Lloyd, and Harry Langdon still had their great talent, the very *sound* of their voices seemed at odds with the eloquence of their expressive physical comedy.

As for Charlie Chaplin, no single voice would have been suitable for his universal figure, the Tramp. The very nature of his comedy demanded silence, demanded that you *watch* his facial gestures and his body movements. Chaplin himself was keenly aware of this, and resisted making a wholly sound film until **The Great Dictator**, released in 1940.

Whereas his contemporaries (Keaton, Lloyd, Langdon) continued to play variations of their silent-era personas, Chaplin abandoned the Tramp after embracing the spoken word. (Ironically, once Chaplin began talking in films he never seemed to stop.) Even without his beloved character, Chaplin continued to explore many of the themes first touched upon in the Keystone and Essanays, and the sprite spirit of the Little Fellow was present in all of his subsequent movies.

While our book is intended for all Chaplin fans, old and (hopefully) new, it is primarily aimed at those who have seen DVD volumes of his Keystones and Essanays for sale or rent, yet aren't quite sure what to make of them. For this reason, we screened DVD copies that are readily available to the average consumer. Better quality prints exist in archives and vaults, but until they are accessible to the general public—and to us, for that matter—there's no point in critiquing material that few will have the opportunity to see.

You may have already seen some of the Keystones or Essanays and have arrived at the conclusion that the rest aren't worth bothering with. Well, that's fine—being a Chaplin fan doesn't necessarily mean you have to be a Chaplin completist. You can still admire the Grand Canyon without jumping into it. We're not making a case that everyone has to watch every scrap of footage concerning Chaplin; even his biggest fans will have to concede that sitting through certain titles requires both the patience of a saint and the curiosity of a cat.

Among the misfires and missteps, however, are isolated moments or entire films containing genuine comic brilliance, revealing a gifted filmmaker honing his skills for great triumphs to come. So if our book helps to explain how an individual film pertains to Chaplin's overall career, or if our commentary intrigues you enough to seek out a title that you might have otherwise ignored, then it has served its purpose.

Note: The life of Charles Spencer Chaplin (1889-1977) has been the subject of numerous books. Since the focus of our volume is on his Keystone and Essanay output, we feel there is no point to reiterate other material that has been covered so extensively elsewhere. So we apologize in advance for giving short shrift to the contributions of his half-brothers Sydney Chaplin (a popular screen comedian in his own right, Syd got Charlie a job with theatrical entrepreneur Fred Karno, which launched Charlie's career in the English music halls) and Wheeler Dryden (who was involved with Charlie's later films for United Artists).

There are many fine Chaplin biographies available and we recommend Jeffrey Vance's *Chaplin: Genius of the Cinema* (Harry N. Abrams, Inc., 2003), David Robinson's *Chaplin: His Life and Art* (McGraw-Hill, 1985), John McCabe's *Charlie Chaplin* (Doubleday & Co., 1978), and Chaplin's own *My Autobiography* (The Bodley Head, 1964) and *My Life in Pictures* (The Bodley Head, 1974). For all things Chaplin, consult Glenn Mitchell's thorough *The Chaplin Encyclopedia* (B. T. Batsford, 1997).

We cannot claim to be the first ones to do a film-by-film examination of Chaplin's Keystone output. That distinction belongs to Harry M. Geduld, whose milestone *Chapliniana Volume 1: The Keystone Films* (University of Indiana Press, 1987) was intended to be the first of three projected volumes of "Commentary on Charlie Chaplin's 81 movies."

Other Chaplin recommendations: Gerald D. McDonald, Michael Conway and Mark Ricci's *The Films of Charlie Chaplin* (Citadel Press, 1965); Eric L. Flom's *Chaplin in the Sound Era: An Analysis of the Seven Talkies* (McFarland & Co., Inc., 1997); Uno Asplund's *Chaplin's Films* (A. S. Barnes, 1976); Denis Gifford's *Chaplin* (Macmillan, 1974); Isabel Quigly's *Charlie Chaplin: Early Comedies* (Studio Vista, 1968); Dan Kamin's *Charlie Chaplin's One-Man Show* (Scarecrow Press, Inc., 1984); Theodore Huff's *Charlie Chaplin* (Henry Schuman, 1951); and Kalton C. Lahue and Terry Brewer's *Kops and Custards: The Legend of Keystone Films* (University of Oklahoma Press, 1968). And for a combination of film history and theory, check out Gerald Mast's *The Comic Mind: Comedy and the Movies* (University of Chicago Press, 1973) and Walter Kerr's *The Silent Clowns* (Alfred A. Knopf, 1975).

THE COMEDY KING AND HIS PRINTS

o o o o o o o o o o o o o o o o o o o o o o o o o o o o o o o o o

"Chaplin's 34 short [Keystone] comedies have over the years been recut and reissued...Unfortunately, each cut and reissue has brought further destruction of the talents he exhibited. The originals contained few and brief titles. The new editions were padded and 'pepped up' by the addition of new, verbose, and often tasteless titles. Sometimes whole sections of the films have been deleted or otherwise destroyed, so much so that an unmutilated original does not exist, to my knowledge, even in the hands of a collector."

—*Kalton C. Lahue, World of Laughter: The Motion Picture Comedy Short, 1910-1930.*

Film historian Lahue made that observation in 1966; four decades later, the situation has changed little. Even now, the biggest challenge in attempting to assess Chaplin's early work is that few of his Keystone comedies are available in their original form. Over the years these films were tampered with to an extent that some are no longer the same pictures. For example, in a 1914 review of ***His Favorite Pastime*** for the *Syracuse Post-Standard*, an unnamed critic wrote:

> *The producer of a Charlie Chaplin film doesn't have to go abroad in search of color and atmosphere. For that matter, the piece of limburger cheese which shares honors with Charlie in **His Favorite Pastime** provides an atmosphere of its own...In the final scene we see him at the top of a telegraph pole while an enemy below is busy with an axe. Charlie lowers the limburger at the end of a string. This drives away the enemy. A typical Chaplin piece.*

This "typical Chaplin piece" is nowhere to be found in the print of *His Favorite Pastime* we viewed. Likewise, a sequence set in a nickelodeon (an early storefront movie theater) is missing from circulating copies of *A Film Johnnie*, another Chaplin Keystone.

Ironically, it was the enormous success of the Chaplin comedies that contributed to the overwhelming number of inferior-quality prints that circulated. Of Chaplin's 35 Keystone comedies (34 shorts and one feature), 28 of them had never been copyrighted, so after their initial release, these films were fair game for any independent distributors or small-time operators who got their hands on them. As a result, duplicate copies were bootlegged from existing copies, to the point where the pictorial quality faded with each trip through the film lab.

Retitling the films only added to the confusion. In addition to bootlegging the Keystones, some distributors deceptively reissued them under different titles, to the confusion of theater operators and the moviegoing public. It was not uncommon to find a Keystone comedy like *The Masquerader* making the rounds under a half-dozen alternate titles. Chaplin was also hugely popular in Europe, where his films were openly bootlegged. In fact, when prints of the Chaplin Keystones became scarce in America—existing copies were worn to the point where they couldn't even be projected—the European bootlegs began to circulate here in the United States. (The only surviving materials on some Chaplin titles are these bootleg copies.)

The Mutual Film Corporation, through an arrangement with the New York Motion Picture Company, originally distributed most of the early Keystone comedies. (Mutual would later sign Chaplin to a 12-picture contract.) In 1915, the New York Motion Picture Company was sold to the Triangle Film Corporation, formed by D. W. Griffith, Thomas Ince, and Mack Sennett. Sennett continued to produce films, which were now released as Triangle-Keystone Comedies. Sennett left Triangle in 1917, and prior to the company's collapse the following year, Harry Aitken, one of its founders, reissued a number of the Keystone films, including several Chaplins.

Several film production companies were shut down during the influenza epidemic of 1918, resulting in a shortage of marketable product, especially where comedies were concerned. Seizing the opportunity, newly-formed "states' rights" companies (that operated on the periphery of the business and got bookings on a state-by-state basis) began reissuing re-edited versions of the Keystone comedies. Two such outfits were Tower Film Corporation and Jans Producing Corporation.

Also in 1918, W. H. ("Wonderful Hits") Productions, another states' rights distributor, re-edited 750 Keystone comedies and reissued them under new titles, including several Chaplin shorts. It wasn't widely known at the time that Harry Aitken and his brother Roy owned and operated both W. H. Productions and Tower Film Corporation. Rival distributors complained to the Federal Trade Commission that these old movies were being passed off as new product, so W. H. Productions agreed to call attention to the fact that they were re-releases. Hence, the title credits for W. H. reissues would read "Charlie Chaplin in *The Good-for-Nothing*, Former Title *His New Profession*" and so forth. The opening titles for W. H. reissues also carried 1918 copyright notices, although many of the films had never been copyrighted to begin with. This was just a ruse on the part of W. H. to deter other distributors from bootlegging its own releases.

Many Keystone comedies survive today thanks to W. H. Productions. Unlike the products of major studios, which were rented to movie theaters and then returned to the studios' vaults, the films of W. H. Productions were sold outright to regional distributors for $80 a reel. Thus the W. H. Keystones "escaped" from the owner's control and passed from hand to hand as time went on.

By 1915 Chaplin had embarked on the Essanay phase of his career. His rising popularity ignited a worldwide "Chaplin Craze" that triggered a flood of newspaper comic strips, animated cartoons, dolls, novelty songs, and lookalike contests. In the United States, as many as 250 prints of each Essanay Chaplin were circulated on their initial run (other comedy shorts averaged 50 to 100 prints in circulation), and they were soon worn out because of exhibitor demand. The Essanay Film Manufacturing Company folded in the 1920s, but its Chaplin comedies remained commercially viable properties. Within a few years it became impossible to find suitable material to make complete replacement copies of the Essanays. Thereafter, good-quality prints were hard to come by.

Regardless of print quality, these titles were still a viable commodity. Chaplin was now producing his own pictures and spending much more time on the creation of them. With three-year gaps between new Chaplin releases, exhibitors filled the void by booking the older Chaplin comedies. The Essanays and the primitive Keystones suffered in comparison to mature efforts like *The Gold Rush* (1925) and *The Circus* (1928), but moviegoers and critics welcomed almost any opportunity to see their beloved Charlie. In reviewing a 1927 revival of *His Prehistoric Past* (Keystone, 1914), *The New York Times* noted that it "has a good many moments of fun, as one might easily imagine when it is said that Chaplin is seen in a caveman's haberdashery." Similarly, the *Times* reported that a 1929 screening of *The Bank* (Essanay, 1915) "provoked gusts of laughter."

Even during the 1930s, after "talking" pictures had obliterated the silent cinema and many of its biggest stars, Chaplin's early films remained marketable. The enormous box office successes of *City Lights* (1931) and *Modern Times* (1936) proved that there was still a huge audience for silent movies that starred Chaplin, which was good news to the independent distributors handling the films. The 12 short comedies Chaplin made for the Mutual Film Corporation (1916-17) were reissued by the Van Beuren Corporation in 1932, with music scores and sound effects. (For more on these reissues, see entry for *The Essanay-Chaplin Revue of 1916*.)

The well-received Van Beuren re-releases may have prompted the New York-based Exhibitors Pictures Corporation to reissue a handful of Chaplin Keystones in the late '30s, hyping them as an opportunity to see "Chaplin as he was 20 years ago!" Exhibitors Pictures also planned to reissue 12 Essanays in 1939. The company renamed itself The King of Comedy Film Corporation in 1940 and reissued 10 Chaplin Essanays, reedited with new subtitles, plus music scores and sound effects. King of Comedy altered the titles on some of the reissues: *The Bank* went out as *In the Bank*, *A Night Out* became *His Night Out*, and *A Night in the Show* was modified to *Night at the Show*. Because Chaplin resisted making sound films for so long (*The Great Dictator*, his first bona fide talkie, wasn't released until 1940), a new generation of moviegoers, who had been weaned on sound movies, readily accepted the notion of a *silent* Chaplin comedy.

Writer-producer Robert Youngson enjoyed great success with *The Golden Age of Comedy* (1958), a compilation that culled footage from comedy shorts of the 1920s. With Chaplin controlling the rights to his films from this period, Youngson was unable to include any Chaplin material in *Golden Age*. (Although *The Gold Rush* [1925] and *The Kid* [1921] now turn up on "public domain" DVD collections, these films were still under copyright in 1958.) For subsequent compilations, Youngson relied on earlier Chaplin movies with lapsed copyright status. *When Comedy Was King* (1960), *Days of Thrills and Laughter* (1961), and *30 Years of Fun* (1963) showcased excerpts from Chaplin's Keystone and Mutual productions.

This revived interest in silent comedies may have been the reason why new 35mm prints of the King of Comedy's Essanay reissues were struck in 1961. They received limited theatrical bookings, and not always in "art house" situations, surprisingly.

In 1965 the syndicated television series *The Charlie Chaplin Comedy Theatre* was broadcast in select markets. The half-hour program showcased Chaplin's Keystone, Essanay and Mutual films; though hardly a ratings smash, it fared better than earlier attempts to air the comedian's work. (See separate entry for ***The Charlie Chaplin Comedy Theatre***.)

But serious Chaplin fans didn't have to depend entirely upon theatrical revivals and television broadcasts. Some of the films were available to private collectors via the home-movie market.

CHAPLIN AT HOME—YOUR HOME

For theatrical distribution, the Keystones and Essanays were printed in the standard-gauge 35mm format, on highly flammable nitrate film stock. The cumbersome projection equipment—to say nothing of the safety hazards—made it impractical for films to be marketed for use in homes, classrooms, and other non-theatrical applications. By the early 1920s, a 28mm format on non-flammable "safety" stock enabled collectors and institutions to obtain copies of early silent movies, including a modest selection of Keystone comedies that were made available from Pathé Laboratories. Movies became more accessible to the private sector when the amateur-gauge 16mm format came along in 1923. With this narrower stock, collectors could now amass a library of licensed films *and* shoot their own movies as well. Novelty Film Company, a New Jersey-based home movie distributor, offered 50-foot 16mm excerpts (running approximately 90 seconds to two minutes) from early Chaplin comedies, though it's hard to determine what the source films were, since they were given generic titles like *The Bashful Lover*. The Keystone Manufacturing Company of Boston (no relation to Mack Sennett's Keystone Film Company) released 100-foot 16mm excerpts from the Chaplin Keystones; their titles included *Bakers Dozen* (from *Dough and Dynamite*) and *Filling a Prescription* (from *Laughing Gas*). An outfit known as Exclusive Movie Studios offered similar 16mm excerpts from Chaplin's Essanay comedies.

Around 1943, Official Films, which was owned by Pathé Industries, issued a handful of Chaplin comedies to the collector's market, including *In the Park* (a retitled version of *Caught in the Rain*), *Laffing Gas* (originally titled *Laughing Gas*) and *Hits of the Past* (a one-reel abridgement of *The Property Man*).

While the more compact and affordable 8mm format was introduced in 1932 (the slightly wider 9.5mm format was manufactured in Europe), the concept of shooting home movies really didn't take off until the late 1940s, when many postwar families purchased 8mm movie cameras and projectors. To add variety to in-home movie presentations, a number of enterprising distributors began catering to 8mm consumers. Castle Films, the largest and most successful of these firms, offered travelogues, newsreels, cartoons, and abridgements of Hollywood features and shorts—but nothing on Charlie Chaplin.

Other companies, however, took advantage of the "public domain" status of certain Chaplin titles. Chaplin controlled the rights to his later films, but he had no legal claim to his Keystone and Essanay comedies, which were no longer protected by copyrights, so home-movie vendors could freely copy and sell prints of any of these films. And they did.

By the 1960s, 8mm movies were staple items in camera shops, department stores, and other retail outlets. Atlas Films, Coast Films and Carnival Films, three New York-based operations, marketed cheaply-priced abridgements of comedies featuring Laurel & Hardy (*Flying Elephants*, *Dirty Work*, and *Thicker Than Water* were among the offerings), Buster Keaton (*Cops*, *The Balloonatic*), and some of Chaplin's Keystones and Essanays. Collectors had their choice of 200-foot editions (running nine to twelve minutes in length) or 50-foot editions (three-minute versions). Many chain store outlets preferred to carry the 50-footers because their compact size made them easier to display (they were frequently dumped in metal bins, like socks and underwear) and they made great "impulse buy" items, priced as low as 79¢ each.

The corporate histories of Atlas, Coast and Carnival remain rather cloudy; they were essentially three limbs sprouting from the same tree. It was not uncommon for a consumer to find a Carnival reel in an Atlas box, or for one of Coast's "Best Of" collections to consist of Carnival-sanctioned titles.

These affordable "toy" editions introduced many a budding film enthusiast to the early work of Chaplin, whose later efforts had been out of circulation for years. But it proved to be a less-than-enchanting viewing experience. These companies weren't concerned about such trifling matters as continuity and coherency; their releases were nothing more than chunks of random footage. This cavalier treatment rendered even the most plotless Chaplin pictures incomprehensible.

Many of the Chaplin films issued to the collectors' market during the 1930s were already of dubious pictorial quality. Some three decades later, the Atlas, Coast, and Carnival merchandise was even more scratchy and grainy, and often unwatchable. Not that you could see the entire image in the first place. Silent movies were photographed in a ratio that produced a square screen image; by design, the apertures of 16mm and 8mm projectors frequently lop off the top of silent-movie actors' heads if the image isn't framed correctly. (This ratio problem is also apparent in VHS and DVD transfers of these films.)

Since a single Chaplin comedy could yield multiple 50-foot excerpts, these companies assigned new titles to their handiwork. One abridgement of the boxing comedy *The Champion* (Essanay, 1915) retained the original title, and others went out as *Sparring Partner*, *Lucky Horseshoe*, *His Lucky Day*, *The Boxer*, and *Battling Charlie*. Children were the target audience for these cutdowns—they were marketed as "kiddie movies"—so no great effort was expended when it came to devising new titles. Accordingly, *His Prehistoric Past* was rechristened *Caveman Charlie*, while *The Property Man* became *Backstage Antics*. Some of these new titles made little to no sense at all. Who, for instance, would have guessed that *The Kidnapped Heiress* and *Diaper Days* both derived from *Easy Street* (Mutual, 1917), or that *Damsel in Distress*, *Charlie's Hot Seat*, and *Scrambled Eggs* were all taken from *The Tramp* (Essanay, 1915)? Equally puzzling were generic titles like *In Trouble*, *Balled Up*, *Charlie Steps Out*, and *Surprise Meetings*; we haven't seen them and couldn't begin to guess which films they were culled from. At least when Walton Home Movies, a British firm, offered retitled abridgements of the Chaplins, their catalogue entries often identified the source movie ("*Charlie on the Farm*, from *The Tramp*").

Other 8mm distributors, such as Select Film Library, Regent Films (a subsidiary of Select), and Ideal Films, usually retained the film's original title, even if they were redone to include their own company identification ("Select Film Library presents Charlie Chaplin in..."). These outfits released some Chaplin shorts in the complete one- and two-reel running times, while a few of the two-reelers were cut down to a one-reel length.

Best of all was Blackhawk Films, which towered above all others in the home-movie field. Founded by Kent D. Eastin, who later partnered with Martin Phelan, this Iowa-based company was the answer to the prayers of every serious collector/student of silent cinema. The Blackhawk catalogue consisted of complete (or as close to complete as possible) versions of many silent movies (Laurel & Hardy, D. W. Griffith, Mack Sennett, Buster Keaton, William S. Hart), including several of Chaplin's Keystone and Essanay comedies. Offering these films in both 8mm and 16mm—and under their *original* titles, thank goodness—Blackhawk made an effort to hunt down good source material. Even when the result wasn't up to Blackhawk's usual standards, it was still leagues ahead of the ratty-looking product offered by other distributors. When the 8mm variant "Super 8" was introduced in 1965, Blackhawk made many of its titles available in that gauge as well. (By 1977, most home-movie manufacturers decided to back the Super 8 format, forcing a near-complete discontinuation of "Standard 8mm" product—in the same manner the DVD format has knocked VHS off the marketplace.)

With the rise of VHS home video in the 1980s, the public-domain status of the Keystones and Essanays made them ideal fodder for independent distributors, which have issued a variety of Chaplin volumes. Like Atlas, Coast, and Carnival before them, most of these operations were content to use whatever material was at hand, regardless of the condition or the quality. Some of the Blackhawk copies were utilized; unfortunately, many inferior prints were also tossed into the mix.

Consumers were lured into the DVD format with the promise of superior picture and sound quality. It's a promise that's been kept, although it doesn't always extend to the public-domain arena, where the results have been distinctly hit-or-miss, especially where silent cinema is concerned. You can purchase a shimmering restoration of **Metropolis** (1926) from Kino On Video, or pick up an edited, blurry version from budget distributors for a fraction of the cost. For the serious collector, the choice is obvious.

Some silent films on DVD have musical accompaniment; some do not. (A few even employ a continuous-loop sound effect of a projector's whirring motor!) Also, many silent films are shown at the wrong speed; in the case of the early Chaplins, the action can appear twice as fast.

When it comes to Chaplin, collectors can select Kino's three-volume **Chaplin's Essanay Comedies**, containing remastered versions of the films (beautifully restored by Blackhawk's David Shepard), or settle for any number of public-domain volumes that offer lesser-quality copies of the same titles. It's a matter of preservation vs. pocketbook. The decision is yours.

Options are limited in regard to the Chaplin Keystones. They are available from several DVD distributors, but the poor-to-mediocre quality of many surviving copies makes it difficult to assess these films properly. On Amazon.com, Chaplin fans and collectors have weighed in on this very subject:

> *"If the originals have deteriorated to the point where they are in poor quality, they simply shouldn't be seen by the average viewer…I believe it does a great disservice to the silent film era. I can't help but feel that most people who [see inferior prints] are going to come away from it with a serious loathing of silent film short comedy. The quality destroys any enjoyment that undoubtedly at one time would have been had…Rarity, for me, is not the issue. These [prints] are beyond watchable quality even if they are the only ones left. This level of deterioration can only be tolerated by the most ardent*

fan. And I don't say that lightly. I am a film student who has seen more than his fair share of poor quality prints."

—j.wade.q (September 15, 2004).

"Some of the Keystones are so many generations removed from a good print that Chaplin appears blurry and scratched."

—Kenneth French (January 12, 2004).

"Now, I'm no film historian or expert, but I was immediately struck by the poor quality of the images, the fact that the actors' heads were chopped off, the framing obviously out of whack…Ick."

—"A viewer" (January 26, 2004).

Even those who are sympathetic to the situation acknowledge the flaws:

"It's not bad quality at all, although it's very hard to get Chaplin's Keystones in good shape because they are so old."

—Thom Eldridge (July 17, 2004).

Whether anyone will embark on a major restoration of all the Chaplin Keystones remains to be seen. (At this writing, archivist David Shepard is working with Lobster Films France to restore a few of them.) When you consider how many silent films have been lost to the ages, perhaps we should just be grateful that *any* material, no matter how shoddy, survives at all.

CHAPLIN AT KEYSTONE

o o o o o o o o o o o o o o o o o o o o o o o o o o o o o o o o o o o

"The reasons for his unprecedented success are not hard to ascertain. Chaplin's Tramp achieves a remarkable blend of humor and pathos, poetry and slapstick that touches a responsive chord in audiences who recognize the humanity upon which the character is based. The broad comedy of these films is executed with such exquisite timing and grace that a fall or a kick in the pants seems as carefully choreographed as a ballet, and a situation as simple as a man falling in love with a pretty girl achieves an unexpected bittersweet quality."

—*Janet E. Lorenz, Charles Chaplin: The Short Films.*

Though typical of the praise awarded Chaplin's work, Lorenz's comments do not necessarily pertain to his early efforts. The "remarkable blend of humor and pathos, poetry and slapstick" were largely absent from his Keystone period and wouldn't begin to blossom until he was at Essanay. But his "exquisite timing and grace" were apparent right from the start.

Born April 16, 1889 in Walworth, a section of London, England, Charles Spencer Chaplin came from an impoverished background. His father was an alcoholic and his mother mentally ill; both had been music hall performers. Chaplin's sad childhood experiences became a source for artistic inspiration. He began performing at an early age, eventually becoming the lead comedian in theatrical impresario Fred Karno's stage company. Karno actually had several troupes that toured England, and it was during this period that Chaplin became a master of the English music hall style.

Chaplin first came to the United States in 1910 as the star comedian of "A Night in an English Music Hall," a road company edition of Karno's popular English revue "Mumming Birds." (Stan Laurel, years before his teaming with Oliver Hardy, understudied Chaplin in the Karno revues.) It was during a second

11

U. S. tour (1912-13) that Mack Sennett, head of the Keystone Film Company in Los Angeles, saw him.

Sennett (1880-1960) began his film career as an actor with the Biograph Company in 1908; within two years, he was directing as well. Sennett launched Keystone in 1912, and by the time he saw Chaplin on stage, he was just beginning to establish his reputation as the leading comedy filmmaker of the era. The rapid-fire pace of the Keystone comedies distinguished them from the competition, and Sennett's roster included such audience favorites as Mabel Normand, Ford Sterling, Roscoe "Fatty" Arbuckle, Mack Swain, Chester Conklin, and Fred Mace. On September 25, 1913, Chaplin signed a one-year contract with Keystone; starting on December 13th of that year, he would receive $150 a week (with a $25 raise after three months) to act in the movies.

Out of necessity, Sennett directed and co-starred in a number of the early Keystones. By mid-1913, he was sharing directorial duties with Mabel Normand, Wilfred Lucas, George Nichols, and Henry Lehrman. Lehrman (1883-1946) had been a streetcar conductor before becoming involved with the motion picture industry. Without any experience in the business, he applied for a job at the Biograph studio, claiming to be M. Henri Lehrman of the Pathé Frères studio in Paris. Legendary director D. W. Griffith, who ran Biograph, saw through Lehrman's charade, but hired him anyway. Griffith also gave Lehrman the nickname "Pathé," which stuck with him for years. (Lehrman would later earn another nickname, "Mr. Suicide," referring to his disregard for the safety of actors.)

Lehrman's claim to cinematic fame is that he directed Chaplin's first film, *Making a Living* (released February 2, 1914), with Charlie playing a conniving "sharper" not unlike one of his English music hall roles. From the very beginning, Chaplin clashed with Lehrman over comedic style. Keystone's roughhouse brand of humor—in which violent acts of retaliation required little or no motivation—was at odds with the character-driven approach favored by Chaplin. Despite some initial misgivings on Sennett's part, Chaplin was soon allowed to shape his own screen persona (which would evolve into his beloved Tramp) and his films. *Twenty Minutes of Love* (released April 20, 1914), Chaplin's eleventh Keystone comedy, marked his directorial debut.

> *"It was this charming alfresco spirit [at Keystone] that was a delight—a challenge to one's creativeness. It was so free and easy—no literature, no writers, we just had a notion around which we built gags, then made up the story as we went along."*
>
> —Charles Chaplin, *My Autobiography*.

"At Keystone, no kick ever needed to be justified. The invitation of an available backside was motivation enough. If one man had a pitchfork in his hand and another man, entirely unoffending, was observed bending over, there was just one thing to do: use the pitchfork."

—Walter Kerr, *The Silent Clowns.*

"Chaplin's Keystone films fell far short of the gentle, sophisticated comedy that would be the hallmark of his later work. Yet, Chaplin injected into the films and, in turn, early film comedy an acute understanding of character and movement that he had refined during his years in the British music halls, and a style of comedy that was polished yet appeared spontaneous at the same time."

—Jeffrey Vance, *Chaplin: Genius of the Cinema.*

"Although Chaplin discovered the components of the tramp character at Keystone, he discovered all the components of the tramp character not there but at Essanay. The side of the tramp that emerged at Keystone was the tough, violent, scrappy, almost sadistic one, not the little man's recognition of a very clear code of human morality…the famed Chaplin 'tramp' figure, the sentimental, warmhearted Everyman, does not yet exist in the Keystones—except for his wiry toughness."

—Gerald Mast, *The Comic Mind.*

"In their haste to discuss Chaplin's later films, scholars and commentators who devote any time at all to the Chaplin Keystones tend to describe them impressionistically rather than accurately or to lump them all together as 'mere slapstick' intermittently enlivened by flashes of Chaplin's comic business."

—Harry M. Geduld, *Chapliniana Volume 1: The Keystone Films.*

Audiences and critics considered the Keystones to be the best screen comedies of the era. However, watching Chaplin's Keystones today is akin to gazing at the blueprints for a grand building—they give an indication of things to come, although the finer details remain sketchy and unformed. As such, it's not surprising that the casual viewer, who is merely in search of a funny movie, will have little tolerance for these raggedy efforts, preferring instead to look at Chaplin's later, more polished efforts.

Not that it's any easier for dedicated Chaplin enthusiasts. It has been rightfully acknowledged that the Keystones represent an important step in Chaplin's evolution as a filmmaker, and several of them contain some undeniably amusing bits of business. Critics and filmgoers immediately hailed Chaplin as someone special. By his fourth film (**Between Showers**), reviewers were enthusiastically calling attention to his work. By his seventh film (**His Favorite Pastime**), exhibitors were clamoring for more Chaplin product.

Naturally, we had this in the back of our minds while watching his Keystones in chronological order, and we kept waiting for the one galvanizing entry that announced the arrival of a certifiable comic genius. Unlike Chaplin observers of that era, we are blessed with hindsight, so it should be easy, we reasoned, to spot the magic moment that started the ball rolling.

But a blessing can also be a curse. While we certainly admire Chaplin and are well aware of the tremendous impact he had on the motion picture industry, most of his Keystone efforts aren't terribly funny from a 21st century perspective. So if you're familiar with the great Chaplin comedies that followed, it may be difficult to comprehend why he stood out from the pack so early on. (Conversely, it's very easy to understand why Mabel Normand and Fatty Arbuckle were audience favorites. They had a warmth and appeal that Chaplin was generally lacking at the time.)

Ultimately, it's a matter of putting these films in their proper historical context. Film historian James L. Neibaur explains:

> Most American film comedians of the early 1910s—people like Fred Mace and Augustus Carney—were superficial talents at best; they wore funny costumes and they ran around and fell down a lot. Their humor wasn't character driven. It isn't surprising that they faded from view as soon as better comedians came along.
>
> Charlie Chaplin was one of those better comedians. His impact was instantaneous because he endeared himself to audiences right from the start. In **Kid Auto Races at Venice**, Chaplin's second Keystone, the Tramp keeps wandering in front of a movie camera and is repeatedly shoved out of the way by the director. Back then, much of the moviegoing public consisted of immigrants—new people in a new land—who still felt out of place in this country. So they identified with this "outsider" who perseveres even though he keeps getting knocked down and pushed aside. They had a rooting interest in Chaplin because they felt he was one of them. And he was. (This one-of-us image also connected Chaplin to Depression-era audiences.)

> *Chaplin also happened to be the freshest comedy talent of 1914. It's easy to take that for granted now, but if you look at other comedies that were being made at the time then look at what Chaplin was doing, he's without a doubt the funniest movie comedian of that era. I've read accounts that audiences roared with laughter during screenings of the Chaplin Keystones, and I don't doubt it one bit.*

In his book *Charlie Chaplin's One-Man Show* (Scarecrow Press, 1984), Dan Kamin had this to say about a modern audience's response during a screening of one of Chaplin's Keystones:

> **The Masquerader** had [the audience] laughing, giggling and roaring throughout. Apparently something was operating beyond the plot and gags, which were rather primitive in this Chaplin film. I realized that the audience was responding much as an audience in 1914 must have—somehow the mere appearance of the Chaplin character was winning them over. Looking at the film more carefully, I noticed that even though he wasn't doing anything particularly ingenious, Chaplin seemed to be totally involved with what he was doing, and further, that his feelings at every moment were communicated to the audience with crystal clarity. A warmth came over the audience. We cared about how this fellow felt and what was happening in the film to affect him.

Nevertheless, some dread the prospect of having to actually sit down and watch a Keystone film. It can be a grim experience for even the most battle-tested historian, as Walter Kerr discovered while researching *The Silent Clowns* (Alfred A. Knopf, 1975): "I have, in the past months, sat through dozens of Keystones—without once being trapped into laughter…There is very little in the Sennett films, for all their breakneck pace and bizarre manhandling of the universe, that one would care to call humor under analytic examination."

Of the 35 films Chaplin made for Keystone, there isn't an enduring comedy classic to emerge from the group. It's important to remember, however, that these efforts represent almost *half* of Chaplin's eventual 81-film output. Collectively speaking, their contribution to Chaplin's evolution is tremendous.

THE CHAPLIN KEYSTONES

All were produced by Mack Sennett for the Keystone Film Company, and originally distributed to theaters through the exchanges of the Mutual Film Company. (Mutual would sign Chaplin to a contract of its own in 1916.)

One reel of film (35mm) was approximately 1,000 feet in length, with a running time of 10 to 14 minutes, depending on the projection speed. (A "split" reel is half of one reel.)

The entries for *Home-movie editions* refer to retitled (and usually abridged) versions issued to the home-movie market. *Working title* is a title assigned to a film during production.

Please note that the "Billy Gilbert" who appears in many Chaplin Keystones is not the same actor who co-starred in Chaplin's *The Great Dictator* (1940).

1. *Making a Living*
(One Reel; Released February 2, 1914)
Working title: *The Reporters*
Reissue titles: *A Busted Johnny*, *Troubles*, *Doing His Best*, *Take My Picture*
Home-movie editions: *A Busted Johnny*, *Doing His Best*
Cast: Charlie Chaplin (*the nervy and very nifty sharper*), Henry Lehrman (*his rival*), Virginia Kirtley (*girlfriend*), Alice Davenport (*mother*), Chester Conklin (*cop*), Minta Durfee (*woman*).
Credits: Directed by Henry Lehrman. Photographed by Enrique Jan Vallejo.
Plot: Chaplin plays a "sharper" who uses his skills as a con artist to borrow money from unsuspecting passerby Lehrman. Later, Charlie woos Lehrman's girlfriend, and the two men become bitter rivals. Lehrman snaps a photograph of an auto accident, hoping the picture will secure him a job as a newspaper reporter. But Charlie steals Lehrman's camera, runs down to the newspaper office, and takes credit for big scoop himself.
Source of print screened: *The Essential Charlie Chaplin Collection Vol. 1* (Delta Entertainment Corporation)

Comments: Well, here it is, Charlie Chaplin's first film.† That fact alone guarantees it a place in motion picture history. Its worth in terms of entertainment value, however, is another matter.

There's nothing in this typically frantic Keystone production that gives any indication Chaplin would become the most beloved movie comedian of his era. In fact, there's nothing even remotely likable about Chaplin's character. His conniving-for-conniving's-sake demeanor lacks the sympathetic edge that could counterbalance his devious actions. (Unlike, for instance, in *The Kid*, where little Jackie Coogan breaks windows so Charlie can make money repairing them.)

With his top hat, frock coat, monocle, and drooping mustache, Chaplin's sinister appearance has all the earmarks of the sort of "Olde Time" villain that an audience would be encouraged to hiss on cue.†† What saves him from total jerkdom is the viewer's complete lack of empathy for the supporting players. Henry Lehrman's character is a victim, not a hero; like the other supporting players, the bland Lehrman makes no impression on the screen. Without any effective comic foils to play against, an energetic Chaplin dominates the proceedings.

Chaplin's skill as an actor is immediately apparent. During his first encounter with Lehrman, Chaplin approaches him amicably, admires his ring, then tells him a tale of woe in order to get a handout. (Charlie keeps watching him out of the corner of his eye to see if the reticent Lehrman is weakening.) When Lehrman finally does take a coin out of his pocket, Charlie displays false pride in refusing it—then quickly snatches it just as Lehrman is about to put the coin back in his pocket. This is pretty subtle stuff, especially by Keystone standards. Some of Chaplin's pantomime bits didn't make it into the finished picture, as Chaplin ruefully recalled in his autobiography: "Although the picture was completed in three days, I thought we contrived some very funny gags. But when I saw the finished film it broke my heart, for the cutter had butchered it beyond recognition, cutting into the middle of all my funny business."

Later, Charlie tries to make his case to a newspaper editor and slaps the man on his knee to drive home his point. When the editor moves his knee, Charlie pulls it back in place so he can continue slapping it. Unfortunately, this and other comic bits aren't fully effective because the viewer isn't rooting for Chaplin's character.

Still, Chaplin's talent as a physical comedian is quite evident. Adept at pratfalls, he employs a scrappy persona that gives a hint of the Tramp-to-come. (In *Making a Living*, it's as if the Tramp got a makeover, then worked his way up to a better street corner.) And he already possesses his trademark cane, which he uses as both a weapon and a third arm.

Making a Living adheres to the basic structure of a generic Keystone comedy: a central comic figure pursues a girl, faces off with a rival, and tries to prove his worth via a job. Chaplin would continue to reuse, reshape, and refine this basic structure long after he left Keystone.

For contemporary viewers, the historic importance of *Making a Living* will be offset by Chaplin's unappealing character and the lack of genuinely funny set-pieces. Prints of the film currently available on DVD don't help matters, either: most are fair-quality copies that don't have any subtitles, which makes the story hard to follow.

Chaplin himself dismissed his debut as a failure. Most viewers who bother to sit through *Making a Living* will share Chaplin's disappointment. Nevertheless, it should be noted there are many silent films now considered "lost," so let us be grateful that this movie milestone is one that has survived.

Other Views and Reviews: "The clever player who takes the role of the nervy and very nifty sharper in this picture is a comedian of the first water, who acts like one of Nature's own naturals. It is so full of action that it is indescribable, but so much of it is fresh and unexpected fun that a laugh will be going all the time almost. It is foolish-funny stuff that will make even the sober-minded laugh, but people out for an evening's good time will howl."—*The Moving Picture World* (1914).

"Viewed today, [*Making a Living*] stands up as one of the better Keystones of the era."—Kalton C. Lahue and Terry Brewer, *Kops and Custards: The Legend of Keystone Films* (1968).

"Certainly it makes no particular impression today: the bouncing 'toff' character has only the slightly weird historical interest of being played by the (barely recognizable) creator of Charlie."—Isabel Quigly, *Charlie Chaplin: Early Comedies* (1968).

"Chaplin's first film is so poorly acted and so unfunny primarily because Chaplin has nothing to play off and against. He simply stands around fuming, and stomping, and fussing; like so many Sennett characters, he demonstrates abstract clichés of passions."—Gerald Mast, *The Comic Mind* (1973).

"The film is full of subtle touches that run throughout Chaplin's later films and shows that much of his comic technique was already intact when he arrived at the Mack Sennett Studio."—Leonard Maltin, *The Great Movie Comedians* (1978).

"In *Making a Living*, the Chaplin costume and makeup are as barren and bizarre as the plot: Fu Manchu mustache, monocle, high hat, frock coat but shirtless, with tie, dickey, and attached collar and cuffs…A distinctive Chaplin hallmark is established in his very first film—his serene belligerence in times of self-need."—John McCabe, *Charlie Chaplin* (1978).

"Almost inevitably, *Making a Living* is a disappointment. Sadly miscast and insensitively directed, Chaplin was, for the most part, singularly unfunny and he knew it."—Harry M. Geduld, *Chapliniana Volume 1: The Keystone Films* (1987).

"*Making a Living* is representative only of the darker side of Charlie…a ruthless Charlie untempered even by the limited degree of humanity found in subsequent Keystones."—Glenn Mitchell, *The Chaplin Encyclopedia* (1997).

†Some sources have noted that Chaplin may have appeared in newsreels at an earlier date. Regardless, *Making a Living* is the first "official" Chaplin film.

††A later home-movie edition of *Making a Living* would claim that "Chaplin wears the villain costume of his pantomime act in English vaudeville." The costume drew upon the appearance of a stage villain and characters Chaplin had played during his years with Fred Karno.

2. *Kid Auto Races at Venice*
Also known as *Kid Auto Races at Venice, Cal.*
(Split Reel†; Released February 7, 1914)
Reissue titles: **The Pest**, **The Kid Auto Race**, **Kid's Auto Race**, **The Children's Automobile Race**
Cast: Charlie Chaplin (*tramp*), Henry Lehrman (*director*), Frank D. Williams (*cameraman*), Billy Jacobs (*boy*), Charlotte Fitzpatrick (*girl*), Thelma Salter (*girl*), Gordon Griffith (*boy*).
Credits: Directed by Henry Lehrman. Photographed by Frank D. Williams (some sources credit Enrique Jan Vallejo as co-photographer).
Plot: In Venice, California, a huge crowd has gathered to watch a children's soap box derby race, and Charlie is one of the spectators. Noticing a movie director and his cameraman trying to shoot footage of the event, Charlie wanders into view, only to be shoved out of the way. Undaunted, he repeatedly tries to get himself into as many shots as possible, to the irritation of the director.
Source of print screened: **The Essential Charlie Chaplin Collection Vol. 1** (Delta Entertainment Corporation)
Comments: It was in this film, his third—made after *Mabel's Strange Predicament*, but released to theaters two days before it††—that Chaplin's Tramp was first seen by movie audiences. Though Chaplin would embellish the character's personality over the next few years, his outward appearance remained basically the same. During this Keystone period, however, Chaplin did not consistently appear as the Tramp, making later non-Tramp efforts such as *Tango Tangles*,

Cruel, Cruel Love, *Mabel at the Wheel*, and *Tillie's Punctured Romance* seem like artistic regressions.

Kid Auto Races at Venice was reportedly improvised within a 45-minute time period, a claim that's entirely plausible judging by the finished product. This is not meant to be a negative assessment. On the contrary, the film comes across as a charming, off-the-cuff screen test for the Tramp, and serves as a much better introduction to Chaplin than *Making a Living* did. It's essentially a one-joke premise, as Charlie repeatedly finds ways to get in front of the camera lens. Yet Chaplin devises a number of amusing variations on this single idea. As a performer, he's become much more assured in front of the camera, and his movements are already subtler than any other Keystone player. (It's worth noting that Chaplin, unknown to the public at this point in his career, was able to stroll anonymously among the huge crowd gathered for the race. Had this film been made a few months later, the Tramp would have been mobbed by hordes of fans.)

In *Kid Auto Races at Venice*, Charlie performs his first onscreen "cigarette kick" (tossing a cigarette butt over his shoulder, then kicking it with the back of his heel before it hits the ground). Watching Chaplin's early Keystones, it's surprising—to us, at least—how much he uses a cigarette as a prop. This facet of the Tramp character would be toned down later on, but in *Mabel's Strange Predicament*, *Between Showers*, *A Film Johnnie*, *The Star Boarder*, *Twenty Minutes of Love*, and other Keystones, he's puffing away like a chimney.

In this film, Chaplin also establishes his relationship with the camera and the moviemaking process. As Walter Kerr states in *The Silent Clowns* (Alfred A. Knopf, 1975):

> [Chaplin] would do this throughout his career, using the instrument as a means of establishing a direct and openly acknowledged relationship between himself and his audience. In fact, he is, with this film, establishing himself as one among the audience, one among those who are astonished by this new mechanical marvel, one among those who would like to be photographed by it, and—he would make the most of this implication later—one among those who are invariably chased away.

Speaking of relationships, the onscreen antagonism between Chaplin and director Henry Lehrman reflects their interaction offscreen. Lehrman, who wanted the comedian to adhere to the strict Keystone regimen, routinely dismissed Chaplin's ideas. They had clashed right from the start, and the bitterness never subsided.

The copies of **Kid Auto Races at Venice** currently available on DVD are taken from a reissue version that made a foolhardy attempt to assign a narrative thread to the film. It opens with the subtitles *"Extracts from a letter from Charlie Chaplin to his best girl: 'I made tracks for the track.'"* After a close-up of the Tramp, the movie concludes with the subtitle *"Your ever so loving Charlie xxxxx—P. S. Just heard my picture won't pass the censor."*

If there's a rational explanation for all of this, we'd like to hear it.

Other Views and Reviews: "**Kid Auto Races** struck us as about the funniest film we have ever seen. Chaplin is a born screen comedian; he does things we have never seen done on the screen before."—*The Cinema* (1914).

"A plotless episode of Chaplin mugging, posturing, gesticulating…All of this is very trivial, yet two vital things happen in the film: Charlie the tramp is born even if only embryonically, and Chaplin, by confronting the camera, joins not the characters in the film but *us*. He joins us, his audience, forever."—John McCabe, *Charlie Chaplin* (1978).

"Anticipating a major theme of **The Circus** (1928), the film contrasts contrived performance (the race) with improvised artistry (Charlie's scene-stealing). We are left in no doubt as to the superiority of the latter…Yet the Tramp in **Kid Auto Races at Venice** is merely a preliminary sketch for a character who was to become more complex with every film in which he would appear."—Harry M. Geduld, *Chapliniana Volume 1: The Keystone Films* (1987).

†The other half of the reel was **Olives and Their Oil**, an educational short purchased from an outside company for distribution by Keystone.

††Many sources claim that **Kid Auto Races at Venice** and **Mabel's Strange Predicament** were released in reverse order. However, in the Spring 1989 issue of *Sight and Sound*, historian Bo Burglund argues that the confirmed date of the actual race (January 10, 1914) indicates otherwise. See the next entry for our opinion.

3. *Mabel's Strange Predicament*
(One Reel; Released February 9, 1914)
Working title: **Pajamas**
Reissue titles: **The Hotel Mix-Up**, **Charlie at the Hotel**
Cast: Charlie Chaplin (*Charlie*), Mabel Normand (*Mabel*), Harry McCoy (*boyfriend*), Chester Conklin (*husband*), Alice Davenport (*wife*), Al St. John (*bellhop*), Billy Gilbert (*bellhop*).

Credits: Directed by Mabel Normand (some sources list Mack Sennett and Henry Lehrman as co-directors). Written by Reed Heustis. Photographed by Hans Koenekamp (some sources credit Frank D. Williams).

Plot: A tipsy Charlie flirts with several women in a hotel lobby, including a disinterested Mabel. Later, a pajama-clad Mabel accidentally gets locked out of her hotel room; in an effort to hide from the still-amorous and intoxicated Charlie, she hides in Chester's room across the hall—to the consternation of Chester's wife and Mabel's boyfriend.

Source of print screened: ***The Essential Charlie Chaplin Collection Vol. 1*** (Delta Entertainment Corporation), under the French title ***Charlot à l'hôtel***

Comments: There's a debate among Chaplin scholars as to whether this film or ***Kid Auto Races at Venice*** marks the first appearance of the Tramp character. It has generally been accepted that ***Mabel's Strange Predicament*** was made before ***Kid Auto Races*** but released afterward. Some, however, claim that the reverse is true.

Watching these films in order of release, we've come to the conclusion that ***Mabel's Strange Predicament*** was made first. We arrived at this conclusion by the simple fact that Chaplin's makeup here differs from any of the Tramp's subsequent appearances—primarily his mustache, which is fuller and slightly longer than it would be in ***Kid Auto Races*** or in all later films. (Chaplin probably felt that a shorter mustache would show his facial expressions to greater advantage and trimmed it accordingly.) Additionally, the overall costume is not as tattered as it would later become; here it's more unkempt than dilapidated.

Although ***Mabel's Strange Predicament*** is bereft of any genuine laughs, it's loaded with Chaplin "firsts." It's his first screen portrayal of a drunk; the inebriate act was a staple of his years with the Fred Karno troupe, and Chaplin would play intoxicated characters throughout his Keystone period (***His Favorite Pastime***, ***The Rounders***) and beyond (***A Night Out***, ***A Night in the Show***, ***One A. M.***, ***City Lights***, ***Limelight***). It's the first film in which Charlie employs his trademark "walk," shuffling along with his feet turned out. It's the first film that shows him tipping his derby, which was an act of salutation and/or flirtation, then twirling his cane and knocking the derby off his head.

It's also the first film to showcase his character's resiliency in dealing with failed romantic conquests. During the opening scenes, Charlie attempts to impress and make small talk with several women. He's rejected each time, and each time he shrugs it off and moves on to the next potential paramour. In later films, Chaplin would add a sentimental touch to this resiliency, as in the final shot of ***The Tramp*** (Essanay, 1915).

For all the firsts on display, the film does not contain Chaplin's first portrayal of an authentic tramp. Although the term "tramp" has always been convenient shorthand in referring to Chaplin's celebrated image, the character is often married and gainfully employed. In *Mabel's Strange Predicament*, he is neither a tramp nor a vagabond; he even has enough cash to bribe the hotel manager.

It's easy to see why Mabel Normand (1894-1930) was one of Keystone's most popular stars. The attractive brunette possessed a natural charm and exuberance that lit up the screen, making her an immensely appealing figure even in her weakest films. (She was often referred to as "the female Chaplin.")

Though Mabel was a more established Keystone player at the time *Mabel's Strange Predicament* was made, Chaplin dominates much of the picture, essentially performing a solo drunk act amidst the usual roughhouse antics. This would seem to support claims that Chaplin's character was added to the film as an afterthought. Mack Sennett allegedly told Chaplin, "We need some gags in here…Put on a comedy makeup. Anything will do."

In his autobiography, Chaplin remembered how he devised what would become his trademark persona:

> *I had no idea what makeup to put on. However, on the way to the wardrobe, I thought I would dress in baggy pants [borrowed from Fatty Arbuckle], big shoes [from Ford Sterling], a cane and a derby hat [from Minta Durfee's father]. I wanted everything to be a contradiction: the pants baggy, the coat tight, the hat small and the shoes large. I was undecided to look old or young…I added a small mustache [trimmed down from Mack Swain's], which, I reasoned, would add age without hiding my expression. I had no idea of the character. But the moment I was dressed, the clothes and the makeup made me feel the person he was. I began to know him, and by the time I walked on to the stage he was fully born.*

While Chaplin's fanciful account makes a ripping good yarn—we desperately *want* to it to be true—other sources have claimed, with great credibility, that the costume was the culled from earlier stage influences. (The "big shoes" were not a part of the costume in *Mabel's Strange Predicament* and some of the other early Chaplin movies.)

For years *Mabel's Strange Predicament* was considered a lost film, until a worn, incomplete French print was discovered in the late 1960s; this is the only version currently available on the collector's market. While Chaplin completists will want to sit through it at least once, it's rough sledding for anyone else. If you want to see the same basic plot better executed, check out *A Night Out* (1915), Chaplin's second film for Essanay.

Other Views and Reviews: "The Keystone Company never made a better contract than when they signed on Chas. Chaplin, the Karno performer. It is not every variety artiste who possesses the ability to act for the camera. Chaplin not only shows that talent; he shows it in a degree which raises him at once to the status of a star performer. We do not often indulge in prophecy, but we do not think we are taking a great risk in prophesying that in six months Chaplin will rank as one of the most popular screen comedians in the world."—*Exhibitors' Mail* (1914).

"Here the mannerisms that were to become so characteristic—the outsize dignity preserved at all costs, the gesture of absurd delicacy in unsuitable situations—began to appear."—Isabel Quigly, *Charlie Chaplin: Early Comedies* (1968).

"One of Chaplin's less successful early comedies...a curiosity piece."—Michael De Zubirira, *The Internet Movie Database* (2001).

4. *Between Showers*

(One Reel; Released February 28, 1914)

Working title: **A Rainy Day**

Reissue titles: **A Rainy Day, The Flirts**†**, In Wrong**††**, Charlie and the Umbrella, Thunder and Lightning**

Home-movie editions: **Roaming Romeo, Stolen Umbrella, Charlie and the Umbrella**

Cast: Charlie Chaplin (*a masher*), Ford Sterling (*another masher*), Chester Conklin (*cop*), Emma Clifton (*girl*), Sadie Lampe (*housemaid*).

Credits: Written and directed by Henry Lehrman (some sources credit Mack Sennett as co-director). Photography by Frank D. Williams.

Plot: Charlie and Ford both try to assist a young lady (Emma Clifton) across a big puddle in the street. Neither succeeds, but they keep pursuing her—Charlie for romantic reasons, Ford to retrieve his umbrella.

Source of print screened: **The Essential Charlie Chaplin Collection Vol. 1** (Delta Entertainment Corporation)

Comments: This is Chaplin's first "park" comedy. Public parks were a favorite setting of the Keystone crew—it was a convenient place to quickly shoot a movie—and Chaplin would make park comedies throughout his Keystone and Essanay years.

Filmed in Westlake Park, **Between Showers** shows Chaplin's trademark appearance falling into place. His mustache has been trimmed a bit further since **Mabel's Strange Predicament** and **Kid Auto Races at Venice**, his jacket is now torn under the arms, and he's wearing really baggy trousers. Though he doesn't have his cane this time, the umbrella becomes a suitable substitute. Ford Sterling also uses the umbrella to strike some surprisingly similar Chaplinesque poses.

The film is standard Keystone fare, which means that all conflicts are resolved via such civilized methods as neck-wringing, brick-throwing, and ass-kicking. Ford Sterling (1883-1939) was Keystone's most popular player before Chaplin joined the company, and here he gives the kind of wild-eyed, gesticulating performance that would become outdated within a few short years. The boisterous Sterling could be very funny under the right circumstances, but like many of his Keystone contemporaries, he never rose to the same heights Chaplin did.

By now, Chaplin was getting into the Keystone spirit, making exaggerated faces for the camera (a practice he would soon abandon) and executing spectacular tumbles (a backwards fall with heels over head) with great enthusiasm. But he's also beginning to develop his own style and attitude as a screen performer. As he flirts with Emma Clifton, you can see that his gestures (tipping his hat, putting on a big smile) have an increasing playfulness to them. For the first time, Chaplin's character acknowledges an authority figure (a cop), smiling at him with a combination of coyness, timidity, and apprehension (Charlie seems to be wondering if the cop is on to him and whether he should stay put or make a run for it). Charlie does a slight variation of what would become a trademark nose-thumbing gesture (referred to as "cocking a snoot") as an act of defiance and disrespect—although he makes sure the cop is out of view when he does it.

Chaplin also performs another one of his trademarks: the 90-degree skidding turn in which he lifts one foot straight off the ground while balances himself and changes directions with the other. In later films he would also hold his hat in place with either his hand or his cane.

This was the last Chaplin Keystone directed by Henry Lehrman. Chaplin and the martinet Lehrman never got along, due to creative differences; they had clashed during the filming of ***Making a Living*** and their relationship continued to sour afterwards. Lehrman's departure would set the stage for Chaplin's eventual elevation to writer and director of his own pictures.

Between Showers will be of great interest to the serious Chaplin scholar; the average viewer will probably remain stone-faced throughout.

Other Views and Reviews: "A screamingly funny comedy."—*The Cinema* (1914). "When Charlie Chaplin started to work for Sennett he had chiefly to reckon with Ford Sterling, the reigning comedian. Their first picture together amounted to a duel before the assembled professionals. Sterling, by no means untalented, was a big man with a florid Teutonic style which, under this special pressure, he turned on full blast. Chaplin defeated him within a few minutes with a wink of the mustache, a hitch of the trousers, a quirk of the little finger."—James Agee, *Life* (1949).

"Under Lehrman's uninspired direction, [Ford Sterling] merely repeated rather mechanically a role he had played in dozens of previous pictures, while Chaplin, obligated to conform to Sterling's style, was reduced to creating an unsubtle caricature, a simplistic version of the masher he had played in ***Mabel's Strange Predicament***."—Harry M. Geduld, *Chapliniana Volume 1: The Keystone Films* (1987).

"Good fun…Not as polished or imaginative as his later films, but a very early gem."—Darren O'Shaughnessy, *The Internet Movie Database* (2000).

†Not to be confused with ***The Flirts***, the working title for ***Getting*** Acquainted (Keystone, 1914).

††Not to be confused with ***In Wrong***, the working title for ***Those Love Pangs*** (Keystone, 1914).

5. *A Film Johnnie*

(One Reel; Released March 2, 1914)

Working title: ***A Movie Bug***

Reissue titles: ***Film Johnny***, ***The Movie Nut***, ***The Million Dollar Job***, ***His Million Dollar Job***

Home-movie editions: ***A Film by Johnny***, ***Charlie the Actor***

Cast: Charlie Chaplin (*a film johnnie*), Roscoe "Fatty" Arbuckle (*himself*), Ford Sterling (*himself*), Edgar Kennedy (*director*), Mack Sennett (*himself*), Virginia Kirtley (*Keystone girl*), Hank Mann (*stagehand*), Henry Lehrman (*himself*); *Missing from print we screened*: Minta Durfee (*nickelodeon patron*), Harry McCoy (*nickelodeon patron sitting next to Chaplin*), George Nichols (*older man on screen*), Billy Gilbert (*nickelodeon usher*).

Credits: Directed by George Nichols. Written by Craig Hutchinson. Photographed by Frank D. Williams.

Plot: Standing out in front of the Keystone studio, a film johnnie ("johnnie" being British slang for a "young fellow") meets Fatty Arbuckle, Ford Sterling, and Mack Sennett as they arrive to work. He then gets past the studio doorman and watches the bustling activity. Charlie is smitten with Keystone player Virginia Kirtley; when he sees an actor giving her a hard time—it's all part of the script—Charlie starts firing a gun to save the damsel-in-distress. A fire breaks out at a neighboring house and the Keystone crew rush to the site, hoping to incorporate footage of the real disaster into one of their productions. But Charlie tags along too, creating further havoc.

Source of print screened: **The Essential Charlie Chaplin Collection Vol. 1** (Delta Entertainment Corporation), under the Exhibitors Pictures Corporation reissue title **Film Johnny**

Comments: **A Film Johnnie** is the first and the weakest of the Chaplin comedies set in a movie studio. In all fairness to the film, however, the muddy-looking print we viewed hardly contributed to our enjoyment of the picture.

Copies currently available on the collector's market are taken from a poor quality Exhibitors Pictures reissue version (from the mid-'30s) which is missing the original opening sequence, which took place in a nickelodeon (a storefront movie theater). In the missing footage, Charlie watches a Keystone film and becomes enamored of Virginia Kirtley, the actress on the screen. After causing a disruption in the theater, he heads for the Keystone Studio to meet Virginia.

At this point, Chaplin's screen appearance is still inconsistent. Oddly, he doesn't have his trademark cane until he picks one up at the studio. His character remains a heavy smoker; the film's best gag has him firing a gun to light a cigarette. Another bit has Chaplin pouring a glass of water in his ear, then spitting water out of his mouth—a gag he would be using as late as **The Great Dictator** (1940).

A Film Johnnie presents Charlie as an outsider, a disruptive spectator on the fringe of the action—as he was in the simpler, funnier **Kid Auto Races at Venice**. Chaplin was adept at executing the comic chaos, but at this point, he was still in search of a distinctive personality.

Edgar Kennedy (1890-1948) plays a director in **A Film Johnnie**. Kennedy would appear in several other Chaplin Keystones, and go on to a successful career as a supporting player for other comedians (Laurel & Hardy, The Marx Brothers, Harold Lloyd, Our Gang) and as the star of his own comedy shorts series for RKO Pictures.

Hank Mann (1887-1971) also appears in the film as a stagehand. Mann would later appear in many other Keystone comedies, including several with Chaplin. His association with Chaplin continued on through **City Lights** (1931; as the tough boxer), **Modern Times** (1936), and **The Great Dictator** (1940).

From today's perspective, **A Film Johnnie**'s most interesting aspect is the behind-the-scenes look at the Keystone operation. When the film crew rushes to the burning house so they can shoot footage of it, you can see the Keystone method in action.

Other Views and Reviews: "The sensation of the year is the success of Chas. Chaplin, whom trade reviewers declare far funnier in Keystones than even in 'Mum-

ming Birds.' One of his films is *A Film Johnnie*...All the Keystone heads are in this and it is packed with indescribably funny incidents."—*The Cinema* (1914).
"Edgar English's [*sic*] work in this picture will keep it amusing."—*The Motion Picture World* (1914).
"*A Film Johnnie* was the first film in which some evolution of the Tramp is discernible; it was also the first film in which Chaplin played the lead in a *preplanned* story film."—Harry M. Geduld, *Chapliniana Volume 1: The Keystone Films* (1987).
"A lightweight and amusing little film [that] captures a time when Chaplin hadn't made the grade just yet."—wmorrow59, *The Internet Movie Database* (2002).

6. *Tango Tangles*
(One Reel; Released March 9, 1914)
Working title: *A Midnight Dance*
Reissue titles: *Charlie's Recreation*†, *The Music Hall*††, *Tango Tangle*
Cast: Charlie Chaplin (*drunk*), Ford Sterling (*trumpet-playing bandleader*), Roscoe "Fatty" Arbuckle (*clarinetist*), Minta Durfee (*hat check girl*), Edgar Kennedy (*bystander who helps Chaplin up off the floor*), Chester Conklin (*dancer in police costume*), Al St. John (*dancer in convict costume*), Glen Cavender (*drummer and dancer*), Hank Mann (*dancer*), George Jeske (*dancer*), Billy Gilbert (*guest in cowboy hat*).
Credits: Written and directed by Mack Sennett. Photographed by Frank D. Williams.
Plot: At a packed dance hall, an inebriated Charlie flirts with the hat check girl (Minta Durfee), which infuriates her boyfriend, the bandleader (Ford Sterling).
Source of print screened: *The Essential Charlie Chaplin Collection Vol. 1* (Delta Entertainment Corporation), under the W. H. Productions reissue title *Charlie's Recreation*
Comments: Chaplin usually played older characters in his stage routines, so when he first met Mack Sennett, the producer was surprised by the 24-year-old's youthful appearance. In his initial films, Chaplin's makeup belied his real age, but in *Tango Tangles*, his sixth Keystone comedy, he and fellow comedians Ford Sterling and Fatty Arbuckle eschew their familiar images, although they still behave in the typical Keystone manner. (Unlike Chaplin and Sterling, however, Arbuckle didn't sport comic mustaches and beards.) Chaplin is neatly dressed, with only a derby and cane to hint at his standard Tramp outfit.

With three rivals (Sterling, Chaplin, Arbuckle) vying for one girl, *Tango Tangles* is merely a Keystone "park" comedy that's been moved to an indoor location. Even though he portrays a smartly-dressed drunk, Chaplin behaves just like the Tramp would in the same situation: smiling, flirting, and using his foot to nudge someone. Once again he's more of a solo performer than an ensemble player, only this time he becomes directly involved in the main action rather than flitting about the periphery.

Chaplin and Sterling resort to fisticuffs to settle their differences, which results in Charlie winding up his arm to deliver a slap to his opponent's face. This and other gestures would be refined and expanded for the boxing match routines in such later Chaplin films as *The Champion* (1915) and *City Lights* (1931). And Chaplin would use intoxication as a source for humor throughout his film career: *His Favorite Pastime* (1914), *A Night Out* (1915), *One A. M.* (1916), *City Lights* (1931), and *Limelight* (1952), to name a few.

Arbuckle appeared briefly with Chaplin in *A Film Johnnie*, and here in *Tango Tangles* they have no real interaction to speak of (throughout the film, it's either Chaplin vs. Sterling or Sterling vs. Arbuckle). Arbuckle would play supporting roles in other Chaplin Keystones (*His Favorite Pastime*, *The Masquerader*, *His New Profession*), and Chaplin returned the favor by appearing as the fight referee in Arbuckle's *The Knockout*. The two comedians would share footage equally in *The Rounders*, one of the better Keystone releases of the period. (For more on Arbuckle, see the entry on *The Knockout*.)

Most of the dance floor scenes were filmed at an actual ballroom, where a crowd of nonprofessionals gets a big charge out of witnessing the impromptu horseplay. (We guess you had to be there.) Though it's an interesting document of an actual event, this footage has an amateur home movie air about it, lacking the technical polish of the studio-lensed inserts that showcase the Keystone regulars.

Overall, *Tango Tangles* is unremarkable Keystone fare. It does, however, have an undeniable novelty value in presenting a fresh-faced young Charlie Chaplin at the beginning of his movie career.

Other Views and Reviews: "The ballroom is soon converted into a battlefield, which results in this Keystone being a real scream!"—*The Cinema* (1914).

"For its glimpse of dapper Chaplin, so young, so handsome, so acrobatic, this little film is unique."—Denis Gifford, *Chaplin* (1974).

†Not to be confused with *Recreation* (Keystone, 1914).

††Not to be confused with *Charlie at the Music Hall*, a home movie edition of *A Night in the Show* (Essanay, 1915).

7. *His Favorite Pastime*
(One Reel; Released March 16, 1914)
Working title: **The Drunk**
Reissue titles: **The Bonehead, Charlie the Bonehead, The Reckless Fling, His Reckless Fling, Charlie's Reckless Fling, Charlie is Thirsty**
Cast: Charlie Chaplin (*drunk*), Roscoe "Fatty" Arbuckle (*drunk*), Peggy Pearce (*wife*), Edgar Kennedy (*drinking companion*), Harry McCoy (*bar patron*), Gene Marsh (*household member*), Billy Gilbert (*shoeshine man*).
Credits: Directed by George Nichols. Written by Craig Hutchinson. Photographed by Frank D. Williams.
Plot: Charlie's favorite pastime is belting 'em down at a neighborhood bar, where he gets into numerous scrapes with the other bar patrons. When he finally staggers outside, Charlie eyes a young woman (Peggy Pearce); he follows her home, which enrages the girl, her husband, and their household staff.
Source of print screened: **The Essential Charlie Chaplin Collection Vol. 1** (Delta Entertainment Corporation), under the French title **Charlot est Trop Galant**
Comments: Chaplin collectors already know that the print quality of the Keystones currently available on DVD varies wildly. Even with lowered expectations, however, this copy of **His Favorite Pastime**, taken from a French reissue, is simply horrendous. The picture is fuzzy and washed out, with the tops of the actors' heads cropped off. This only compounds our negative reaction to this tedious effort, which encapsulates everything that's wrong with Keystone's fly-by-the-seat-of-your-pants style of moviemaking. Free-wheeling improvisation is one thing—just going through a series of motions to fill out a reel of film is another.

After appearing *au naturel*, so to speak, in **Tango Tangles**, Chaplin is back in his Tramp outfit. He plays a drunk once again, and for the first time he's the central figure who creates the action rather than one who feeds off another player. Unfortunately, his obnoxious behavior negates the appeal of the physical humor, particularly one otherwise impressive moment when tipsy Charlie attempts to walk up a flight of stairs, falls over the banister, lands on a chaise lounge, then nonchalantly lights a cigarette as though nothing out of the ordinary has occurred. Throughout **His Favorite Pastime**, Charlie is an ill-tempered inebriate whose antagonism toward others results in his first cinematic free-for-all in which he pummels multiple opponents.

Unlike later Chaplin films, his romantic interest in the young lady has a decidedly foul air about it. He's a nasty drunk who follows a married woman back to her home...did they use the term "stalker" back in 1914? When he gets his final come-uppance†, the audience feels he's gotten his just desserts—hardly the desired effect of Chaplin's later work!

Chaplin does add a new bit to his repertoire: smashing the top of his hat with a cane to create a crease down the middle, transforming his derby into a make-shift homburg. (This bit would be repeated in *Twenty Minutes of Love*, *His New Profession*, and other Keystones.)

Other Views and Reviews: "It is absolutely the funniest thing the Keystone Company has ever put out, and this is not written by a press agent."—*Motion Picture News* (1914).

"Chaplin has created an entirely new variety of screen comedian—a weird figure in whom one may recognize elements of the dude, the tramp, the acrobat, and, flavoring all, the 'silly ass' of whom the drunken swell in 'Mumming Birds' was so perfect a type. This extraordinary character wanders through the recent Keystone releases—there is no other word to describe the Chaplin touch—and indulges in escapades which are side-splitting in their weird absurdity and their amazing suddenness."—*Kinematograph Weekly* (1914).

"This is the prototype of the 'unpleasant' tough film of which so many are found in Chaplin's 1914 output."—Uno Asplund, *Chaplin's Films* (1976).

"'Gentle, lovable, pathetic Charlie' is a much later development...*His Favorite Pastime* contains one of the comedian's more intriguing virtuoso performances and compares favorably with some of his Essanay comedies."—Harry M. Geduld, *Chapliniana Volume 1: The Keystone Films* (1987).

†This version of *His Favorite Pastime* ends with Charlie getting thrown out of the house. A *Syracuse Post-Standard* review from 1914 mentions a different conclusion in which Charlie drives his enemy away with a piece of limburger cheese. This scene is not in any circulating copy of the film.

8. *Cruel, Cruel Love*
(One Reel; Released March 26, 1914)
Working title: **Poison**
Reissue title: **Lord Helpus**
Cast: Charlie Chaplin (*a gentleman†*), Minta Durfee (*fiancée*), Edgar Kennedy (*butler*), Alice Davenport (*maid*), Hank Mann (*gardener*), Glen Cavender (*doctor*), Billy Gilbert (*ambulance attendant*). (Some sources list Chester Conklin in the cast—we didn't spot him.)
Credits: Directed by George Nichols (some sources credit Mack Sennett). Written by Craig Hutchinson. Photographed by Frank D. Williams.

Plot: Charlie's fiancée jumps to the wrong conclusion when she sees him massaging her maid's ankle (the maid had fallen; Charlie was merely making sure she was okay) and breaks off their engagement. Despondent, Charlie attempts suicide by taking poison. In the meantime, his fiancée learns the truth behind the incident and lets him know all is forgiven. A frantic Charlie phones his doctor and discovers that the supposed poison was only water.

Source of print screened: ***The Essential Charlie Chaplin Collection Vol. 2*** (Delta Entertainment Corporation)

Comments: Forsaking his Tramp costume, Charlie appears in a modified version of his outfit from ***Making a Living***, wearing a mustache that's been trimmed down from the drooping one he sported in his first film. For most of its length, ***Cruel, Cruel Love*** is farcical, with much footage devoted to Chaplin's deliberately overplayed reactions to his supposed suicide attempt. Chaplin would eventually abandon this sort of broad facial gesturing; nonetheless, he seems to be enjoying himself immensely and it's fascinating to watch him spin completely out of control. Though more story-driven than usual, this is still a Keystone comedy, and it ends with a frantic free-for-all.

Seen here as Charlie's fiancée, Minta Durfee (1891-1975) was a Keystone regular who was married to Roscoe "Fatty" Arbuckle during this period. She appeared in several Arbuckle films, as well as the Chaplin Keystones ***Making a Living***, ***The Star Boarder***, ***Caught in a Cabaret***, ***The New Janitor***, ***Tillie's Punctured Romance***, ***A Film Johnnie***, ***Tango Tangles***, ***The Masquerader***, ***The Knockout***, and ***The Rounders*** (the latter five also featured Arbuckle).

In his later films, Chaplin would reuse or embellish an idea that dated back to his Keystone days. In this instance, Charlie's false-poison hysterics in ***Cruel, Cruel Love*** would be reworked to greater comic effect in his brilliant ***Monsieur Verdoux*** (1947). (In ***Cruel, Cruel Love***, Chaplin even looks like a younger version of his Henri Verdoux character.)

Despite some interesting flourishes—including a brief fantasy scene of Charlie taunted by devils in Hell—***Cruel, Cruel Love*** is strictly for Chaplin completists who will cross this one off their list after they've viewed it. (One down, eighty to go.)

Other Views and Reviews: "Slight in texture, but it makes a pleasing, laughable picture."—*The Moving Picture World* (1914).

"***Cruel, Cruel Love*** is far from the subtlest of Chaplin's early performances. During most of the film he deliberately overacts for comic effect. But he does give us a few finer brush strokes, mainly in the 'wooing' sequence that opens the picture."—Harry M. Geduld, *Chapliniana Volume 1: The Keystone Films* (1987).

"Chaplin is enjoyably hammy in this very early role...an unusually funny Keystone comedy."—wmorrow59, *The Internet Movie Database* (2002).

†Chaplin's character is unidentified in the print we viewed. Other versions cite his character name as "Lord Helpus" and "Mr. Dovey."

9. *The Star Boarder*

(One Reel; Released April 4, 1914)

Reissue titles: **The Landlady's Pet**, **The Hash-House Hero**, **The Fatal Lantern**, **In Love with His Landlady**

Cast: Charlie Chaplin (*the landlady's pet*), Minta Durfee (*the landlady*), Edgar Kennedy (*the landlord*), Gordon Griffith (*son*), Alice Davenport (*the lady friend*), Harry McCoy (*boarder who assists the magic lantern show*), Billy Gilbert (*boarder*).

Credits: Directed by George Nichols (some sources credit Mack Sennett). Written by Craig Hutchinson. Photographed by Frank D. Williams.

Plot: Charlie is the apple of his landlady's eye and is always given preferential treatment—a fact that doesn't sit too well with her husband, their young son, and the other boarding house tenants. While Charlie flirts with the landlady and her husband spends some quality time with his lady friend, the son snaps incriminating photos of both couples. Their dalliances are exposed when the boy puts on a magic lantern show for the boarders.

Source of print screened: **The Essential Charlie Chaplin Collection Vol. 2** (Delta Entertainment Corporation), under the W. H. Productions reissue title **The Landlady's Pet**

Comments: **The Star Boarder** isn't a particularly funny outing, but it does represent a marked improvement over most of his previous Keystones. Once again he's the central figure, and this time there's a more logical progression of events than you'd normally find in a Sennett comedy. Perhaps Chaplin's influence was finally taking hold. And though he's dressed as the Tramp, his character is not perceived as one nor does he perceive himself as one.

The film marks the first time a child figures prominently in a Chaplin comedy. Gordon Griffith (1907-1958), who plays the landlady's son, also appeared with Chaplin in the Keystones **Kid Auto Races at Venice**, **Caught in a Cabaret**, **The Fatal Mallet**, and **Tillie's Punctured Romance**. Children would have significant roles in later Chaplins, such as "Dinky" Dean Riesner in **The Pilgrim** (1923) and Michael Chaplin (one of Charlie's sons) in **A King in New York** (1957). But no child actor made more of an impact in a Chaplin film than Jackie Coogan did in **The Kid** (1921). Under Chaplin's direction, Coogan matches his co-star's performing brilliance.

In *The Star Boarder*, Chaplin shows he was beginning to develop his own comedic personality, as evidenced in a scene where he merrily prances toward a beer-filled icebox or later when he nervously tries to conceal a stolen pie. Little moments like these distinguish this minor effort from other early Keystones.

(Unfortunately, a persistent video scratch during the middle portion of the film mars the copies of *The Star Boarder* available from Delta Entertainment and Brentwood Home Video.)

Other Views and Reviews: "A very funny comedy."—*Motion Picture News* (1914). "Up to this point—his ninth film—no specific Charlie persona had really emerged. Although in most of these one-reel films the tramp costume is present and the free-wheeling, audacious, confident charm dominates, this is not yet the Tramp."—John McCabe, *Charlie Chaplin* (1978).

"The most charming of this group of films supervised by Sennett…has the verve and simplicity of a comic strip."—David Robinson, *Chaplin: His Life and Art* (1985).

"The comedy emphasis is on situation rather than character. Accordingly, the film is one of Chaplin's lesser Keystones."—Harry M. Geduld, *Chapliniana Volume 1: The Keystone Films* (1987).

10. *Mabel at the Wheel*

(Two Reels; Released April 18, 1914)

Working title: **Racing Queen**

Reissue titles: **A Hot Finish, His Daredevil Queen**

Cast: Mabel Normand (*Mabel*), Charlie Chaplin (*the villainous sportsman*), Harry McCoy (*Mabel's boyfriend*), Chester Conklin (*Mabel's father*), William Hauber (*Mabel's co-driver*), Mack Sennett (*bumpkin*), Edgar Kennedy (*spectator*), Mack Swain (*spectator*), Alice Davenport (*spectator*), Charles Parrott [Charley Chase] (*spectator*), Al St. John (*henchman*), William A. Seiter (*henchman*), Joe Bordeaux (*dubious character*).

Credits: Written and directed by Mabel Normand and Mack Sennett.

Plot: Charlie kidnaps Mabel's boyfriend right before the start of the Vanderbilt Cup auto race. Mabel takes his place at the wheel; despite Charlie's efforts to sabotage her, Mabel wins the race.

Source of print screened: **Charlie Chaplin Keystone Shorts Vol. 5** (Golden Hollywood Video)

Comments: Just when it looked as though Chaplin's film career was beginning an upward climb, along came **Mabel at the Wheel**, his first two-reeler, which marked a huge regression. Some historians have speculated that his role was originally intended for Ford Sterling, which would be in keeping with the kind of comic villains Sterling often played. Chaplin even wears Sterling's trademark goatee and frock coat; however, it's a poor fit, and an awkward throwback to his first film, **Making a Living**. Not that Chaplin is bad in the role; his dastardly deeds are often quite humorous. But he's clearly being forced to operate on a level below his potential.

Ironically, **Mabel at the Wheel** is an above-average vehicle for star comedienne Mabel Normand, who registers well as the plucky heroine. Many Chaplin books have recounted the oft-told tale of the friction between Charlie and Mabel during the production of this film…so who are we to buck tradition? As the story goes, Charlie suggested a gag that was roundly dismissed by Mabel, who was acting as the nominal director. This led to harsh words, a tearful reaction from Mabel, and Chaplin's refusal to work with her. Mack Sennett—romantically involved with Mabel at the time—reprimanded Charlie, who contemplated quitting the studio. (Chester Conklin persuaded Chaplin to stick around; see entry on **Dough and Dynamite**.) The next day, the situation was smoothed over when Sennett agreed to let Chaplin direct his own films if he'd cooperate with Mabel. (Chaplin would later discover that Sennett's immediate change in attitude stemmed from a telegram he received from the New York office, requesting more Charlie Chaplin product.)

The rift between Chaplin and Normand was resolved amicably, and they would continue to appear together in additional Keystone films, such as **Caught in a Cabaret**, **The Fatal Mallet**, **Mabel's Busy Day**, **Mabel's Married Life**, **His Trysting Place**, **Getting Acquainted**, and **Tillie's Punctured Romance**. In Samuel Goldwyn's book *Behind the Screen* (G. H. Doran, 1923), Mabel Normand remembered Chaplin fondly:

> *They didn't really appreciate Charlie in those early days. I remember numerous times when people in the studio came up and asked me confidentially, "Say, do you think he's so funny? In my mind he can't touch Ford Sterling." They were just so used to slapstick that imaginative comedy couldn't penetrate.*

In later years, Chaplin would also recall Normand with great affection. (For more on Mabel Normand, see entry on **Tillie's Punctured Romance**.)

William A. Seiter (1892-1964) plays one of Chaplin's henchmen in **Mabel at the Wheel**. Seiter would become a noted director of comedies, working with Laurel & Hardy (**Sons of the Desert**, 1934), The Marx Brothers (**Room Service**,

1938), Abbott & Costello (*Little Giant*, 1946), and Wheeler & Woolsey (*Girl Crazy*, 1932; *Diplomaniacs*, 1933).

Other Views and Reviews: "This is a Keystone comedy, having said which you proceed to qualify by all the adjectives standing for funny, burlesque, grotesque, farcical or screaming that you can think of, and leave with the fear that you have not done it justice."—*New York Dramatic Mirror* (1914).

"The addition of a rather obnoxious goatee and some notably vicious behavior suggest his role to be as substitute for Ford Sterling, who had recently left Keystone."—Glenn Mitchell, *The Chaplin Encyclopedia* (1997).

11. *Twenty Minutes of Love*
(One Reel; Released April 20, 1914)
Working title: **Passing of Time**
Reissue titles: **He Loved Her So**, **Cops and Watches**, **The Love-Fiend**
Cast: Charlie Chaplin (*tramp*), Chester Conklin (*pickpocket*), Emma Clifton (*pickpocket's girlfriend*), Minta Durfee (*woman*), Edgar Kennedy (*her lover*), Josef Swickard (*rightful owner of watch*).
Credits: Written and directed by Charlie Chaplin. Photographed by Frank D. Williams.
Plot: During a stroll in the park, Charlie steals a watch from a pickpocket, then gives it to the pickpocket's girlfriend in an effort to impress her, leading to altercations with the thief, the rightful owner of the watch, and the law.
Source of print screened: **The Essential Charlie Chaplin Collection Vol. 2** (Delta Entertainment Corporation)
Comments: So why did they call this **Twenty Minutes of Love** when it only runs ten minutes? Granted, a film's title and running time don't necessarily have to correspond with each other. **Nine ½ Weeks** doesn't run as long as its title…though it sure feels like it.

Anyway, this was Chaplin's directorial debut, although other sources, including his autobiography, give that distinction to **Caught in the Rain**. During the making of **Mabel at the Wheel**, Mack Sennett agreed to let Chaplin start writing and directing his own comedies, with an additional payment of $25 per film for his directorial services. In return for this creative freedom, Chaplin volunteered a $1500 deposit (which was his entire life's savings at the time) in the event his efforts failed to produce a releasable picture.

Fortunately for Chaplin and Sennett, **Twenty Minutes of Love** was releasable and proved popular with critics and moviegoers alike. It doesn't seem all that funny today, but it indicates that Chaplin was honing his skills on both sides of the camera. Even though it was completed in a single afternoon, the film shows more care in its conception and execution than most other Keystones. Chaplin the director allows Charlie the comedian more time for pantomime. He's still quick to kick someone, but now he reacts before doing so. Before relieving the pickpocket of the watch, Charlie looks into the camera and indicates his intentions to us. The gracefulness of his gestures in this and other scenes are a hint of better things on the horizon.

However, the Tramp characterization is still rough around the edges. In the opening sequence, two lovers are smooching on a park bench, and Charlie mocks them by hugging a tree and kissing its trunk. The later, fully mature Tramp would never mock love (though he playfully imitates a giddy married couple in **Modern Times**), and often envied it from afar. True love would become something the Tramp would aspire to, a condition of the heart he would hold sacred.

While **Twenty Minutes of Love** isn't one of Chaplin's crowning achievements, it shows that he was establishing a unique character in a sea of Keystone caricatures. He was no longer an interchangeable cog in the Sennett wheel of mayhem.

Other Views and Reviews: "Plenty of the comic element is introduced and the person who does not laugh at the peculiar antics of Chas. Chaplin—well, must be hard to please."—*Kinematograph Weekly* (1914).

"One of the slightest of [Chaplin's] 'park' films. Nevertheless there are developing traits of the later Charlie character. There is a sweetness about his mischief and flirtations, and a touch of the romantic."—David Robinson, *Chaplin: His Life and Art* (1985).

"The most inventive of all Chaplin's Keystones to date."—Harry M. Geduld, *Chapliniana Volume 1: The Keystone Films* (1987).

12. *Caught in a Cabaret*
(Two Reels; Released April 27, 1914)
Working title: **The Waiter**
Reissue titles: **The Waiter†, The Jazz Waiter, Faking with Society**
Home-movie editions: **Charlie the Waiter, Prime Minister Charlie, Café Society**
Cast: Charlie Chaplin (*Charlie, alias O. T. Axle, Ambassador for Greece*), Mabel Normand (*Mabel*), Chester Conklin (*waiter*), Harry McCoy (*Count Rendered*), Edgar Kennedy (*café owner*), Minta Durfee (*dancer*), Josef Swickard (*father*), Alice Davenport (*mother*) Mack Swain (*man in park* and *tough guy in cabaret*),

Gordon Griffith (*boy*), Hank Mann (*dancer with eye patch*), Glen Cavender (*pianist*), Gene Marsh (*maid*), Billy Gilbert (*cabaret patron*).

Credits: Written and directed by Mabel Normand and Charlie Chaplin. (Normand also received producer's credit.) Photography by Frank D. Williams.

Plot: Charlie works as a waiter in a seedy cabaret. While walking his dog, he saves a society girl from a robbery and impresses her further by passing himself off as a foreign diplomat. The deception works. Invited to a society party, Charlie has a grand time, then hurries back to the cabaret. In the meantime, a jealous rival has discovered Charlie's true identity and suggests a "slumming" party. He takes the society folks down to the cabaret, where Charlie is exposed as a fraud and all hell breaks loose.

Source of print screened: ***The Essential Charlie Chaplin Collection Vol. 2*** (Delta Entertainment Corporation)

Comments: The first two-reel comedy Chaplin directed (or, more precisely, co-directed), ***Caught in a Cabaret*** introduces themes that would recur in his later work. It's a prototype for the superior ***The Count*** (Mutual, 1916) and ***The Rink*** (Mutual, 1916), and echoes of it can be found in ***The Adventurer*** (Mutual, 1917), ***The Idle Class*** (First National, 1921), and ***City Lights*** (United Artists, 1931). Unlike those films, however, Charlie's deception in ***Caught in a Cabaret*** is for purely self-indulgent reasons; it doesn't yield any gallant or altruistic results.

   Caught in a Cabaret is also the first film in which Chaplin's character is gainfully employed, and establishes the kind of combative relationships he would have with his onscreen co-workers. His encounter with a large cabaret patron foreshadows the David-Goliath altercations that would figure prominently throughout his career.

   At this juncture, his onscreen relationship with animals is perfunctory; they're just props or convenient plot devices. Here, Charlie's pet dog, a dachshund, is around because it's funny-looking and walking it gives his character a reason to be away from the cabaret. In later films like ***The Champion*** (Essanay, 1915) and ***A Dog's Life*** (First National, 1918), Charlie's dogs would be more than ornaments—they'd be allies and companions in a cold, cruel world, and Charlie would treat them with extreme tenderness.

   Caught in a Cabaret reveals the progress Chaplin had made within such a short duration. He seems far more comfortable in front of the camera, and there's even time for some quietly charming moments between Charlie and Mabel. But these scenes are undermined by a reliance on typically frenetic—and pointless—Keystone chaos that ends without a satisfying narrative resolution. (To add insult to injury, the reissue version we viewed had a "gagged up" ending in which reverse printing is used to make it look like Mabel keeps knocking Charlie to the floor and he keeps springing back up again. *Har-de-har-har.*)

Fortunately, Chaplin was destined to rise above this kind of formulaic film-making.

Other Views and Reviews: "Superlatives are dangerous epithets, especially when dealing with pictures. For that reason it is unwise to call this the funniest picture that has ever been produced, but it comes mighty close to it."—*New York Dramatic Mirror* (1914).

"Charlie's adventures as a poseur in this early film are far less funny and far less pointed than in later films with the same motif."—Gerald Mast, *The Comic Mind* (1973).

"There was something of the dundreary dude from his first film [*Making a Living*] here, but with greater depth. Charlie was no longer the con man out for cash at any cost, he was looking for love."—Denis Gifford, *Chaplin* (1974).

"Mabel Normand and Charlie Chaplin together! A joy! Their playing is far subtler and wittier than that of their contemporaries at Keystone or at the other comedy studios. Their chemistry is great together."—Tom Sanchez, *The Internet Movie Database* (2002).

†Not to be confused with the 8mm home movie condensations of *The Rink* (Mutual, 1916) which were retitled *The Waiter* and *Waiter!*

13. *Caught in the Rain*
(One Reel; Released May 4, 1914)
Working title: *All Wrong*
Reissue titles: *At It Again*, *Who Got Stung?*
Home-movie editions: *In the Park*†, *Day's End*, *Sleepless Night*, *Charlie and the Sleepwalker*
Cast: Charlie Chaplin (*Charlie*), Mack Swain (*husband*), Alice Davenport (*wife*), Alice Howell (*woman*).
Credits: Written and directed by Charlie Chaplin. Photographed by Frank D. Williams.
Plot: Charlie meets a woman in the park and flirts with her until her irate husband comes along. Charlie then checks into a hotel and gets a room, as luck would have it, right across the hall from the husband and wife he encountered earlier. The wife is a sleepwalker; during her unconscious state, she wanders into Charlie's room and winds up in his bed. Charlie wakes her up and takes her back to her own room, only to run afoul of the jealous husband once again.

Source of print screened: **The Essential Charlie Chaplin Collection Vol. 5** (Delta Entertainment Corporation), under the Official Films title **In the Park**

Comments: **Caught in the Rain** was released to the home-movie market by Official Films as **In the Park**, which was also the title of one of Chaplin's later comedies for Essanay. It's been a source of confusion ever since, because several distributors have used the Official Films version for video and DVD transfers, identifying it as the Essanay picture.

Chaplin's second directorial effort begins as a "park" comedy and turns into a standard Keystone marital farce, with all the usual elements firmly in place (i.e., running around hallways, slamming doors, hyperactive cops). Under Chaplin's guidance, his character was becoming the focal point of the action. While there's nothing new going on here, Chaplin is already adept at setting up a situation and keeps the action moving at a brisk pace.

One memorable scene has an apparently drunk Charlie attempting to walk up the hotel staircase. Before he can reach the top, he tumbles backwards, landing at the foot of the stairs. Undaunted, he tries again and again until he finally makes it all the way. Chaplin would expand upon this idea in two of his later comedies for Mutual, **The Floorwalker** (1916) and **One A. M.** (1916).

Other Views and Reviews: "The climax comes when [Chaplin] takes part in a comical sleep-walking scene at the hotel. His explanations cause a riotous finale."—*Bioscope* (1914).

"This remains one of the most accomplished films of Chaplin's year at Keystone. The film has clarity, verve, a musical or balletic rhythm in the rapid cutting; it is still entertaining and amusing after seventy years."—David Robinson, *Chaplin: His Life and Art* (1985).

"Although this is not an earth-shaking classic, this is a very pleasant little film. But if you're looking for a work of a comic genius, this is not it. Chaplin never did any of those at Keystone. Their brand of farce did not really suit him."—boblipton, *The Internet Movie Database* (2002).

†Not to be confused with **In the Park**, the working title for **Recreation** (Keystone, 1914), and **In the Park** (Essanay, 1915).

14. *A Busy Day*
(Split Reel†; Released May 7, 1914)
Working title: **San Pedro**
Reissue titles: **The Militant Suffragette, Busy As Can Be, Lady Charlie**
Cast: Charlie Chaplin (*wife*), Mack Swain (*husband*), Mack Sennett (*movie director*), Billy Gilbert (*cop*).

Credits: Written and directed by Charlie Chaplin (some sources credit George Nichols as the director). Photographed by Frank D. Williams.

Plot: While watching a military parade, a jealous wife (Chaplin) catches her husband sneaking off with a young lady.

Source of print screened: *The Essential Charlie Chaplin Collection Vol. 2* (Delta Entertainment Corporation), under the W. H. Productions reissue title *The Militant Suffragette*

Comments: *A Busy Day* is another example of the Keystone crew attending an actual event (in this case, a military parade celebrating the opening of the harbor in San Pedro, California) and having the actors improvise something—*anything*—around the proceedings. This is Keystone filmmaking at its emptiest, scraping the bottom of the comedic barrel in an effort to grind out yet another movie (a split reel, for cryin' out loud) as quickly as possible, with Chaplin and Mack Swain putting on a human Punch-and-Judy show.

However, it is notable for being only one of three films in which Chaplin appeared in drag. Unlike the other two—*The Masquerader* (Keystone, 1914) and *A Woman* (Essanay, 1915)—Charlie portrays a female character, not a man disguised as a woman. There's also an interesting scene that recalls *Kid Auto Races at Venice*, in which the jealous wife notices a director and his cameraman filming the event and tries to get herself into many of the shots, only to be repeatedly shoved out of the way. It's just a throwaway bit, but in a picture like *A Busy Day*, it's a major highlight.

Although it is generally assumed that Chaplin directed this effort, some observers suspect that this may actually be the work of one of the stock Keystone directors, like George Nichols. Whoever it was, we doubt that anyone was eager to take credit—or assume blame—for this endeavor.

Other Views and Reviews: "[Chaplin] gives an amazing exhibition of acrobatic humor."—*Bioscope* (1914).

"Chaplin's first on-screen female impersonation follows the knockabout tradition of British pantomime dame, in which respect it differs from later examples in *The Masquerader* and *A Woman*."—Glenn Mitchell, *The Chaplin Encyclopedia* (1997).

"Even by [Keystone's] slapdash methods, this was a cursory effort...It's not especially funny, but it has some historical value as an early example of on-the-fly filmmaking."—F. Gwynplaine MacIntyre, *The Internet Movie Database* (2003).

†The other half of the reel was *The Morning Papers*, an educational short purchased from an outside company for distribution by Keystone.

15. *The Fatal Mallet*

(One Reel; Released June 1, 1914)

Working title: ***The Knockout***†

Reissue titles: ***The Pile Driver***, ***Hit Him Again***, ***The Rival Suitors***

Cast: Charlie Chaplin (*Charlie*), Mabel Normand (*Mabel*), Mack Sennett (*suitor*), Mack Swain (*suitor*), Gordon Griffith (*little boy*).

Credits: Written and directed by Mack Sennett (some sources credit Charlie Chaplin and Mabel Normand as co-directors). Photographed by Frank D. Williams.

Plot: Charlie and Mack Sennett both have romantic designs on Mabel. When Mack Swain, a third rival, enters the picture, they resort to using a mallet and bricks to get rid of the competition.

Source of print screened: ***The Essential Charlie Chaplin Collection Vol. 2*** (Delta Entertainment Corporation)

Comments: If you thought ***A Busy Day*** was the pinnacle of creative desperation, it looks like ***Some Like It Hot*** compared to ***The Fatal Mallet***. A tired rehash of the standard "park" comedy formula, this is the sort of film that gives Keystone and early Chaplin a bad reputation, with Sennett's heavy-handed "technique" hitting an all-time low. In one particularly nasty exchange, Chaplin kicks a kid in the stomach; by contrast, this makes the brick-throwing and mallet-swinging seem positively genteel. (Curiously, we're not bothered by the physical abuse Charlie heaps on his elderly assistant in ***The Property Man***, a later Keystone effort. Go figure.)

The Three Stooges had the rare ability to raise violence to a comedic art form; as an actor and director, Sennett had no such gift. When he turned up as a performer in his own films, Sennett invariably chose to play rubes and bumpkins. Evidently, he found this type of humor appealing. No wonder he and Chaplin were oceans apart in their views on comedy.

If you've never seen a Chaplin Keystone—or *any* Chaplin film, for that matter—we beg you not to start with ***The Fatal Mallet***. Trust us. After all, wouldn't you warn someone about ***Freddie Got Fingered***?

Other Views and Reviews: "This one-reeler proves that hitting people over the head with bricks and mallets can sometimes be made amusing."—*The Moving Picture World* (1914).

"Whatever else it may be, ***The Fatal Mallet*** is unique in presenting Chaplin's only onscreen confrontation with Sennett. It is also the only film appearance of the quartet of Chaplin, Mabel, Sennett, and Mack Swain."—Harry M. Geduld, *Chapliniana Volume 1: The Keystone Films* (1987).

"Rough stuff, even by Keystone-Chaplin standards…*Fatal Mallet*'s reliance on one-dimensional violence was adequate in 1914 [but] posterity takes a different view."—Glenn Mitchell, *The Chaplin Encyclopedia* (1997).

"A nice little comedy."—boblipton, *The Internet Movie Database* (2002).

†Not to be confused with *The Knockout* (Keystone, 1914).

16. *Her Friend the Bandit*

(One Reel; Released June 4, 1914)

Working title: *The Italian*

Reissue titles: *Mabel's Flirtation, A Thief Catcher*

Cast: Charlie Chaplin (*the bandit*), Mabel Normand (*Mabel De Rocks*), Charles Murray (*Count De Beans*), Glen Cavender, William Hauber, Charlotte Singleton, Phillip Tryon.

Credits: Written and directed by Charlie Chaplin (some sources list Mabel Normand as co-director). Photography by Frank D. Williams.

Plot: Count De Beans is captured by a bandit, who assumes the Count's identity and attends a swanky party thrown by Mabel De Rocks. The bandit wrecks havoc with the upper class until the police are called in to take him away.

Source of print screened: Currently unavailable on DVD

Comments: As of this writing, there is no surviving print of *Her Friend the Bandit*. This is the only "lost" Chaplin film. Forty years ago, *Mabel's Strange Predicament*, *A Busy Day*, and *Cruel, Cruel Love* were also considered to be lost, so there's always a chance that a print of *Her Friend the Bandit* will eventually turn up. The plot has similarities to such later Chaplins as *A Jitney Elopement* (Essanay, 1915), *The Count* (Mutual, 1916), *The Rink* (Mutual, 1916), and *The Adventurer* (Mutual, 1917).

In *The Chaplin Encyclopedia* (B. T. Batsford, 1997), Glenn Mitchell notes that some scholars express doubt as to whether Chaplin is in the film at all, a mystery that won't be cleared up until *Her Friend the Bandit* resurfaces.

Other Views and Reviews: "This farce [is] a bit thin; but it has the rough whirling of happenings usually found in farces of this well-marked type."—*The Moving Picture World* (1914).

"An arousing farce."—*Bioscope* (1914).

17. *The Knockout*

(Two Reels; Released June 11, 1914)

Working title: *A Fighting Demon*

Reissue titles: *The Pugilist, Counted Out*

Home-movie editions: **In Training**, **In the Ring**
Cast: Roscoe "Fatty" Arbuckle (*Pug*), Minta Durfee (*his girl*), Al St. John (*rival suitor*), Edgar Kennedy (*Cyclone Flynn*), Charlie Chaplin (*referee*), Hank Mann (*hobo who impersonates Cyclone Flynn*), Mack Swain (*gambler*), Mack Sennett (*fight spectator*), George "Slim" Summerville (*fight spectator*), Charles Parrott [Charley Chase] (*fight spectator*), Billy Gilbert (*vocalist*).
Credits: Directed by Charles Avery (some sources claim Mack Sennett or Roscoe Arbuckle may have been the director). Photographed by Frank D. Williams.
Plot: Egged on by others, Pug enters a "Winner Take All" boxing match against prizefighter Cyclone Flynn. In the ring, Pug and Flynn deliver powerful punches, although the referee receives most of the blows. Pug grabs a pair of guns and begins firing; he chases Flynn out of the arena and across the rooftops. The Keystone Kops try to lasso Pug, but he drags the hapless law enforcers down to the ocean and they all wind up in the water.
Sources of prints screened: **The Forgotten Films of Roscoe "Fatty" Arbuckle** (Laughsmith Entertainment) and **The Essential Charlie Chaplin Collection Vol. 2** (Delta Entertainment Corporation)
Comments: **The Knockout**† is actually a starring vehicle for Fatty Arbuckle, with Chaplin making a brief appearance (although in subsequent reissues, Chaplin was billed as the main attraction, relegating Arbuckle to co-star status). Despite Charlie's limited screen time, the film is a clear-cut example of how his distinctive style outshone standard Keystone antics. As the referee during the boxing sequence, Chaplin uses his dexterity and comic invention to devise seemingly endless variations on the single theme of getting clobbered whenever he gets near the fighters. Not surprisingly, he grabs the viewer's attention the moment he arrives onscreen and keeps it until he departs.

Charles Avery (who gave Chaplin his tiny jacket for the Tramp costume in **Mabel's Strange Predicament**) is often credited as the film's director, although some sources speculate that Arbuckle and Mack Sennett had a hand in the direction. In *Chapliniana Vol. 1: The Keystone Films* (University of Indiana Press, 1987), Harry M. Geduld offers his opinion that Chaplin choreographed the boxing match. This is entirely credible, as the sequence possesses a verve and punch (literally!) lacking from the rest of the film.

Chaplin winds up stealing the picture. With a few short minutes, he's knocked to the canvas, knocks Fatty to the canvas, hangs from the ropes, and slides across the boxing ring using the lower rope like a pulley system. He darts between Arbuckle and Edgar Kennedy, and frequently receives the blows intended for the other fighter. At one point, it's Charlie and Fatty who exchange punches as Kennedy tries to break them apart. This expertly choreographed chaos anticipates *The Champion* (Essanay, 1915) and the boxing scene in *City Lights* (United Artists, 1931).

By all accounts, Fatty Arbuckle was that rare comedian who was never bothered by having another performer upstage him, as Chaplin does here. Arbuckle wisely knew that a funny performance would enhance the overall production, regardless of who was getting the laughs. For further proof of his onscreen generosity, just take a look at his later comedies in which he gives full range to the talents of a young supporting player named Buster Keaton. (Also see *The Rounders*, a later Keystone that showcases a full-fledged Chaplin-Arbuckle teaming.)

Aside from Chaplin's participation, *The Knockout* is pretty flat. To its credit, the gags are motivated by narrative, rather than being a series of isolated skirmishes. But in typical Keystone fashion, the plot is never resolved, as the picture ends with an obligatory chase sequence. While one admires the high spirits and energy level of the Keystone players, the results are exhausting instead of amusing.

Roscoe "Fatty" Arbuckle (1887-1933) was one of the screen's most beloved comedians when Chaplin began at Keystone. Though much of his early work is frenzied and unfocused, Arbuckle established an appealing and sympathetic persona long before Chaplin did. Even in a film as weak as *The Knockout*, Arbuckle endears himself to the audience from his first scene, in which he lets his dog have a piece of his sandwich. (The Keystone Charlie would have kicked the dog rather than give up a portion of his meal.)

Like Chaplin, Arbuckle would eventually leave Keystone, and his later films became much more polished. Arbuckle was one of the greatest comedians of the silent era, and his popularity continued unabated until 1921 when he became the center of one of Hollywood's most notorious celebrity trials. Arbuckle was accused of raping Virginia Rappe, an obscure actress and well-known "party girl." When she died—allegedly as a result of the comedian's physical abuse—the press had a field day, dragging Arbuckle's name through the mud. (Chaplin was among the many loyal friends who called the charges "ludicrous.") Although Arbuckle was acquitted, none of the Hollywood studios supported him and the court of public opinion condemned him. As a result, his once-thriving career was completely destroyed.

Overnight, Arbuckle saw his reputation as the world's favorite fat funnyman dissolve into one of evil personified. Unemployable as a performer, he directed several films under the pseudonym "William Goodrich." Finally, in 1932, the

Warner Brothers studio felt that enough time had passed to take a chance on hiring Arbuckle as an actor. He starred in a series of well-received comedy shorts and was on the verge of a major comeback when he died of a heart attack in 1933 at the age of 46.

Al St. John (1893-1963), Arbuckle's real-life nephew who had a prolific film career (he's "Fuzzy" St. John in many '40s B-Westerns), appears in *The Knockout* as a rival for Minta Durfee's affections. Incidentally, Keystone player Durfee (1891-1975) was married to Arbuckle at the time. For those of you who've seen *Girlfight* (2000) and *Million Dollar Baby* (2004), two recent films dealing with female boxers, it's interesting to note that Durfee's character in *The Knockout* has to disguise herself as a man in order to get in to see the fight, a reminder of an era when women weren't allowed to participate in the male-dominated sport, even as spectators.

The Knockout was reissued in 1920 as *Counted Out*, with Chaplin deceptively given top-billing over Arbuckle. By the following year, the film was withdrawn from circulation—along with all other Arbuckle titles—due to the murder scandal. Not even Chaplin's enormous popularity could override the notoriety.

The DVD copies of *The Knockout* we viewed are a study in extreme contrasts. The version on Delta's *The Essential Charlie Chaplin Collection Vol. 2* is typical of most circulating prints: grayish and somewhat fuzzy. Laughsmith Entertainment's *The Forgotten Films of Roscoe "Fatty" Arbuckle* is a superlative collection of beautifully restored Arbuckle comedies, including *The Knockout* and the later Chaplin-Arbuckle teaming *The Rounders*. *The Knockout* remains one of the lesser Arbuckle efforts, but Laughsmith's restoration is a joy to behold.

Other Views and Reviews: "Roscoe Arbuckle, ably supported, makes barrels of fun in this two-reel comedy release…a big chase, as well as a comedy prize fight, is unusually funny."—*The Moving Picture World* (1914).

"Why isn't this film, which is actually a good bit better than the standard Keystone product of the time, truly funny today? [The Keystones] are successful agitations, successful explorations of elaborate visual possibilities; if laughter once accompanied them, it has to have been the laughter of breathlessness, not the laughter of perception."—Walter Kerr, *The Silent Clowns* (1975).

"Chaplin's refereeing is balletic, and introduces gags of a sophistication alien to the rest of the film."—David Robinson, *Chaplin: His Life and Art* (1985).

"This is one of Chaplin's best although he doesn't star in this film…Charlie is the hilarious referee."—Daniel Dopierala, *The Internet Movie Database* (2002).

†Not to be confused with **The Knockout**, the working title for **The Fatal Mallet** (Keystone, 1914).

18. *Mabel's Busy Day*
(One Reel; Released June 13, 1914)
Working title: **Wiener Story**
Reissue titles: **Hot Dogs, Charlie and the Sausages, Love and Lunch**
Home-movie edition: **Hot Dog Charlie**
Cast: Mabel Normand (*Mabel*), Charlie Chaplin (*sharper*), Chester Conklin (*cop*), Mack Sennett (*customer in straw hat*), George "Slim" Summerville (*cop*), Billie Bennett (*spectator*), Gene Marsh (*spectator*), Harry McCoy (*thief*), Edgar Kennedy (*spectator*), Glen Cavender (*customer*), Al St. John (*bit*), Charles Parrott [Charley Chase] (*bit*).
Credits: Written and directed by Mabel Normand (some sources list Chaplin as co-director). Photographed by Frank D. Williams.
Plot: Mabel, a hot dog vendor, tries to peddle her wares at an auto race, with little success. Charlie has pushed his way past the admissions gate; he protects Mabel from a bully, then steals some of the hot dogs. After altercations with rowdy customers and the police, a now-contrite Charlie comforts a weeping Mabel.
Source of print screened: **Chaplin: The Legend Lives On** (Madacy Home Video)
Comments: **Mabel's Busy Day** doesn't have a plot—it's merely a series of scenes set against a (genuine) motor race. In this respect, it's like an expanded version of **Kid Auto Races at Venice**, Chaplin's second Keystone. Only this time, Charlie reverts to playing a sharper, which probably explains why he's wearing a double-breasted frock coat with a carnation instead of the Tramp costume.

Because this is one of those improvised, fly-by-the-seat-of-your-pants Keystone productions, no time is spent on establishing a narrative. Everyone just runs amuck until a reel of film has elapsed. Mabel is spunky and gets by on the sheer force of her personality. Charlie manages to inject some nice bits of physical comedy; this is the first film in which he rolls his hat down the length of his arm and catches it in his hand. But the frenzied performances only serve to magnify the paucity of material. You know a film isn't working when you spend just as much time watching the real-life spectators in the background as you do the lead actors.

Frantic doesn't equal funny, and **Mabel's Busy Day** is more of an artifact than it is art.

Other Views and Reviews: "Any comedy with Charles Chaplin and Mabel Normand [as] the leads is sure to be an immense success. There is no plot at all, but the events that transpire in the one reel are side-splitting."—*Motion Picture News* (1914).

"A rough and rowdy little piece."—David Robinson, *Chaplin: His Life and Art* (1985).

"One of the nastier Chaplin Keystones. The only funny thing in it is Chaplin's dance around the cops who pursue him onto the racetrack."—Harry M. Geduld, *Chapliniana Volume 1: The Keystone Films* (1987).

19. *Mabel's Married Life*
(One Reel; Released June 20, 1914)
Working title: **His Wife's Birthday**
Reissue titles: **The Squarehead, When You're Married, Charlie and the Mannequin**
Cast: Mabel Normand (*Mabel*), Charlie Chaplin (*her husband*), Mack Swain (*big bully*), Eva Nelson (*bully's wife*), Hank Mann (*bar patron*), Charles Murray (*bar patron*), Al St. John (*deliveryman*), Alice Davenport (*neighbor*).
Credits: Directed by Charlie Chaplin (some sources list Mabel Normand as co-director). Written by Charlie Chaplin and Mabel Normand. Photographed by Frank D. Williams.
Plot: Mabel is dismayed when her husband, Charlie, is unable to subdue a big bully who's been flirting with her. She purchases a boxing dummy from a sporting goods store, hoping he will use it to improve his fighting ability. Charlie comes home drunk, sees the dummy and thinks it's the bully. The intoxicated Charlie is no match for the inanimate object, which keeps knocking him over. To Mabel's amusement, Charlie's jealously subsides once he realizes his mistake.
Source of print screened: **Tillie's Punctured Romance and Mabel's Married Life** (Image Entertainment)
Comments: It's difficult to believe that a film as innovative and assured as **Mabel's Married Life** could follow hot on the heels of something as unfocused and undisciplined as **Mabel's Busy Day**, but it did. This was easily Chaplin's best Keystone effort to date.

By this time, Charlie and Mabel had established an easy rapport as a screen couple. Mabel's subtle comic timing is used to good advantage. Her winsome facial expressions and body language convey a variety of moods; at one point she even does a precise imitation of Chaplin's shuffling walk. **Mabel's Married Life** is one of her finest Keystone vehicles and a prime example of why she was referred to as "the female Chaplin."

Chaplin plays Charlie the married man instead of Charlie the Tramp, which probably explains why he's wearing a top hat instead of his customary derby. (Other than that, the costume is the same.)

The centerpiece of *Mabel's Married Life* is Charlie's drunken encounter with the boxing dummy. Here Chaplin gives his most sustained comic performance thus far. Charlie comes home and, through a drunken haze, mistakes the dummy for the bully he encountered earlier. Ordering the "stranger" out of the apartment, he gives it a swift kick; because the dummy is mounted on a rounded base, it rebounds and strikes Charlie, who is taken aback by this retaliatory gesture. So Charlie tries reasoning with it, cajoling it, and finally using strong-arm tactics to remove the intruder from the premises.

Bolstered by Chaplin's pantomimic skills, this simple idea works beautifully because Charlie never reacts like he's the one who's drunk. On the contrary, he thinks the dummy is intoxicated, and makes a "drinking" gesture with his hand as if to ask the dummy if he's had one too many. While trying to engage the inanimate object in small talk, Charlie belches, then registers disgust, as though the dummy is responsible for such rude behavior. It's a memorable set-piece that anticipates his astonishing solo performance in *One A. M.* (Mutual, 1916).

As the big bully, Mack Swain appears without his trademark (fake) mustache and gives a jaunty performance quite unlike his usual "Ambrose" character. (For more on Swain, see the entry on *His Musical Career.*)

The print of *Mabel's Married Life* we viewed is the edition available from Image Entertainment; it's on the same DVD as the restored *Tillie's Punctured Romance*, Chaplin's feature-length Keystone comedy. Image's copy has been restored and looks great, which certainly added to our enjoyment of the film. Unfortunately, most copies in circulation derive from an inferior, poorly framed French print titled *Charlot et le mannequin.*

Maybe if we saw a pristine copy of *Mabel's Busy Day*, we would hold that one in higher esteem…maybe.

Views and Reviews: "The mix-up between Mabel, Charles and the dummy is extremely funny…Mr. Chaplin gives a very excellent study in inebriation. This is certainly one of the best of the Keystone comedies."—*Bioscope* (1914).

"In *Mabel's Married Life* [Chaplin] had discovered the comic value of believing with intense seriousness in whatever he was doing. What he is doing [is] having a conversation with a dummy…it should be noticed that the sequence would not be possible without its silence; in a talking film, the dummy's failure to speak would destroy the impression that it is responding."—Walter Kerr, *The Silent Clowns* (1975).

"The authenticity of Charlie's drunkenness is an acting lesson. Unlike other comics who cleverly simulate drunkenness, Chaplin—like a real drunk—summons up his thoughts in an attempt to be *sober*…Chaplin looks at the drunk he is portraying from the *drunk's* point of view, not from the view of a skilled comedian trying to be drunk."—John McCabe, *Charlie Chaplin* (1978).

20. *Laughing Gas*
(One Reel; Released July 9, 1914)
Working title: **Dentist Story**
Reissue titles: **The Dentist, Down and Out, Tuning His Ivories**
Home-movie editions: **Laffing Gas, Laffin' Gas, Busy Little Dentist, Filling the Prescription, Filling a Prescription, At the Drug Store, Pulling Teeth**
Cast: Charlie Chaplin (*dentist's assistant*), Fritz Schade (*Dr. Pain*), Mack Swain (*burly bystander*), Alice Howell (*Mrs. Pain*), Gene Marsh (*female patient*), George "Slim" Summerville (*patient*), Josef Swickard (*patient*), Joseph Sutherland (*assistant*).
Credits: Written and directed by Charlie Chaplin. Photographed by Frank D. Williams.
Plot: Charlie works at a dental office run by Dr. Pain. The dentist sends Charlie to the pharmacy to have a prescription filled. During the errand, Charlie gets into a brick-throwing fight with a burly bystander, then flirts with a woman and winds up tearing her skirt off. Unbeknownst to Charlie, the woman is Mrs. Pain, who telephones her husband and tells him to come home immediately. Taking advantage of the dentist's absence, Charlie flirts with a female patient. Having had some teeth knocked out by flying bricks, the burly man goes to the dentist's office; when he spots Charlie, their fight resumes. Then the Pains show up and get involved in the mêlée.
Source of print screened: **The Essential Charlie Chaplin Collection Vol. 3** (Delta Entertainment Corporation), under the Official Films title **Laffing Gas**
Comments: **Laughing Gas** marks the first time we feel as though we're watching a Chaplin Keystone film as opposed to a Keystone film with Chaplin. His Tramp character is the focal figure, with the action revolving entirely around him. Not that the picture represents any particular artistic progress—unless you consider Charlie kicking Mack Swain in the ass *and* the stomach artistic progress.

Laughing Gas exploits the universal fear of having to go to the dentist. Reporting to work, Charlie displays a brazen lack of compassion for the anguished patients waiting in the office, and even winds up slapping a couple of them in the mouth. After a patient has been anaesthetized with "laughing gas,"

Charlie tries to revive him with one of those large mallets that always seem to be within arm's reach in Keystone comedies. Despite the comic potential of the setting, the gags are more outrageous than they are laugh-provoking. Chaplin performs some amusing bits—such as a well-executed "hat roll" (he tips his head, his hat rolls down the length of his arm and he catches it with his hand)—but as a director, he remains overly dependent on the brick-hurling school of Keystone humor.

Dentistry has been a favorite subject for comedians; it certainly underscores the old adage that defines comedy as pain that's being inflicted on someone else. Laurel & Hardy went to the dentist's office in *Leave 'Em Laughing* (1928) and *Pardon Us* (1931), Abbott & Costello made a similar trip in *The Noose Hangs High* (1948), and tooth-extraction was an ingredient of The Three Stooges' *All the World's a Stooge* (1941), *I Can Hardly Wait* (1943), *Pardon My Clutch* (1948), and *Mummy's Dummies* (1948).

Quite often, as in *Laughing Gas*, the comedians were administering the abuse rather than being on the receiving end of it. "Painless" dentist Bob Hope took his practice to the Wild West in *The Paleface* (1948), as did Wheeler & Woolsey in *Silly Billies* (1936), The Three Stooges in *The Tooth Will Out* (1951), and Don Knotts in *The Shakiest Gun in the West* (1968; the remake of *The Paleface*). W. C. Fields was his usual cantankerous self in the title role of *The Dentist* (1932); like *Laughing Gas*, this comedy short was produced by Mack Sennett. Bob Monkhouse was the *Dentist in the Chair* (1960), then the *Dentist on the Job* (1961). Steve Martin pulled out all the stops as a sadistic dentist in the remake of *Little Shop of Horrors* (1986); Bill Murray was his masochistic patient, a role played by Jack Nicholson in the 1960 original. (Martin played a dentist again in *Novocaine* [2001].)

Two of the funniest dental routines weren't even in motion pictures, but on television: befuddled dentist Tim Conway examined an exasperated Harvey Korman on an episode of *The Carol Burnett Show*, while Rowan Atkinson paid a riotous visit to his dentist on *Mr. Bean*. In both instances, the results were inventive and sidesplitting, two virtues lacking, unfortunately, in *Laughing Gas*.

Other Views and Reviews: "This is an uproarious farce of a kind which is likely to create unrestrained mirth for its particular class of audience."—*Bioscope* (1914).

"*Laughing Gas* is one of Chaplin's most anarchic early films: a wholesale mockery of order, dignity, and respectability...The variety of the comic business is impressive."—Harry M. Geduld, *Chapliniana Volume 1: The Keystone Films* (1987).

"While Charlie's brick-throwing seems gratuitous, the dental savagery is executed with the exaggeration and finesse that is essential to remove the sting from this kind of comedy."—Glenn Mitchell, *The Chaplin Encyclopedia* (1997).

"Even making allowances for the poor condition of surviving prints, this one is hard to follow and doesn't offer much in the way of solid laughs."—wmorrow59, *The Internet Movie Database* (2003).

21. *The Property Man*

(Two Reels; Released August 1, 1914)

Reissue titles: **The Roustabout, Getting His Goat, Props, Vamping Venus**

Home-movie editions: **Vodvil Days, Hits of the Past, Backstage Antics, The Baggage Man, Charlie on the Boards**

Cast: Charlie Chaplin (*Props*), Fritz Schade (*Garlico the strong man*), Gene Marsh (*Garlico's wife*), Josef Swickard (*elderly stagehand*), Phyllis Allen (*Ham Lena Fat*), Alice Davenport (*actress*), Charles Bennett (*Ham Lena's husband*), Mack Sennett (*boisterous audience member*), Norma Nichols (*vaudeville artist*), Joe Bordeaux (*old actor*), Harry McCoy (*drunk*), Chester Conklin (*spectator*), Lee Morris (*spectator*), Vivian Edwards (*Goo Goo sister*), Cecile Arnold [Cecile Arley] (*Goo Goo sister*), George "Slim" Summerville (*audience member*), Frank Opperman (*audience member*), Dixie Chene (*spectator*).

Credits: Written and directed by Charlie Chaplin. Photographed by Frank D. Williams.

Plot: As the property man in a smalltime vaudeville theater, Charlie causes plenty of commotion on and off stage. When he's not physically abusing an elderly stagehand, he's tangling with the guest acts, especially Garlico the strong man. Garlico's wife gets knocked unconscious; Charlie takes her to the dressing room and tries to revive her. Garlico walks in, jumps to the wrong conclusion, and starts chasing Charlie all over the theater, disrupting the stage performance. Tempers flare, and Charlie has to turn on the fire hose to cool everyone off.

Source of print screened: **The Chaplin Collection Vol. 1** (Madacy Home Video), under the French title **Charlot, Garcon de Théâtre**

Comments: **The Property Man** was (and still is) singled out as one of the most mean-spirited Chaplin Keystones, due to Charlie's abuse of his elderly assistant. And yes, Charlie does pummel the poor guy at every opportunity, repeatedly kicking him in the face. But these and other moments of comic violence are performed in such a gleefully unpretentious manner that this exaggerated savagery transcends the pain inflicted and becomes outrageously humorous, as in a Three Stooges comedy. Aesthetically, the film is the kind of Stooge-like endeavor Charlie would have made had he wound up working for director Jules White at Columbia Pictures. In fact, the White-directed Three Stooges shorts *Three Hams on Rye* (1950) and *Loose Loot* (1953) contain backstage antics reminiscent of this Chaplin effort. As Chaplin biographer John McCabe has accurately noted, *The Property Man* is funny in the same way an animated cartoon is funny, because the sadism is so patently unreal.

Charlie forsakes his usual Tramp costume here. He still wears the derby and baggy pants, but he has no jacket and smokes a pipe. While his character is gainfully employed, his loutish behavior indicates that he doesn't give a damn as to whether he keeps his job or not. He knows he's not going to rise to a loftier position so he doesn't feel the need to kiss anyone's butt. As in other Keystones, he maintains a combative relationship with his co-workers, and would much rather spend his time flirting with women and tormenting his assistant.

We've seen plenty of slapstick comedies, so the abuse Charlie heaps upon his elderly assistant is impossible for us to take seriously. It's the sort of outlandish comic cruelty that's evident on Benny Hill's television programs. When Hill regulars Jackie Wright and Bob Todd take their lumps, we don't cringe, we laugh—as we do during *The Property Man* when the assistant is crushed under the weight of a heavy trunk and Charlie casually strikes a match on the trunk to light his pipe before making any effort to rescue his co-worker.

The Property Man is also of interest because of its vaudeville setting. Although the action unfolds within the confines of the Keystone studio rather than a genuine theater, it nevertheless utilizes an emerging entertainment form (motion pictures) to document one that would fade from view. This was the first Chaplin film to deal with the world of vaudeville and music halls—a world he would return to in later efforts such as *A Night in the Show* (1915) and, in a more melancholy vein, *Limelight* (1952).

Raucous and unrefined, *The Property Man* is, strangely enough, more entertaining than some of the highly regarded Chaplin Keystones.

Other Views and Reviews: "There are very few people who don't like these Keystones. They are thoroughly vulgar and touch the homely strings of our own vulgarity. There is some brutality in this picture and we can't help feeling that this is reprehensible. What human being can see an old man kicked in the face and count it fun?"—*The Moving Picture World* (1914).

"A cheerful cruelty characterized many of Sennett's films [and] Charlie became master of the process…*The Property Man* is no exception. In his short films, Charlie's sadism is incessant. One does not laugh at a cartoon—which is what

The Property Man is—because it is real, but precisely because it is unreal, a caricature of life's troubles."—John McCabe, *Charlie Chaplin* (1978).

"Genuinely unpleasant…[Chaplin plays] a sadistic bully who torments his elderly assistant…This movie isn't merely bad, it's a blot on Chaplin's reputation, but fortunately he outgrew stuff like this pretty quickly."—wmorrow59, *The Internet Movie Database* (2002).

22. *The Face on the Bar Room Floor*
(One Reel; Released August 10, 1914)
Reissue titles: **The Ham Artist, The Ham Actor**
Home-movie editions: **Barroom, The Artist, Face on the Barroom Floor, Charlie Loses His Girl, Charlie Goes Mad**
Cast: Charlie Chaplin (*the artist*), Cecile Arnold [Cecile Arley] (*Madeline*), Fritz Schade (*client who stole Madeleine*), Vivian Edwards (*model*), Charles Bennett (*sailor*), Chester Conklin (*drinker*), Harry McCoy (*drinker*), Hank Mann (*drinker*), Wallace MacDonald (*drinker*), Josef Swickard (*drinker*).
Credits: Written and directed by Charlie Chaplin. Based on the poem "The Face Upon the Floor" written in 1887 by Hugh Antoine D'Arcy. Photographed by Frank D. Williams.
Plot: Down-and-out, Charlie walks into a bar; in exchange for drinks, he tells the gathered crowd his sad life story. He was, he explains, a talented painter whose descent into alcoholism began when he lost his true love, Madeline, to one of his clients. Then, with a piece of chalk, he draws a simplistic sketch on the bar room floor, and a violent brawl erupts.
Source of print screened: **The Essential Charlie Chaplin Collection Vol. 3** (Delta Entertainment Corporation), under the Official Films title *Face on the Barroom Floor*
Comments: It isn't fair for us to judge **The Face on the Bar Room Floor** by the Official Films copy that's widely available. This version, which was issued to the home-movie collector's market, has very few subtitles and several scenes are reportedly presented out of order. So not only is the narrative difficult to follow, but the artistic intent of Chaplin's original is ruined.

Even in this butchered edition we can tell that this was Chaplin's most ambitious effort to date in terms of acting and storytelling, with its use of flashbacks and dramatic set-pieces. However, because of the concentration on dramatic narrative, there's no real comedy content.

Chaplin biographer John McCabe claims that **The Face on the Bar Room Floor** is the first film to depict Charlie as a genuine tramp. We don't entirely agree with McCabe's assessment, although we can see where he's coming from. Charlie's character enters the bar room with even less than usual: no cane, no necktie, and filled with despair. Like the Tramp in the final scenes of **City Lights** (1931), just before he's reunited with the flower girl, his spirit has been broken. His true love ran off with another, and after seeing her with the man and their children, he realizes that happiness is no longer attainable to him. In this respect, the drunken artist has reached a level *below* the Tramp; he has lost more than the Tramp ever had an opportunity to have.

(Chaplin conveys the idea that Madeline is a less-than-pure picture of womanhood by showing her *smoking a cigarette*—gasp!—an interesting comment on his Victorian-era mindset.)

Though ultimately an unsuccessful attempt to elicit sympathy from an audience, **The Face on the Bar Room Floor** is a breakthrough effort in that Chaplin clearly had more on his mind than filling a picture with wall-to-wall brick-tossing and ass-kicking. As he matured as a filmmaker, Chaplin would develop a firmer grasp of how to blend heartbreaking emotion with uproarious comedy. **The Face on the Bar Room Floor** represents the first step in this new direction.

Other Views and Reviews: "Will evoke screams of laughter…Extremely broad in its humor, but never offensive."—*Bioscope* (1914).

"One of the most direct anti-romantic statements from the Keystone period."—Raoul Sobel and David Francis, *Chaplin: Genesis of a Clown* (1977).

"Technically the least interesting of Chaplin's films."—David Robinson, *Chaplin: His Life and Art* (1985).

23. *Recreation*

(Split Reel†; Released August 13, 1914)

Working title: **In the Park**††

Reissue title: **Spring Fever**

Home-movie editions: **Fun Is Fun, His Recreation**†††

Cast: Charlie Chaplin (*tramp*), Gene Marsh (*girl*), Charles Bennett (*sailor*).

Credits: Written and directed by Charlie Chaplin. Photographed by Frank D. Williams.

Plot: Broke and alone, Charlie contemplates jumping off a bridge—until a young lady strolls by. Her boyfriend, a sailor, doesn't appreciate all the attention Charlie is paying her, and a brick-throwing mêlée ensues. Before long, the police get involved, and everyone winds up in the lake.

Source of print screened: **The Essential Charlie Chaplin Collection Vol. 3** (Delta Entertainment Corporation)

Comments: Creatively, Charlie's running on empty in **Recreation**. This hastily-made "park" comedy was just another mercenary attempt on the part of the Keystone Company to get another Chaplin movie into the hands of exhibitors as quickly as possible. (It was turned out so quickly that Charlie's jacket bears the same paint stain seen in his previous picture, **The Face on the Bar Room Floor**.)

The only interesting scene in the film shows Charlie about to jump off a bridge. He lifts up his right left, with his foot over the railing, then lifts up his left leg, and tumbles to the ground. It's a great bit of physical comedy, and a routine that Buster Keaton would use throughout his career. Other than this fleeting moment, **Recreation** contains nothing to recommend it.

Even viewing the film is a challenge. The wretched-quality print we watched was extremely blurry, and the unformatted framing cut off the tops of the actors' heads. **The Fatal Mallet** is starting to look good by comparison.

Other Views and Reviews: "Charlie has a peculiar manner entirely his own, and the way he tries to extricate himself from an awkward position is very whimsical."—*The Cinema* (1914).

"The violence in this little film is performed with such grace and rhythm that it seems to become a ballet of bricks and brawling."—Gerald D. McDonald, Michael Conway and Mark Ricci, *The Films of Charlie Chaplin* (1965).

"In its composition the film is so extremely like the earlier **Twenty Minutes of Love**…that one may almost suspect it of using up a certain amount of leftover material from the earlier film, to which new takes have been added."—Uno Asplund, *Chaplin's Films* (1976).

"Improvisational doesn't always equal inspiration…the results are nothing special."—wmorrow59, *The Internet Movie Database* (2002).

†The other half of the reel was **The Yosemite**, a travel short purchased from an outside company for distribution by Keystone.

††Not to be confused with **In the Park**, the home movie title for **Caught in the Rain** (Keystone, 1914), and **In the Park** (Essanay, 1915).

†††**His Recreation** is a composite of **Recreation** and **Laughing Gas** (Keystone, 1914).

24. *The Masquerader*
(One Reel; Released August 27, 1914)
Working title: **Queen of the Movies**
Reissue titles: **Putting One Over**, **The Picnic**, **A Female Impersonator**, **The Female Impersonator**, **The Female**, **The New Janitor**†, **The Perfumed Lady**
Home movie editions: **The Female Impersonator**, **Charlie at the Studio**

Cast: Charlie Chaplin (*Charlie, a.k.a. Senorita Chapelino*), Roscoe "Fatty" Arbuckle (*himself*), Charles Murray (*movie director*), Mabel Normand (*movie actress*), Minta Durfee (*leading lady*), Cecile Arnold [Cecile Arley] (*movie actress*), Vivian Edwards (*movie actress*), Gene Marsh (*movie actress*), Fritz Schade (*movie actor*), Harry McCoy (*movie actor*), Charles Parrott [Charley Chase] (*movie actor*), Billy Gilbert (*cameraman*).

Credits: Written and directed by Charlie Chaplin. Photographed by Frank D. Williams.

Plot: Charlie works as an actor at the Keystone studio. He causes such a disruption during filming that the director fires him. Charlie gets back on the lot by disguising himself as "Senorita Chapelino" and the director is quite taken by "her" charms. Charlie eventually reveals his masquerade, and his co-workers chase him around the lot.

Source of print screened: **The Essential Charlie Chaplin Collection Vol. 3** (Delta Entertainment Corporation)

Comments: **The Masquerader** is one of the better Chaplin Keystones, though that hardly ranks it with his best later efforts. For film buffs, there's the added interest of setting the action at the Keystone studio. This was his first real satire of moviemaking (in the earlier **A Film Johnnie** he was an observer rather than a participant), and points the way to his later parodies **His New Job** (Essanay, 1915) and **Behind the Screen** (Mutual, 1916).

The Masquerader is the second of three films in which Chaplin donned women's clothing. In the first, **A Busy Day** (Keystone, 1914), Charlie's character was supposed to be female; in **The Masquerader** and **A Woman** (Essanay, 1915), he's in disguise.

Although comments about **The Masquerader** usually begin and end with his drag bit, the most interesting sequence in the picture is the one that shows Chaplin (sans mustache) and Fatty Arbuckle putting on their make-up and costumes in the Keystone dressing room. (This scene predates a similar one in **Limelight** [1952], with Charlie and Buster Keaton getting ready to go onstage.) As in every instance where Charlie is gainfully employed, he has a combative relationship with his co-workers. There's some good by-play between the two comedians (Fatty switches a bottle of beer with a bottle filled with gasoline, which Charlie drinks; Charlie gets talcum powder all over Fatty), paving the way for their full-fledged teaming two films down the road in **The Rounders**.

This is also the first film we've seen where Chaplin does his trademark "hat bounce" (using both hands, he's about to place the derby on his head, only to have it "pop" off when he's startled). Chaplin performed this bit throughout his career, and even did it when he was presented with an honorary Oscar at the Academy Awards ceremony in 1972.

Other Views and Reviews: "[Chaplin] gives a really remarkable female impersonation. The makeup is no less successful than the characterization, and is further proof of Mr. Chaplin's undoubted versatility."—*Bioscope* (1914).

"[His masquerade is] remarkably, undatedly attractive at this distance, in contrast to many of the actresses of the time, whose charm it is hard to see fifty years later."—Isabel Quigly, *Charlie Chaplin: Early Comedies* (1968).

"Definitely one of Chaplin's more entertaining and amusing short comedies."—Michael De Zubiria, *The Internet Movie Database* (2001).

†Not to be confused with another Chaplin Keystone titled *The New Janitor* (1914), and the non-Keystone *The New Janitor* (1916) starring Dave Don and Patsy De Forest.

25. *His New Profession*
(One Reel; Released August 31, 1914)
Working title: **The Rolling Chair**
Reissue titles: **The Good-for-Nothing, Helping Himself, Charlie the Nurse Maid**
Cast: Charlie Chaplin (*Charlie*), Charles Parrott [Charley Chase] (*nephew*), Gene Marsh (*nephew's girlfriend*), Fritz Schade (*uncle*), Cecile Arnold [Cecile Arley] (*girl*), Roscoe "Fatty" Arbuckle (*bartender*), William Hauber (*cop*), Vivian Edwards (*nurse*), Charles Murray (*drinker*), Glen Cavender (*drinker*). (Some sources list Minta Durfee in the cast, but this is disputed by Chaplin scholars.)
Credits: Written and directed by Charlie Chaplin. Photographed by Frank D. Williams.
Plot: A young man wants to spend time with his girlfriend, but first he needs to find someone to take care of his ill-tempered uncle who is confined to a wheelchair because of gout. The nephew meets Charlie in the park and hires him to push the uncle around, for which he'll be paid later. But the deferred payment plan doesn't do Charlie any good when he wants to get a drink at a bar. On the pier, Charlie spots a one-armed beggar asleep in a wheelchair; the man has a tin cup and a sign that reads "HELP A CRIPPLE." Charlie places the cup and sign on the now-dozing uncle. After a charitable passerby drops money into the cup, Charlie scoops it up and heads straight for the bar. The nephew and his girlfriend find the snoozing uncle and are shocked to see the "CRIPPLE" sign—but not as shocked as the one-armed beggar, a con artist who actually has both limbs.

Source of print screened: **The Essential Charlie Chaplin Collection Vol. 3** (Delta Entertainment Corporation), under the W. H. Productions reissue title **The Good-For-Nothing**

Comments: Viewing the films in chronological order, **His New Profession** is the first Keystone that we feel provides Chaplin with a proper showcase. The sadism inherent in his first two dozen films is still evident, but Charlie's screen character has evolved from an opportunistic sharper into an incorrigible rascal. The "HELP A CRIPPLE" sequence is certainly in dubious taste (Charlie even peers into the one-armed beggar's coat sleeve to verify the limb is missing), but it's perfectly in keeping with the nature of Charlie's character here. He has a simple goal—to obtain money for a drink—and will go about achieving it in the most expedient manner possible. The sequence is not executed in a mean-spirited fashion, and the fact that the beggar is exposed as a fraud takes some of the harsh edge off the situation. Besides, there's more bad taste on display in a single minute of any random comedy of the last 30 years than there is in all of **His New Profession**.

On the other hand, Charley Chase (1893-1940), a.k.a. Charles Parrott, was a comedian of exquisite taste. Unfortunately, **His New Profession** is typical of the bland supporting roles he played at Keystone, where his considerable comedic talents went untapped. It wasn't until Chase signed with producer Hal Roach during the 1920s that his career as a writer, director and performer blossomed, resulting in some of the funniest—and classiest—comedy shorts ever made.

Under Chaplin's direction, **His New Profession** is a marked improvement over his earlier Keystones in terms of the staging of the gag sequences. Chaplin's cinematic technique was becoming much more assured; in a charming introduction to his character, he opens the film with a close-up of the Tramp reading the *Police Gazette*.

Oddly, Charlie's costume varies from his standard garb; he sports a bow tie and a solid vest, looking very much like a waiter. Was this a plot element dropped from the final cut or just another Keystone inconsistency? Or are we spending way too much time mulling this over? Perhaps we're the ones who need a drink.

Gout-affliction would later figure into **The Cure** (1917), one of Chaplin's funniest Mutual comedies, with Eric Campbell's outrageously over-bandaged foot the prime target of abuse.

Other Views and Reviews: "Charlie Chaplin appears in this picture and as usual, whenever he appears it is a laugh throughout."—*Motion Picture News* (1914).

"The boozy, self-interested Charlie of Keystone days is given full reign on this occasion, though as always there are indications of better things."—Glenn Mitchell, *The Chaplin Encyclopedia* (1997).

"Refined, it ain't, but somehow it's more enjoyable than some of the other Keystones. It's well paced and despite the low comedy stuff the atmosphere is light-hearted."—wmorrow59, *The Internet Movie Database* (2002).

26. *The Rounders*
(One Reel; Released September 7, 1914)
Working title: **The Two Drunks**
Reissue titles: **Revelry, Two of a Kind, Going Down, The Love Thief, Tip Tap Toe, Greenwich Village, Oh, What a Night**
Cast: Charlie Chaplin (*Charlie*), Roscoe "Fatty" Arbuckle (*Wilfred*†), Phyllis Allen (*Charlie's wife*), Minta Durfee (*Wilfred's wife*), Al St. John (*bellhop* and *waiter*), Fritz Schade (*diner*), Charles Parrott [Charley Chase] (*diner*), Wallace MacDonald (*diner*), Dixie Chene (*diner*), Gene Marsh (*diner*), Cecile Arnold [Cecile Arley] (*guest*), Edward F. Cline (*man in lobby*), Billy Gilbert (*doorman in blackface* and *man in boat*), Edgar Kennedy (*bit*).
Credits: Written and directed by Charlie Chaplin. Photographed by Frank D. Williams.
Plot: An inebriated Charlie staggers back to his hotel room, incurring the wrath of his angry wife. Across the hall, an identical scenario is being played out with a tipsy Wilfred and his spouse. The quarreling couples cross paths, and Charlie and Wilfred realize they're lodge members. The two drunkards head for a posh café, and their rowdy antics infuriate the diners. Pursued by their wives and irate diners, Charlie and Wilfred flee to the park, where they set sail in a rowboat that winds up sinking. Not that it matters to them; they're peacefully dozing as they disappear under the water.
Sources of prints screened: **The Forgotten Films of Roscoe "Fatty" Arbuckle** (Laughsmith Entertainment) and **The Essential Charlie Chaplin Collection Vol. 3** (Delta Entertainment Corporation)
Comments: Although Chaplin and Arbuckle appeared together in other Keystones, **The Rounders**†† marks the only time they were a full-fledged team. It's a swiftly paced, gracefully executed comedy that showcases their natural rapport.

In his top hat, cape, and evening attire, Chaplin's character is closer to the inebriate portrayal from his Fred Karno days; the only hint of the Tramp is his omnipresent cane. Under Chaplin's direction, Arbuckle gives a smoother performance than in, say, **The Knockout**, and Chaplin gives him plenty of opportunity to display his considerable gifts as a physical clown. Like Arbuckle, Chaplin realized that another funny performance only served to enhance the overall picture. Their rough-and-tumble shenanigans anticipate Arbuckle's later comedies with

Buster Keaton (*Coney Island, The Cook, The Garage*, et al.) and Chaplin's later teaming with Keaton in *Limelight* (1952).

The Rounders is one of the best Keystone comedies. What makes the film click is the obvious and infectious joy Chaplin and Arbuckle have working together. Both are perfectly in synch, as if they had been teammates for years. Chaplin's good mood is particularly evident in the closing scene (filmed on location at Echo Lake Park): as the rowboat sinks, a supposedly unconscious Charlie has trouble keeping a straight face while submerging.

Minta Durfee, a prolific Keystone player and Mrs. Arbuckle offscreen, plays his onscreen wife in *The Rounders*. Phyllis Allen (1861-1938), cast as Charlie's formidable spouse, was already a veteran of many Keystone comedies, including several with Chaplin.

Edward F. Cline (1892-1961), who has a bit part in the film, became a writer and director for Buster Keaton's production company in the 1920s, and was often seen in supporting roles in the Keaton shorts (*The Boat, The Playhouse*, etc.). During the sound era, Cline directed numerous feature films, including comedies starring W. C. Fields (*The Bank Dick, Never Give a Sucker an Even Break, You Can't Cheat an Honest Man* [uncredited], *My Little Chickadee*), The Ritz Brothers (*Behind the Eight Ball*), Olsen & Johnson (*Crazy House, Ghost Catchers, See My Lawyer*), and Wheeler & Woolsey (*Hook, Line and Sinker, So This is Africa, Cracked Nuts, On Again-Off Again, High Flyers*).

The Rounders is more indicative of Fatty Arbuckle's Sennett efforts than it is of a maturing Charlie Chaplin. Nevertheless, it's superior to the general run of Keystone product and represents a time capsule that preserves the comedians' only genuine teaming.

About his work with Chaplin, Arbuckle would later remark: "I have always regretted not having been his partner in a longer film than these one-reelers we made so rapidly. He is a complete comic genius, undoubtedly the only one of our time, and he will be the only one who will be still talked about a century from now." (For more on Arbuckle, see the entry for *The Knockout*.)

For years now, many people only know Arbuckle because of the scandal that ruined his career rather than for the wonderful comedies that made him one of the silent screen's most popular performers. This situation will hopefully be corrected with Laughsmith Entertainment's release of *The Forgotten Films of Roscoe "Fatty" Arbuckle*, a four-disc DVD collection containing 32 restored films starring and/or directed by Arbuckle. The collection includes *The Rounders* and it's easily the finest quality copy available, although the reissue edition on Delta's *The Essential Charlie Chaplin Collection Vol. 3* isn't bad.

If you've never seen Arbuckle at his best, Laughsmith's *The Forgotten Films of Roscoe "Fatty" Arbuckle* provides a perfect introduction to the work of this unsung comic legend.

Other Views and Reviews: "It is a rough picture for rough people, that people, whether rough or gentle, will probably have to laugh over while it is on the screen."—*Moving Picture World* (1914).

"Chaplin and Arbuckle made a remarkable team in this film."—Gerald D. McDonald, Michael Conway and Mark Ricci, *The Films of Charlie Chaplin* (1965).

"This very effective teaming of Chaplin and Arbuckle was, sadly, their only such excursion, their other collaborative appearances being rather less focused."—Glen Mitchell, *The Chaplin Encyclopedia* (1997).

†Most cast listings for *The Rounders* credits Chaplin as "Mr. Full" and Arbuckle as "Mr. Fuller." However, the reissue print in Delta Entertainment's *The Essential Charlie Chaplin Collection Vol. 2* refers to Arbuckle as "Wilfred," while Chaplin's character is unnamed.

††The term "rounder" derives from "rogue" and "bounder"—in other words, a scoundrel or mischievous fellow.

27. *The New Janitor*

(One Reel; Released September 24, 1914)

Working title: *Caught*

Reissue titles: *The New Porter*, *The Porter*, *The Blundering Boob*, *The Custodian*

Home-movie editions: *The Window Washer*, *Capturing the Robber*, *Charlie the Janitor*

Cast: Charlie Chaplin (*the new janitor*), Fritz Schade (*president*), John Francis "Jack" Dillon (*manager*), Minta Durfee (*secretary*), Glen Cavender (*Luke Connor*), Al St. John (*elevator operator*).

Credits: Written and directed by Charlie Chaplin. Photographed by Frank D. Williams.

Plot: Charlie loses his new job as janitor when he drops a bucket of water on his employer's head. Later, the office manager tries to steal company funds to pay off gambling debts, but Charlie thwarts his scheme and saves the day.

Source of print screened: *The Essential Charlie Chaplin Collection Vol. 4* (Delta Entertainment Corporation)

Comments: With *The New Janitor*†, Chaplin delivered his most subdued performance to date, adding new dimensions to his character. The Charlie seen in earlier Keystones like **Laughing Gas** and **The Property Man** had no work ethic and could have cared less whether he kept his job or not. This time, however, he is conscientious about his duties, even though simple tasks such as collecting waste paper baskets (he holds them upside down and spills the contents) and window washing (he dumps a bucket on his boss) are beyond his limited capabilities.

When he gets fired, Charlie briefly attempts to plead his case, then bows respectfully to his boss and backs out of the office. For a Keystone film, it's a surprisingly understated scene, with Chaplin's graceful pantomime giving it a touch of pathos†† and civility. And in sharp contrast to his usually combative relationships with co-workers, Charlie doesn't cause a stir when the elevator operator denies him access to the lift.

The New Janitor is the first film to present Charlie as a heroic figure. The secretary catches the office manager trying to abscond with company funds; in the ensuing struggle, the secretary pushes an intercom button that signals the janitor. Charlie has just been dismissed, but he takes it upon himself to answer one final call. Entering his ex-employer's office, Charlie sees the manager with a gun and knocks it to the floor. Charlie then reaches down to recover it; although he's bent over and has turned his back on his adversary, Charlie is able to keep him covered by aiming the weapon through his legs.

This also marks the first time Chaplin makes observations regarding deceptive appearances and mistaken identity. When the boss enters the office and sees Charlie wielding a gun, he assumes that the scruffy ex-janitor is threatening the honest, smartly-groomed manager. Just as Charlie is about to be whisked away by a cop, the secretary explains who the real culprit is. The don't-judge-a-book-by-its-cover theme would recur throughout Chaplin's career, as in **City Lights** (1931; in which the Tramp befriends a blind girl who mistakenly believes he's wealthy), and **Monsieur Verdoux** (1947; with Chaplin as a serial killer who is also a compassionate family man).

The New Janitor is one of Chaplin's more noteworthy Keystone efforts. The workplace-intrigue storyline would serve as the prototype for **The Bank** (Essanay, 1915), **The Floorwalker** (Mutual, 1916), and **The Pawnshop** (Mutual, 1916).

John Francis "Jack" Dillon (1887-1934), who plays the crooked manager in **The New Janitor**, later became a director himself; his credits include **Sally** (1929), **Spring is Here** (1930), **The Cohens and the Kellys in Hollywood** (1932), and **Call Her Savage** (1932). Sometimes crime *does* pay.

Other Views and Reviews: "A ripping good comedy number, with Chas. Chapman [*sic*] playing the part of the janitor. He interpolates a lot of his inimitable funny business and the plot is better than usual."—*The Moving Picture World* (1914).

"A significant departure from Chaplin's previous Keystones. The film's slapstick is relatively inconsequential. The new emphasis is on a fusion of character comedy and melodrama."—Harry M. Geduld, *Chapliniana Volume 1: The Keystone Films* (1987).

"Chaplin's dismissed janitor displays a hitherto unseen vulnerability and grace…and this new dimension, though seldom explored in subsequent Keystones, would be further developed in the following year's series for Essanay."—Glenn Mitchell, *The Chaplin Encyclopedia* (1997).

†Not to be confused with the reissue title for another Chaplin Keystone, **The Masquerader** (1914), or **The New Janitor** (1916) starring Dave Don and Patsy De Forest.

††In his autobiography, Chaplin cited this please-don't-fire-me scene in **The New Janitor** as the moment he realized he could "evoke tears as well as laughter." However, his description of the scene differs from what actually occurs. As noted in Glenn Mitchell's *The Chaplin Encyclopedia*, the scene Chaplin described turns up in one of his later films, **The Pawnshop** (Mutual, 1916).

28. *Those Love Pangs*
(One Reel; Released October 10, 1914)
Working title: **In Wrong**†
Reissue titles: **The Rival Mashers, Busted Hearts, Oh, You Girls**
Home-movie editions: **Love Pangs, Love Pains, Busted Hearts, Charlie and His Rival**
Cast: Charlie Chaplin (*masher*), Chester Conklin (*rival masher*), Cecile Arnold [Cecile Arley] (*pretty blonde*), Vivian Edwards (*brunette*), Fred Fishback (*brunette's boyfriend*), Harry McCoy (*cop*), Gene Marsh (*landlady*), Fritz Schade (*movie patron*), George "Slim" Summerville (*movie patron*), Billy Gilbert (*movie patron*).
Credits: Written and directed by Charlie Chaplin. Photographed by Frank D. Williams.
Plot: Lovesick and suicidal (what a combination!), Charlie can't believe his eyes when he sees Chester, his rival, cuddling with a pretty blonde. Charlie decides to go to a bar, until a brunette catches his attention. He follows the blonde and brunette into a movie theater, where he sits between them. But Chester and the brunette's boyfriend catch up with Charlie and throw him through the movie screen.

Source of print screened: ***The Essential Charlie Chaplin Collection Vol. 4*** (Delta Entertainment Corporation), under the W. H. Productions reissue title ***The Rival Mashers***

Comments: ***Those Love Pangs*** opens in a boarding house, where Charlie and Chester are both trying to score with their landlady. The following events were supposed to depict the rivals going to their jobs as waiters in a bakery. But when the sequence seemed to gain a life of its own—Chaplin found that the bakery milieu yielded much more potential than the boarding house rivalry did—it was developed into a separate short, which eventually became ***Dough and Dynamite*** (see next entry).

This left Chaplin to conceive another conclusion for the original film. Evidently all of his inspiration went into ***Dough and Dynamite*** because ***Those Love Pangs*** is one of his emptiest Keystones. All of the flirting, fighting, and undisciplined mugging brings back memories of his earlier "park" comedies—and not the pleasant memories, either. Chaplin does add a meager touch of pathos to the scene where he catches Chester spooning with Cecile, and the movie theater finale is nicely executed. Other than that, the whole enterprise has an air of indifference about it. Without the pivotal bakery sequence, ***Those Love Pangs*** has as much substance as a hollowed-out éclair.

In *The Chaplin Encyclopedia*, Glenn Mitchell makes this interesting observation about the roles played by Cecile Arnold and Vivian Edwards:

> Intriguingly, ***Those Love Pangs*** contains the intimation that both girls may be prostitutes. When Charlie decides to follow the brunette instead of buying a drink, he examines his money as if to decide which commodity to purchase. Similarly, one might query Chester's status with blonde Cecile Arnold (herself sporting a stereotypical "streetwalker" kiss-curl) when she gives him a sum of money retrieved from her shoe. Such references appear in several non-Chaplin Keystones of the period, and must have been quite shocking to contemporary audiences.

And people call Charlie a tramp!

Other Views and Reviews: "In a comparatively short time Charles Chaplin has earned a reputation as a slapstick comedian, second to none. His odd little tricks of manner and his refusal to do the most simple things in an ordinary way are essential features of his method, which thus far has defied successful imitation."—*New York Dramatic Mirror* (1914).

"Few of Chaplin's one-reel Keystones are as rich in comic business as ***Those Love Pangs***. The film includes most of the already familiar gags and a few new ones.

And even the familiar gags are sometimes given a new wrinkle."—Harry M. Geduld, *Chapliniana Volume 1: The Keystone Films* (1987).

"Neither the best nor the worst of the Keystone series...just another one-reeler cranked out while he was learning his craft, but there are a couple of funny bits."—wmorrow59, *The Internet Movie Database* (2002).

†Not to be confused with *In Wrong*, a reissue title for *Between Showers* (Keystone, 1914).

29. *Dough and Dynamite*
(Two Reels; Released October 26, 1914)
Working title: *In Trouble*
Reissue titles: *The Doughnut Designers*, *The Cook*†, *The New Cook*
Home-movie editions: *Bakers Dozen*, *Charlie Caught Out*, *Charlie's Hot Spot*
Cast: Charlie Chaplin (*waiter*), Chester Conklin (*waiter*), Fritz Schade (*bakery owner*), Norma Nichols (*owner's wife*), Cecile Arnold [Cecile Arley] (*waitress*), Vivian Edwards (*waitress*), Phyllis Allen (*customer*), Charles Bennett (*customer*), John Francis Dillon (*customer*), Edgar Kennedy (*striking baker*), George "Slim" Summerville (*striking baker*), Charles Parrott [Charley Chase] (*striking baker*), Wallace MacDonald (*striking baker*), Glen Cavender (*striking baker*).
Credits: Written and directed by Charlie Chaplin. Photographed by Frank D. Williams.
Plot: Charlie and Chester are waiters in a bakery. When the bakers go on strike, the owner makes the waiters fill in for them. Plotting revenge, the bakers plant a stick of dynamite in a loaf of bread, which Charlie innocently places in the oven. The owner mistakenly thinks Charlie is taking romantic liberties with his wife and chases him all over the bakery. During the fracas, the oven explodes, covering poor Charlie in a gooey pile of dough.
Source of print screened: *The Essential Charlie Chaplin Collection Vol. 5* (Delta Entertainment Corporation)
Comments: *Dough and Dynamite* is generally considered to be Chaplin's best picture to date and one his finest Keystone comedies.

Gerald Mast singles it out for praise in *The Comic Mind* (The University of Chicago Press, 1973):

> *Despite the purely Sennett premise of the film, it is dominated by the Chaplin style of paying close attention to what he can do with a bit of inanimate matter...In this film Chaplin creates one of his classic bits. Holding aloft a whole tray of bread loaves, he runs, dances, twirls, pirouettes, and somersaults without spilling a single loaf. Then, when he stoops down casually to pick one loaf off the floor, the whole*

*tray of loaves slips and falls. Charlie does the supremely difficult balancing act with great ease; it is the simple, ordinary task that boggles him. This balancing act would be reincarnated over and over again in Chaplin films like **Shanghaied** (1915) and as late as **Monsieur Verdoux** (1947), where he tumbles with a tea-cup in his hand without spilling a drop.*

With **Dough and Dynamite**, Chaplin reveals his most sophisticated filmmaking techniques thus far. The editing is particularly ambitious: there is a lot more intercutting within scenes, as he uses close-ups for comic effect and to complement the narrative. Chaplin is no longer just filming the action—here he's using cinematic technique to enhance the visuals, as he does when he shakes the camera the moment the dynamite explodes.

The gags and gag sequences show better construction and more imagination than usual. In his aforementioned bread-tray balancing act, full range is given to his gifts as a physical comedian. There's plenty of broad comedy—flour and dough fly fast and free—but there are also distinct Chaplinesque touches. In one scene, Charlie makes doughnuts by flinging the dough around his wrist. In another, Charlie gazes at a hip-swinging young lady then looks at a sign reading "Assorted FRENCH TARTS"; grinning slyly, he does an exaggerated imitation of her movements. The antics are effectively integrated into the film's storyline; the plot points may be thin, but it's a vast improvement over the Keystone crew showing up at a public event and trying to ad-lib a story to fit the surroundings.

Not that **Dough and Dynamite** is a perfect film. The trademark Keystone gesticulating is still at odds with Chaplin's comic sensibilities, and the picture concludes without resolving the plot twists. However, the latter may be the result of Chaplin having to wrap up the production *posthaste*. After nine days of filming, Chaplin had spent $1,800 ($800 over budget); Sennett, denying Chaplin his $25 director's bonus, had the footage fashioned into two reels instead of one. Chaplin wound up scoring an artistic and financial victory when **Dough and Dynamite** garnered rave reviews and grossed more than $135,000 on its initial release.

As they do in other Keystone comedies, Chaplin and walrus-mustached Chester Conklin (1888-1971) work well together. Although Conklin was often the lead player in other Keystones, he knows he's "second banana" to Charlie and willingly plays the comic foil. **Dough and Dynamite** is the best of the Chaplin-Conklin pairings, and Conklin reportedly helped Chaplin devise the plot for the film.

Unlike their onscreen counterparts, Charlie and Chester enjoyed a good working relationship. In fact, it was Chester who persuaded Charlie not to quit Keystone after quarreling with Mabel Normand during the making of *Mabel at the Wheel*. Conklin would later play supporting roles in Chaplin's *Modern Times* (1936) and *The Great Dictator* (1940).

As mentioned in the previous entry, *Dough and Dynamite* was expanded from a bakery sequence originally planned for *Those Love Pangs*. A similar situation occurred with the Three Stooges short *Merry Mavericks* (1951). Although a dentistry sequence in the Stooges film ran too long, it went over gangbusters at a preview screening, so producer Hugh McCollum excised it and had writer-director Edward Bernds concoct an additional short, *The Tooth Will Out* (also released 1951). As in the case of the Chaplin films, the secondary effort turned out to be superior to what remained of the original.

Dough and Dynamite was the first Chaplin Keystone to fully showcase the comedic style that would further evolve at Essanay and reach maturity at Mutual. *Other Views and Reviews*: "Two reels of pure nonsense, some of which is very laughable indeed. This is well-pictured and very successful for this form of humor."—*The Moving Picture World* (1914).

"The film shows Chaplin developing new sophistication in his deployment of studio sets and restricted camera set-ups."—David Robinson, *Chaplin: His Life and Art* (1985).

"Filled with wonderful comedy touches…In both characterization and structure, *Dough and Dynamite* is much finer than other comedy films of the time."—Jeffrey Vance, *Chaplin: Genius of the Cinema* (2003).

"*Dough and Dynamite* drags too much for a short piece—as an example of how to do set pieces of comedy, it's fine, but it is hard going for audiences today compared to the rest of Charlie's work."—didi-5, *The Internet Movie Database* (2004).

†Not to be confused with *Charlie the Cook*, a home-movie edition of *Shanghaied* (Essanay, 1915).

30. *Gentlemen of Nerve*
(One Reel; Released October 29, 1914)
Working title: **Attending the Race**
Reissue titles: **Some Nerve†, Charlie and Mabel at the Races**
Home-movie editions: **Charlie at the Races, A Gentleman with Nerve, Gentleman with Nerves, Charlie Sneaks In**
Cast: Charlie Chaplin (*Mr. Wow-Wow††*), Mabel Normand (*Mabel*), Mack Swain (*Ambrose*), Chester Conklin (*Mr. Walrus†††*), Phyllis Allen (*his wife*), Glen Cavender (*cop*), Alice Davenport (*waitress*), Cecile Arnold [Cecile Arley] (*specta-*

tor), George "Slim" Summerville (*spectator*), Gene Marsh (*spectator*), Charles Parrott [Charley Chase] (*spectator*), Harry McCoy (*spectator*), Billy Gilbert (*spectator*), Joe Bordeaux (*spectator*), Tammany Young (*spectator*).

Credits: Written and directed by Charlie Chaplin. Photographed by Frank D. Williams.

Plot: Mr. Wow-Wow and Ambrose sneak into an auto race by squeezing through an open space in a wooden fence. Mabel and her companion, Mr. Walrus, are also in attendance. Wow-Wow spends more time flirting with Mabel than he does watching the event, provoking a fight with Walrus. Ambrose also shows an interest in Mabel. In the ensuing ruckus, Walrus and Ambrose are escorted out by the police, leaving Wow-Wow and Mabel to pursue their romance uninterrupted.

Source of print screened: **The Chaplin Collection Vol. 2** (Madacy Home Video), under the French title **Charlot et Mabel aux Courses**

Comments: **Gentlemen of Nerve** is basically a standard "park" comedy set at an auto race. Though the film is better photographed and edited than most Chaplin Keystones, it's not much funnier than the rest of them.

Substance-wise, it's the same old formula, with plenty of aggressive sadism (Charlie bites Chester Conklin's nose, Charlie burns Mack Swain's nose with a cigarette, Charlie kicks a spectator in the head, etc.). This time, however, Chaplin does attempt to bring new variations to the hoary material. Before getting into a fight with Chester, Charlie sets down his cane, removes his coat and derby, limbers up, moves Mabel out of harm's way, positions Chester with his left hand, then smacks him with his right.

There are also lighter moments amid the mayhem. While sitting in the stands, Charlie surreptitiously takes sips from a spectator's soda, not unlike the way he stole bites of a child's hot dog in **The Circus** (United Artists, 1928).

The most memorable shots in the film are not gag sequences but a couple of close-ups of Chaplin with Mabel Normand. Their smiles and laughter appear to be genuine, providing the viewer with a candid glimpse of two performers who are enjoying each other's company—a far cry from their experience making **Mabel at the Wheel**.

Other Views and Reviews: "Charlie, Chester and Mabel attend an auto race. Results? As laughable as ever were pictured."—*Motion Picture News* (1914).

"Primitive burlesque farce, which is hardly worth either Chaplin or his art."—Uno Asplund, *Chaplin's Films* (1976).

"Slight of construction and long on violence. There are a few good gags...but inspiration is otherwise lacking, although, as always, Chaplin's customary bits of business frequently enliven a commonplace idea."—Glenn Mitchell, *The Chaplin Encyclopedia* (1997).

"Excellent sight gags."—Daniel Dopierala, *The Internet Movie Database* (2002).

†Not to be confused with *Some Nerve* (1913), a Keystone comedy starring Ford Sterling.

††Most sources credit Chaplin's character as "Mr. Wow-Wow," although he was not referred to by name in the print we viewed. In some home-movie editions he is referred to as "Mr. Nervo."

†††Not referred to by name in the print we viewed. In some home-movie editions he is referred to as "Mr. Dusty Furnace."

31. *His Musical Career*
(One Reel; Released November 7, 1914)

Working title: *The Piano Movers*

Reissue titles: *Musical Tramp*, *The Piano Movers*

Home-movie edition: *Charlie as a Piano Mover*

Cast: Charlie Chaplin (*Charlie*), Mack Swain (*piano mover*), Fritz Schade (*Mr. Rich*), Cecile Arnold [Cecile Arley] (*Mrs. Rich*), Frank Hayes (*Mr. Poor*), Gene Marsh (*Mrs. Poor*), Charles Parrott [Charley Chase] (*piano-store manager*), William Hauber (*servant*). (Although Billy Gilbert is pictured in a publicity photo for this film, he wasn't in the print we viewed.)

Credits: Written and directed by Charlie Chaplin. Photographed by Frank D. Williams.

Plot: A piano-store manager instructs employees Charlie and Mack to deliver a new piano to 666 Prospect Street and repossess one from 999 Prospect Street. Naturally, they get the addresses switched, to the delight of Mr. Poor and the outrage of Mr. Rich.

Source of print screened: *The Essential Charlie Chaplin Collection Vol. 4* (Delta Entertainment Corporation), under the reissue title *Musical Tramp*

Comments: While *His Musical Career* bears passing resemblance to Laurel & Hardy's piano-moving classic *The Music Box* (1932), it's debatable as to whether it can be considered a true forerunner. There are similarities, particularly in a scene where Charlie and Mack attempt to deliver a piano up a staircase. But whereas Chaplin uses it for a brief gag, Laurel & Hardy based their whole picture around moving a piano up a ridiculously long flight of stairs.† One thing, however, isn't debatable: *The Music Box* is a far funnier film.

Nevertheless, *His Musical Career* is an above-average Keystone effort thanks to Chaplin's directorial touches. The interaction between Charlie and Mack is sharper and more inventive than usual (Mack is Chaplin's full-fledged teammate here, not just a convenient comic accessory), and their gag sequences are very well staged. After carrying a piano up the aforementioned staircase (Charlie futilely attempts to push it with his cane), Charlie hoists the heavy instrument on his shoulders, only to have his knees buckle when Mr. Poor can't make up his mind exactly where he should set it down. In another scene, their mule-drawn cart tilts backwards, causing the critter to hang in mid-air; this gag would be repeated in *Work* (Essanay, 1915), with Charlie taking the place of the mule.

Much of *His Musical Career* was shot outdoors, and crowds gathered to watch the filming; if you look closely, you can see their reflection in the windows of the piano shop and a trolley.

Mack Swain (1876-1935) was seen in many Keystone comedies, usually as a broom-mustached character named "Ambrose." Swain is also in several Chaplin Keystones, as well as later Chaplin films for First National, such as *The Idle Class* (1921), *Pay Day* (1922), and *The Pilgrim* (1923). But he's best known for his role as prospector "Big Jim McKay," Chaplin's Klondike buddy in *The Gold Rush* (United Artists, 1925). Chaplin often had former associates like Chester Conklin and Hank Mann play supporting roles in his later features, but Mack Swain was the only ex-Keystone comic to ever figure so prominently in one of his later works.

His Musical Career isn't what you'd call a laugh riot, but Chaplin fans should get a few good chuckles out of it.

Other Views and Reviews: "One of the best short comedies in a month. Funny piano moving skit."—*Variety* (1914).

"The staircase sequence is a major episode of *The Music Box* but a fairly brief one in *His Musical Career*. Chaplin's plot is more elaborate and his characters and themes are quite different."—Harry M. Geduld, *Chapliniana Volume 1: The Keystone Films* (1987).

"*His Musical Career* has frequently been cited as a prototype for the classic Laurel & Hardy short, *The Music Box* (1932), but in truth they share few ideas that were not essentially common property. Transporting the instrument on a cart was standard procedure at the time, and the idea of delivering to the wrong address was and is a staple of farce."—Glenn Mitchell, *The Chaplin Encyclopedia* (1997).

†The comic idea of making deliveries up a long flight of stairs also figured in Laurel & Hardy's *Hats Off* (1927) and The Three Stooges' *An Ache in Every Stake* (1941).

32. *His Trysting Place*
(Two Reels; Released November 9, 1914)
Also known as *His Trysting Places*†
Working title: *Ingratitude*
Reissue titles: *His Trysting Places*, *The Family House*, *Family Home*, *Very Much Married*, *The Henpecked Spouse*, *The Ladies' Man*
Home-movie editions: *His Trysting Places*, *Papa Charlie*
Cast: Charlie Chaplin (*Charlie*), Mabel Normand (*Mabel*), Mack Swain (*Ambrose*), Phyllis Allen (*Ambrose's wife*), Gene Marsh (*Camomile*), Glen Cavender (*cook* and *cop*), Nick Cogley (*old man with beard*), Frank Hayes (*diner wearing bowler hat*), Vivian Edwards (*woman outside restaurant*), Billy Gilbert (*diner*).
Credits: Written and directed by Charlie Chaplin. Photographed by Frank D. Williams.
Plot: After writing a love letter to her "Snooky Ookums," Camomile asks fellow tenant Ambrose to mail it for her. In the meantime, Charlie tells his wife Mabel that he's stepping out to buy a bottle for their baby son. Charlie and Ambrose wind up at the same café; after an altercation, they wind up with each other's overcoat. When Charlie gets home, Mabel finds the love letter in his pocket and flies into a rage. Ambrose's wife also thinks the worst after finding the baby bottle in her husband's coat pocket. Eventually, Ambrose returns the bottle to Charlie, and Mabel is relieved. But Ambrose is still in hot water because his wife now thinks the love letter was intended for *him*.
Source of print screened: ***Chaplin: The Legend Lives On*** (Madacy Home Video), under the Hollywood Film Enterprises title *His Trysting Places*
Comments: A "park" comedy variant with a few more twists than usual, *His Trysting Place* shows the great strides Chaplin had made as a filmmaker since his raggedy directorial debut, *Twenty Minutes of Love*. The Keystone rowdiness is still evident, but now Chaplin takes time to introduce the characters, set up the situation, and provide some rationale for their behavior. As a result, there is sharper interaction between Charlie, Mabel Normand, and Mack Swain.

The café sequence reveals how Chaplin took a standard Keystone situation and put his own stamp on it. There are no available seats when Charlie enters the café, but he notices an old man with a scraggly beard (Nick Cogley) sitting at the end of the counter. Charlie proceeds to eat food off the man's plate, then wipes his hands on the man's beard. Disgusted, the old man departs and Charlie takes his seat, next to Mack Swain. Mack's sneezing and soup slurping offend a suddenly genteel Charlie, who puts his finger in his ears to drown out the noise. Reaching across the counter, Mack shoves his arm in front of Charlie's face.

Charlie, who has been gnawing on a hambone, retaliates by biting Mack's arm and throwing the bone into Mack's soup bowl. In an instant, all hell breaks loose.

In earlier films, Chaplin would have clobbered Mack after the first slurp. Here, he lets the situation build, as his bemused annoyance turns into full-blown anger. Also memorable is a later bit in the park where Charlie and Mack cease fighting and strike nonchalant poses (which seem more effeminate than tranquil) when a policeman passes by.

His Trysting Place marks the first time Charlie played a family man. Such domestic portraits would be rare in his films; *A Day's Pleasure* (First National, 1919), about a Chaplin family outing, is the only other one that comes to mind.

Chaplin acknowledged French comedian Max Linder (1883-1925) as one of his great influences. The films of the debonair, top-hatted Linder deftly combined subtle farce with imaginative visual gags. Though Chaplin's later comedies would be closer to Linder's style, *His Trysting Place* clearly reveals the Linder influence taking hold.

Other Views and Reviews: "Chaplin does some particularly amusing stunts in this and the fun runs high through the entire two reels."—*The Moving Picture World* (1914).

"Arguably Chaplin's best Keystone."—James L. Neibaur, *Movie Comedians* (1986).

"In terms of comic characterization *His Trysting Place* is one of Chaplin's more effective and mature Keystones...The editing of most of the film seems unexceptionally Keystone, but the eating scene, filmed in an extended two-shot, would not have looked out of place in one of Chaplin's Mutual comedies."—Harry M. Geduld, *Chapliniana Volume 1: The Keystone Films* (1987).

†Accounts vary as to the exact title of this film. It is most frequently listed as *His Trysting Place*, while other reliable sources state that it was originally released by Keystone as *His Trysting Places*, a title that was also used for theatrical reissues and home-movie editions.

33. *Getting Acquainted*
(One Reel; Released December 5, 1914)
Working title: *The Flirts*†
Reissue titles: *A Fair Exchange*, *Exchange Is No Robbery*, *Hello Everybody*
Cast: Charlie Chaplin (*Charlie*), Mabel Normand (*Mabel*), Mack Swain (*Mabel's husband*), Phyllis Allen (*Charlie's wife*), Cecile Arnold [Cecile Arley] (*pretty blonde*), Glen Cavender (*Turk*), Edgar Kennedy (*cop*), Gene Marsh (*girl in park*), Harry McCoy (*flirt*).

Credits: Written and directed by Charlie Chaplin. Photographed by Frank D. Williams.

Plot: He may be in the park with his wife, but that doesn't stop Charlie from flirting with other women. First, it's the comely Cecile—until her boyfriend, a knife-wielding Turk, chases him away. Then it's Mabel, who sets a cop after him. In the meantime, Mabel's husband begins flirting with Charlie's wife, who also notifies the cop. When both couples finally meet, there are red faces all around.

Source of print screened: **The Essential Charlie Chaplin Collection Vol. 4** (Delta Entertainment Corporation), under the W. H. Productions reissue title **A Fair Exchange**

Comments: **Getting Acquainted** is yet another "park" farce straight off the Keystone assembly line, which turned out comedies faster than Oscar Mayer cranks out bologna. Under Chaplin's supervision, however, the results are slicker than usual.

Charlie is a total horndog in this one, literally chasing anything in a skirt. At one point, he even stares intently at Cecile Arnold's posterior while she's bending over. Perhaps we should call him the *Scamp*. (We can understand why Charlie, married to battle-axe Phyllis, would chase after cute little Mabel, but why would Mabel's husband pursue Phyllis? No man's hormones are *that* out of control.)

In the film's best scene, Charlie not-so-accidentally lifts Mabel's skirt with his cane. Feigning outrage, Charlie spanks the cane then scolds it for misbehaving. For a minor effort like **Getting Acquainted**, this moment represents a major highpoint.

Other Views and Reviews: "Yet another fine Charles Chaplin number, including the celebrated Mabel Normand."—*The Cinema* (1914).

"As a farce it is astonishingly primitive to have been made so late in the Keystone series."—Uno Asplund, *Chaplin's Films* (1976).

"Even such an undistinguished outing as **Getting Acquainted** shows great distinction in Chaplin's grasp of comedy film making [calling upon] his surefooted knowledge of film construction as well as general comedy know-how."—Leonard Maltin, *The Great Movie Comedians* (1978).

"A 'park' film without either brick throwing or a watery finale, and with one significant difference, unlike **Twenty Minutes of Love**, **Recreation**, and **Those Love Pangs**, **Getting Acquainted** involves the interaction of married couples…Instead of mere flirtations, you see molestations and male impulses to commit adultery."—Harry M. Geduld, *Chapliniana Volume 1: The Keystone Films* (1987).

†Not to be confused with *The Flirts*, a reissue title for *Between Showers* (Keystone, 1914).

34. *His Prehistoric Past*
(Two Reels; Released December 7, 1914)
Working title: *A Prehistoric Villain*
Reissue titles: *A Dream*, *The Hula-Hula Dance*, *King Charlie*
Home-movie editions: *I Am King*, *The Caveman*, *Caveman Charlie*, *Happy Dreams*, *Hoola-Hoola Dance*
Cast: Charlie Chaplin (*Weakchin*), Mack Swain (*King Low-Brow*), Gene Marsh (*Sum-Babee, King Low-Brow's favorite wife*), Fritz Schade (*Ku-Ku the medicine man*), Cecile Arnold [Cecile Arley] (*cavewoman*), Vivian Edwards (*cavewoman*), Al St. John (*caveman*), Frank D. Williams (*bit*), Syd Chaplin (*cop*).
Credits: Written and directed by Charlie Chaplin. Photographed by Frank D. Williams.
Plot: King Low-Brow welcomes a lone caveman named Weakchin into his tribe. Things are fine until Weakchin takes a fancy to Sum-Babee, Low-Brow's favorite wife. Weakchin kicks Low-Brow over a cliff, then appoints himself the new king. But Low-Brow survives the fall, and returns to clobber Weakchin over the head with the rock. At this point, we see a cop hitting Charlie over the head with his nightstick. Charlie had fallen asleep on a park bench and his Stone Age adventure was just a dream.
Source of print screened: *Chaplin: The Legend Lives On* (Madacy Home Video)
Comments: For his final Keystone film (made after *Tillie's Punctured Romance* but released a week before it), Chaplin concocted this lame Stone Age variation of a standard "park" comedy. Reportedly, Chaplin's concentration was strained during production because he was weighing a number of business propositions, contemplating life after Keystone. This may explain why *His Prehistoric Past* doesn't offer much beyond the sight of a derby-crowned Charlie clad in bearskin (instead of a club, he wields a cane, and smokes a pipe in place of a cigarette). Aside from that, it's business as usual, with the Keystone players whacking each other with clubs and rocks instead of mallets and bricks.

    His Prehistoric Past parodies D. W. Griffith's Stone Age tale *Man's Genesis* (1912) and its sequel, *Brute Force* (1914)—a fact that will be lost on most 21st century viewers. In *Man's Genesis*, Robert Harron (who appeared other Griffith productions, such as *Intolerance* [1916] and *Hearts of the World* [1918]) stars as a caveman named Weakhands, who wins his true love, Lilywhite (Mae Marsh, who appeared in *Intolerance* and *The Birth of a Nation* [1915]) by conquering the villainous Bruteforce (Wilfred Lucas). (It's worth noting that Lucas, who is best known for his role as the prison warden in Laurel & Hardy's **Pardon Us** [1931], was directing Keystone comedies during Chaplin's year with Sennett.) Lacking the physical strength of his opponent, Weakhands gets the upper hand by inventing the club. In **Brute Force**, he invents the bow and arrow and saves his tribe from their enemies.

Other comedians have used the Stone Age setting as a source for anachronistic humor. Buster Keaton played a caveman in one of a trio of stories that comprise his very funny **Three Ages** (1923), and The Three Stooges (Moe, Larry, Shemp) mined prehistory for belly laughs in **I'm a Monkey's Uncle** (1948) and its stock-footage-infested remake, **Stone Age Romeos** (1955). Laurel & Hardy had a less successful go at it in **Flying Elephants** (1928), an early effort made before they had jelled as a team.

The copy of **His Prehistoric Past** we viewed was a Hollywood Film Enterprises reissue that was missing an opening sequence showing Charlie falling asleep on a park bench. In *The Chaplin Encyclopedia*, historian Glenn Mitchell is convinced that Charlie's half-brother Syd, a fine comedian in his own right, plays the cop who wakes Charlie up at the conclusion. And if Mitchell says its so, that's good enough for us.

Dream sequences would recur throughout Chaplin's film work, as slumber would provide idyllic escapes from cold reality in **The Bank** (1915), **Shoulder Arms** (1918), **The Idle Class** (1921), **The Gold Rush** (1925), and **Modern Times** (1936). Yet he experienced peaceful dreams that turned unpleasant in **The Kid** (1921), **Sunnyside** (1919), and **Limelight** (1952).

The funniest thing about **His Prehistoric Past** has nothing to do with the actual content: in France, the film was called **Charlot nudiste...Charlie the nudist**! Evidently the French were unaware of paleontology back in 1914.

Other Views and Reviews: "Charles Chaplin and other members of the Keystone Company have outdone all their previous fun-provoking efforts."—*San Francisco Call and Post* (1914).

"An early Keystone product of the time when, apparently, Chaplin's mastery of pantomime had not been developed or discovered. It is purely a rough and tumble reel and those who relish Chaplin's artistry of today are glad that it belongs to his past, wishing only that it was prehistoric."—*The New York Times* (reviewing a 1919 revival).

"An old comedy of Chaplin's [that] has a good many moments of fun, as one might easily imagine when it is said that Chaplin is seen in a caveman's haberdashery."—*The New York Times* (reviewing a 1927 reissue).

"When a reissue of *His Prehistoric Past* turned up at a 'comedy week' in New York's Rivoli Theater during March 1919, the *New York Times* found anachronism in more than the setting…Posterity takes a gentler view of *His Prehistoric Past*, but this review provides insight into the degree to which Chaplin's methods—and those of the industry in general—were thought to have progressed in the intervening half-decade."—Glenn Mitchell, *The Chaplin Encyclopedia* (1997).

35. *Tillie's Punctured Romance*
(Six Reels; Released December 14, 1914†)
Pre-production titles: **She Was More Sinned Against Than Necessary, Dressler No. 1**
Reissue titles: **Charlie's Big Romance, Marie's Millions, Tillie's Big Romance, Tillie's Love Affair, Tilly's Love Affair, For the Love of Tillie, The Adventures of Tillie**
Home-movie editions: **The City Slicker, Married for Money, Love Riot, Their New Home, Two-Timing Charlie, Tillie's Flirtation, Charlie and Tillie's Elopement, Charlie Ditches Tillie, Charlie the Fortune Hunter**
Cast: Marie Dressler (*Tillie Banks*), Charlie Chaplin (*the city slicker*), Mabel Normand (*Mabel*), Mack Swain (*John Banks* and *man on street*), Charles Bennett (*Donald Banks, Tillie's rich uncle*), Charles Murray (*detective*), Charles Parrott [Charley Chase] (*detective in movie theater*), Chester Conklin (*Mr. Whoozis*), Edgar Kennedy (*restaurant owner* and *servant*), Harry McCoy (*pianist*), Glen Cavender (*pianist* and *cop*), Gene Marsh (*maid*), Phyllis Allen (*prison matron* and *restaurant patron*), Alice Davenport (*guest*), Fred Fishback (*servant*), Gordon Griffith†† (*newsboy*), Frank Opperman (*Rev. D. Simpson*), Hank Mann (*cop*), George "Slim" Summerville (*cop*), Al St. John (*cop*), Wallace MacDonald (*cop*), Joe Bordeaux (*cop*), G. G. [Grover] Liggon (*cop*), Billie Bennett (*girl at party*), Alice Howell (*guest*), A. Edward Sutherland (*cop*).
Credits: Directed by Mack Sennett. Written by Hampton Del Ruth. Based on the 1910 play "Tillie's Nightmare" by A. Baldwin Sloane and Edgar Sloane.
Plot: A city slicker sweet-talks Tillie Banks, a naive country girl, into grabbing her father's money and running away with him. Shortly after hitting the big city, Tillie gets drunk and is arrested, while the slicker makes off with her dough and meets up with Mabel, his old partner-in-crime. Upon her release from jail, the disgraced Tillie finds employment as a waitress. Tillie's rich uncle Donald, "a well-known pie manufacturer," is lost during a mountain-climbing expedition; when the newspapers declare Tillie the sole heir to a $3,000,000 fortune, the

crafty slicker ditches Mabel and proposes to Tillie, who foolishly forgives his previous trespass. The newlyweds move into Uncle Donald's mansion and throw a lavish party to announce their arrival in high society. Not to be undone—or cut out of the action—Mabel crashes the event by getting a job as a maid. But the news of Uncle Donald's death is premature. He only sustained a bad fall, and returns home just as Tillie catches her new husband kissing Mabel. All hell breaks loose and the cops are summoned. After a wild chase, the slicker is apprehended as Tillie and Mabel come to the realization that the cad has victimized both of them.

Source of print screened: ***Tillie's Punctured Romance and Mabel's Married Life*** (Image Entertainment)

Comments: ***Tillie's Punctured Romance***'s primary claim to fame is that it was the first feature-length comedy film. It's also notable as the last starring film in which Chaplin was directed by someone else. As a Chaplin movie, it marks a regression back to earlier non-Tramp efforts like ***Making a Living*** and ***Mabel at the Wheel***. But as a Keystone comedy, it's one of the best, and certainly the best one Mack Sennett personally directed, although the rough edges of his style are readily apparent.

Tillie's Punctured Romance had a 14-week shooting schedule (late April 1914 to late July), extravagant by Keystone terms. To the casual observer, the film may seem to be just another (albeit longer) Keystone farce, but viewing it within the context of Sennett's work to date, it's a very ambitious production that benefits from surprisingly assured direction and slick location work.

Chaplin's city slicker bears little outward resemblance to the Tramp, though he retains his trademark cane and shuffle. With a spiffy jacket and trimmed mustache, Charlie's gentlemanly appearance here seems like a hybrid of his characters in the earlier ***Making a Living*** and the much later ***Monsieur Verdoux***. (He also bears a slight resemblance to actor Douglas Fairbanks, a close friend of Chaplin's.) Yet beneath the somewhat tidier exterior there beats the heart of the Tramp, who still gets intoxicated at social gatherings and who still spanks a leopardskin rug after he's tripped over it.

The passage of time and numerous theatrical reissue/home video incarnations have obscured the fact that ***Tillie's Punctured Romance*** was designed as a starring vehicle for Marie Dressler, with Chaplin and Mabel Normand in support. Dressler (1869-1934) had gained national fame in the play "Tillie's Nightmare" (1910), from which the film was (very) loosely adapted. When he was embarking on a theatrical career, Mack Sennett sought the advice of Dressler, an experienced stage actress; now, Sennett arranged for her to star in the most ambitious production that he ever tackled.

The broad facial expressions and body gestures Dressler employed onstage made her an ideal candidate for a Keystone heroine. Dressler had a knack for delivering boisterous performances that never became overbearing. Though middle-aged and overweight, she was certainly up to the physical demands of the role; she's a comic powerhouse who gives Charlie and Mabel a good run for their money.

Portions of *Tillie's Punctured Romance* have overtones of a typical Keystone effort. Marie and Charlie's initial encounter occurs on a farm, but the resulting flirtation, slapping, and brick-tossing could have just as easily taken place at a park, a hotel lobby, or an auto race. Dressler and Chaplin establish an immediate rapport, and the by-play between the con artist and his unwitting dupe foreshadows Chaplin's empty-promises relationship with Martha Raye in *Monsieur Verdoux*. (Marie and Charlie's society party also predates the frantic wedding reception in *Verdoux*.)

Aside from Dressler, the rest of the cast is comprised of familiar Keystone faces: Mack Swain, Charlie Murray, Edgar Kennedy, Chester Conklin (who has his usual combative relationship with Charlie), Phyllis Allen, Glen Cavender, Alice Davenport, Hank Mann, and Al St. John all turn up at various junctures, some doing double duty. Chaplin is once again paired with Mabel Normand, and it's arguably their best teaming, as they have a greater opportunity to interact with one another. It's definitely one of Mabel's finest hours; on several occasions her deft clowning manages the near-impossible feat of drawing attention away from Dressler and Chaplin!

One of the film's highlights finds Charlie and Mabel hiding out in a movie theater after they've purchased new clothes with Marie's money. The picture flashing on the screen is titled "A Thief's Fate," and they both squirm as they realize the movie's plot bears a strong similarity to their current situation. To complicate matters, a detective just happens to be sitting next to them. The detective is played by Charley Chase, who, for once, gets an opportunity to be funny in a Keystone comedy (he was usually cast as a straight man for other Keystone players). Unfortunately, this entire interlude is missing from most bargain-priced video and DVD copies of this movie.

To Sennett's credit, *Tillie's Punctured Romance* never feels like an elongated one-reel short. Much of the humor seems dated, but the film barrels along at a merry pace, so one is never bored with the proceedings. Sennett is more at home with the comedy set-pieces than he is with the rudiments of storytelling. Particularly clumsy is his handling of the subplot involving Tillie's Uncle Donald (Charles Bennett), who falls down the side of a mountain and is rescued by a guide. As presented by Sennett, it takes longer for the guide to journey several feet down a hill than it does to print *and* distribute a newspaper containing an article about Uncle Donald's death!

Though *Tillie's Punctured Romance* was an enormous hit, Marie Dressler did not derive any immediate benefits from it. She starred in two quasi-sequels, *Tillie's Tomato Surprise* (Lubin, 1915) and *Tillie Wakes Up* (Peerless-World, 1917), neither of which created much of a stir at the box office. In addition, Dressler unsuccessfully tried to bring legal action against the Keystone Company, charging that she had been promised half ownership in *Tillie's Punctured Romance* and that her husband was supposed to have handled the distribution of the film. Her movie career was increasingly erratic until the advent of "talking" pictures. Under contract to Metro-Goldwyn-Mayer, Dressler became one of Hollywood's best loved and most popular actresses (she was the number one box-office star in the early '30s), delivering beautifully rendered seriocomic performances in *Anna Christie* (1930), *Min and Bill* (1931; for which she won an Oscar as Best Actress), *Emma* (1932), *Tugboat Annie* (1933) and *Dinner at Eight* (1933).

For Mack Sennett (1880-1960), *Tillie's Punctured Romance* was the crowning achievement of his Keystone period. In 1915 Sennett joined D. W. Griffith, and Thomas Ince to form the Triangle Film Corporation; in 1917, he formed his own company, Mack Sennett Comedies. By the time he ceased producing and directing in the mid-'30s, Sennett was credited with nurturing the film careers of Gloria Swanson, Carole Lombard, Harry Langdon, W. C. Fields, and Bing Crosby. Acknowledged as the "King of Comedy," Sennett was given a special Academy Award in 1937. In later years he made cameo appearances—as himself—in movies dealing with the by-gone era of silent cinema (*Hollywood Cavalcade*, *Down Memory Lane*, *Abbott and Costello Meet the Keystone Kops*). His autobiography, *King of Comedy*, was published in 1954.

For Mabel Normand (1894-1930), *Tillie's Punctured Romance* was one of the high points in the sad career of the troubled actress. While her offscreen love affair with Mack Sennett came to an abrupt end, she continued to star in numerous Keystone comedy shorts with Roscoe "Fatty" Arbuckle (*Fatty and Mabel Adrift*, *Fatty and Mabel at the San Diego Exposition*, et al.), as well as feature films like *Mickey* (1917) and *The Extra Girl* (1923). In 1922, her reputation as a comedienne was overshadowed by her involvement in the murder of film director William Desmond Taylor (Mabel was the last known person to see him alive); she was absolved, but the scandal dogged her for years. The Queen of the Keystone Studio died of tuberculosis in 1930.

For Chaplin, the success of ***Tillie's Punctured Romance*** cemented his position as the premier comedy star in motion pictures. The film hardly represents any artistic advancement for the comedian, but it does represent the culmination of his 34 short films, neatly wrapping up and putting a bow on the entire Keystone package.

(It would be seven years before the release of another feature-length comedy starring Charlie Chaplin. ***The Kid*** [First National, 1921], the first *real* Chaplin feature, was made when he had complete creative control over his work.)

Note: The version of ***Tillie's Punctured Romance*** we screened—and the version we recommend—is the restoration available on DVD from Image Entertainment. This edition was assembled from multiple sources; despite occasional shifts in pictorial quality, this is the best-looking and most complete print on the market. (It even includes a final shot of stage curtains closing, which is missing from every other copy we've seen.) If you're planning to add this title to your collection, be sure to get the Image release, which also comes with an excellent-quality bonus Chaplin Keystone, ***Mabel's Married Life***.

This restoration serves as a reminder that most people who think they've seen ***Tillie's Punctured Romance*** really haven't. For years, a complete copy wasn't even available for screening. The film was reissued throughout the silent era, under a variety of different titles, including ***Tillie's Big Romance***, ***Charlie's Big Romance*** (to capitalize on Chaplin's popularity), and ***For the Love of Tillie***. With each reissue, the film's running time was compromised. In the early 1920s, it was whittled down to a three-reel version titled ***Tillie's Love Affair*** (a.k.a. ***Tilly's Love Affair***). ***Marie's Millions***, a souped-up "sound" revision with music and sound effects, was released in 1929.

The 8mm home movie market produced editions that were further truncated. Retitled abridgements like ***The City Slicker***, ***Love Riot***, ***Charlie Ditches Tillie***, and ***Their New Home*** had running times ranging from three to twelve minutes!

Today, the version of ***Tillie's Punctured Romance*** most commonly available derives from the truncated Monogram Pictures reissue. Monogram was one of Hollywood's "Poverty Row" operations, specializing in cheaply-produced B-movie fare like comedies with The East Side Kids (later regrouped as The Bowery Boys), Charlie Chan mysteries (after lead actor Sidney Toler's stint as Chan at 20th Century Fox), and Bela Lugosi horror thrillers. In 1941 Monogram released a 38-minute condensation of ***Tillie's Punctured Romance*** with a tinny music score and non-stop narration. (If you think Chaplin's narration for his 1942 reissue of *The Gold Rush* is needlessly verbose, it's the model of restraint compared to the filibustering in the Monogram edition.) Burwood Pictures, an obscure independent distributor, reissued the Monogram condensation in 1950, and it's this version that budget-priced DVD manufacturers offer to consumers. Sitting through this awful edition is a migraine-inducing ordeal you wouldn't wish on anyone. Worse yet, it does a tremendous disservice to silent-era cinema in general, reinforcing the misconception that all silent movies are of similarly poor quality.

Six Degrees of Separation: A. Edward Sutherland (1895-1974), who plays a cop in *Tillie's Punctured Romance*, worked as an assistant director on Chaplin's *A Woman of Paris* (United Artists, 1923) and *The Gold Rush* (United Artists, 1925). Later, Sutherland became a full-fledged director, working with comedians such as Eddie Cantor (*Palmy Days*, 1931), W. C. Fields (*International House*, 1933; *Mississippi*, 1935; *Poppy*, 1936), Laurel & Hardy (*The Flying Deuces*, 1939), and Abbott & Costello (*One Night in the Tropics*, 1940). Intriguingly, Sutherland also directed an in-name-only remake of *Tillie's Punctured Romance* (Paramount, 1928) starring Louise Fazenda, W. C. Fields, and Chester Conklin. At this writing, no print of the film is known to have survived.

Other Views and Reviews: "Marie Dressler breaks into the story at the first jump. She fits into the Keystone style of work as to the manner born. Charlie Chaplin plays opposite Marie Dressler. The two constitute a rare team of funmakers. Chaplin outdoes Chaplin; that's all there is to it. Mack Sennett has done well."—*The Moving Picture World* (1914).

"Miss Dressler is the central figure, but Chaplin's camera antics are an essential feature in putting the picture over."—*Variety* (1914).

"It is more than mere slapstick. It is a smart take-off of the old city slicker-country maiden cliché adding some pointed thrusts at the 'high society' of the period."—Theodore Huff, *Charlie Chaplin* (1951).

"It was pleasant working with Marie, but I did not think the picture had much merit."—Charles Chaplin, *My Autobiography* (1964).

"Elaborately and luxuriously staged for the time, the film was free swinging in all aspects. Filled with earthy humor and somewhat vulgar in places...rather static and stagelike at the outset, the film gradually became more cinematic in tone as it progressed."—Kalton C. Lahue and Terry Brewer, *Kops and Custards: The Legend of Keystone Films* (1968).

"*Tillie's Punctured Romance* is still vital comedy, perhaps too vital. It is funny although much of its basic appeal may be to folks who enjoy cockfights and mud-wrestling."—John McCabe, *Charlie Chaplin* (1978).

"Behind the slapstick and extravagant farce, there is a realistic and quite affecting theme of a stupid, good-natured country girl duped by a ne'er-do-well sharper…At moments Chaplin's characterization of the deft, funny, heartless adventurer anticipates Verdoux [the central character in Chaplin's **Monsieur Verdoux**]."—David Robinson, *Chaplin: His Life and Art* (1985).

"A historical curiosity, necessary for your Chaplin collection out of a sense of completeness rather than for great comic enjoyment."—Lawrance M. Bernabo, *Amazon.com* (2001).

"The thing that really makes this movie great is Marie Dressler. The way she carries her considerable girth is a major element in the comedy and her big face and huge eyes are strictly for howling."—Taz Delaney, *The Internet Movie Database* (2003).

†Many sources give the release date for **Tillie's Punctured Romance** as November 14, 1914. The December 14 date that we decided to go with is the one given in Jeffrey Vance's *Chaplin: Genius of the Cinema* (Harry N. Abrams, Inc., 2003) and Kalton C. Lahue and Terry Brewer's *Kops and Custards: The Legend of Keystone Films* (University of Oklahoma Press, 1968).

††For years, Milton Berle claimed to have played the role of the newsboy. Although Berle did appear in some silent films, he is not in **Tillie's Punctured Romance**. The newsboy is clearly Gordon Griffith, who was seen in other Chaplin Keystones.

In *Making a Living* (Keystone, 1914), Charlie Chaplin makes his film debut not as the Tramp, but as a "nervy and very nifty sharper."

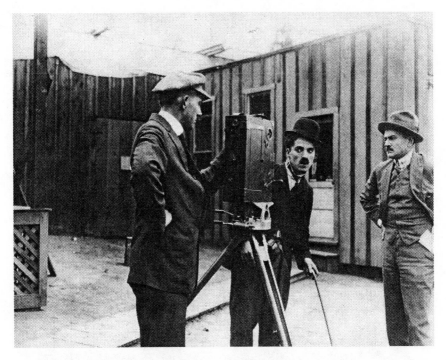

Movie audiences were introduced to the Tramp in *Kid Auto Races at Venice* (Keystone, 1914). Here Chaplin poses with cameraman Frank D. Williams (left) and director Henry Lehrman (right). (*Courtesy of Jamie Brotherton.*)

Poster for *Cruel, Cruel Love* (Keystone, 1914), in which Chaplin forsook his trademark Tramp costume. (*From the collection of David Maska.*)

This poster for *Laughing Gas* (Keystone, 1914) also depicts Joseph Swickard as Charlie's hapless patient. In these early days, it was standard practice for Keystone not to identify the performers, so Chaplin's name does not appear on the poster. (*From the collection of David Maska.*)

Charlie and Keystone favorite Mabel Normand co-starred in *Caught in a Cabaret* (1914), which they also co-wrote and co-directed. Charlie and Mabel appeared in a total of 12 films together.

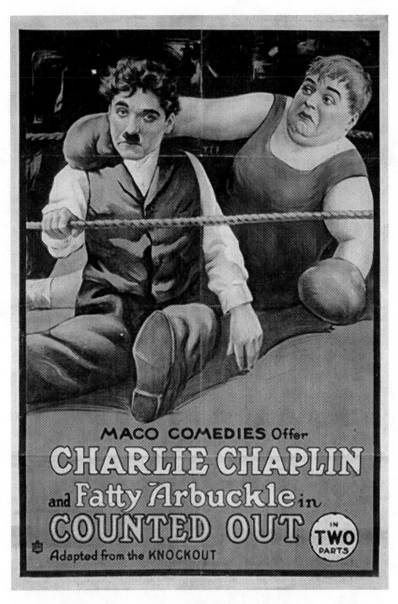

Chaplin made a brief appearance in *The Knockout* (Keystone, 1914), which starred Roscoe "Fatty" Arbuckle. When the film was reissued as *Counted Out*, Chaplin was given top billing. (*From the collection of David Maska.*)

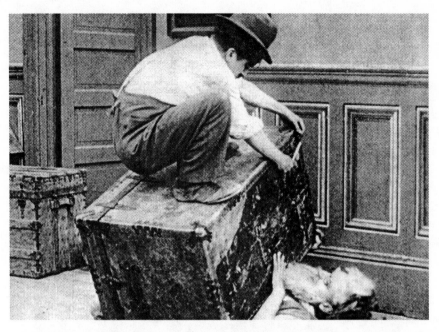

Charlie's counterproductive efforts to help his assistant (Josef Swickard) in *The Property Man* (Keystone, 1914). (*Courtesy of Jamie Brotherton.*)

Although Chaplin and Roscoe "Fatty" Arbuckle appeared together in several Keystones, *The Rounders* (1914) represents their only full-fledged teaming.

Phyllis Allen and Mack Swain catch Mabel Normand and Charlie in the
act of *Getting Acquainted* (Keystone, 1914).
(Courtesy of Jamie Brotherton.)

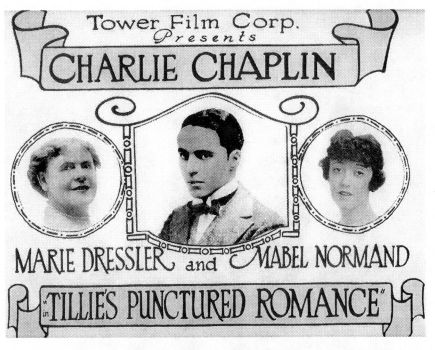

For a 1920 reissue of *Tillie's Punctured Romance* (Keystone, 1914), Chaplin was given top billing over Marie Dressler, the original star of the picture. (*From the collection of Ted Okuda.*)

Exhibitors displayed this life-sized cutout alongside theater box offices to promote Chaplin's Essanay releases. (*From the collection of David Maska.*)

In 1915, lovely Edna Purviance (1895-1958) began appearing in Chaplin's films and quickly established herself as his finest leading lady. (*From the collection of Ted Okuda.*)

Charlie and cross-eyed comic Ben Turpin square off in *His New Job* (Essanay, 1915). (*Courtesy of Jamie Brotherton.*)

Drunk and very disorderly, Ben Turpin and Charlie incur the wrath of Leo White during *A Night Out* (Essanay, 1915). (*Courtesy of Jamie Brotherton.*)

Charlie with his faithful companion Spike the bulldog in *The Champion* (Essanay, 1915). (*Courtesy of Jamie Brotherton.*)

Edna Purviance gets caught between Charlie, a phony Count, and Leo White, the real deal, in *A Jitney Elopement* (Essanay, 1915). (*Courtesy of Jamie Brotherton.*)

Charlie hits the road at the conclusion of *The Tramp* (Essanay, 1915),
which many consider to be Chaplin's first masterpiece.

Edna Purviance and Charlie both take a break from *Work* (Essanay, 1915). (*Courtesy of Jamie Brotherton.*)

A heartbreaking moment from *The Bank* (1915), one of Chaplin's finest Essanay films. (*From the collection of David Maska.*)

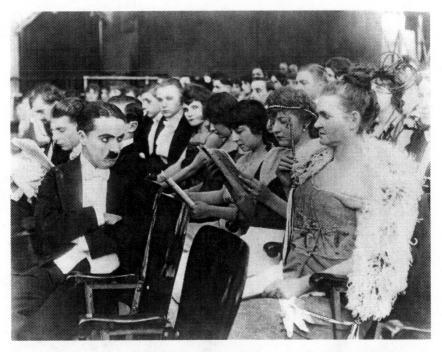

The inebriated Mr. Pest creates pandemonium in the audience and on the stage when he spends *A Night in the Show* (Essanay, 1915). (*Courtesy of Jamie Brotherton.*)

Dashing soldier Darn Hosiery (Chaplin) falls under the spell of the exotic gypsy Carmen (Edna Purviance) in *Burlesque on "Carmen"* (Essanay, 1915-16). Chaplin's original two-reel version is arguably his best film for Essanay. (*From the collection of David Maska.*)

Essanay took leftover footage from Chaplin's uncompleted feature film *Life* and concocted an ersatz Chaplin short, *Triple Trouble* (1918). *Top*: Assistant cook Charlie meets servant Edna Purviance. *Above*: Charlie spends an eventful evening in a flophouse. (*Frame enlargements from the collection of David Maska.*)

During the 1960s, companies like Coast Films made 8mm abridgements of Chaplin's Keystones and Essanays available to the home-movie collectors market. (*From the collection of Ted Okuda.*)

The Essanay Studio located at 1345 W. Argyle Street in Chicago was des-
ignated as a landmark on March 26, 1996. Note the trademark terra-
cotta Indian heads flanking the building's entrance. (*Photographed in
2004 by David Maska.*)

CHAPLIN AT ESSANAY

By the end of 1914, Chaplin was not only the most popular comedian at Keystone, he was on his way to becoming the most popular comedian in motion pictures. Ironically, because the Keystone comedies didn't identify the performers in the credits, some moviegoers and critics didn't even know his proper name; it was not uncommon to read a review that referred to Chaplin as Charlie Chapman, Charlie Englishman, or Edgar English.

As his one-year contract neared its expiration date, Chaplin tried to arrange a more lucrative deal with Mack Sennett. Sources differ as to the exact terms of their negotiations; reported offers vary from $400 to $750 per week. Sennett painted a bleak picture, cautioning Chaplin that leaving Keystone would have a disastrous effect on his newfound stardom. Privately, Chaplin was concerned that no other studio would be interested in his services. Yet a rumor began circulating that he was seeking a salary of $1,250 per week plus a $10,000 bonus. The Essanay Film Manufacturing Company agreed to those terms—Chaplin happily accepted, even though he wasn't making those demands to begin with—and Sennett lost his biggest attraction. (Although, in Sennett's defense, Chaplin had asked for more money than Sennett made.)

Established in 1907, Essanay (pronounced *S-and-A*) got its name from the initials of its founders, George K. *Spoor* and Gilbert M. *Anderson*. Spoor was the one who ran the company, while Anderson was better known as movie cowboy star "Broncho Billy" Anderson. Essanay was advertised as "The House of Comedy Hits," and turned out some moderately successful comedies with Ben Turpin and Wallace Beery; in 1912, Essanay's most popular comedian was the now-forgotten Augustus "Alkali Ike" Carney. Unlike Keystone, Essanay was never able to develop a major comic talent of their own, and the studio seized the opportunity to sign Chaplin.

Chaplin closed the deal with Essanay in November 1914, and by the following January, the studio placed advertisements in exhibitor journals that proudly proclaimed "Millions Are Laughing With CHARLES CHAPLIN—The Greatest Comedian is now with ESSANAY." Chaplin's first Essanay comedy, the aptly named **His New Job**, was released on February 1, 1915. Essanay even provided exhibitors with an extremely short promotional film called ***Introducing Charlie Chaplin***, which heralded their star attraction. (There is no documentation as to what this promotional film actually consisted of.)

Despite this ballyhoo, however, Chaplin clashed with Essanay management. George K. Spoor claimed he never heard of the comedian, and Chaplin bristled when Spoor tried to renege on the agreed-upon $10,000 bonus. The studio expected Chaplin to work from scripts prepared by their scenario department, which was headed by Louella Parsons (who later became a powerful Hollywood gossip columnist); Chaplin vehemently refused, insisting he would create his own material. Additionally, Chaplin was horrified when he wanted to look at daily "rushes" (the footage completed thus far) and discovered that it was a standard practice at Essanay to screen the original camera negative instead of positive prints. And later, after leaving Essanay, Chaplin unsuccessfully sued the company for re-editing films with his permission. (It didn't seem to bother Chaplin that Keystone also mangled his films; perhaps he wasn't upset because he never thought much of those pictures to begin with.)

For the rest of his life, Chaplin would remain bitter about his Essanay period. That's a pity, because his work for them represents one of the most important chapters in his career. These are the movies that made Charlie Chaplin an international star.

"Like Borneo and Uruguay, Charles Chaplin's Essanay comedies are well-known but seldom-visited, even by the comedian's many passionate devotees. In part perhaps this is because Chaplin is thought to have improved upon their outstanding moments in his later work, but the series is actually rich in ideas and routines to which he never returned."

—David Shepard, *liner notes for Kino's **Chaplin's Essanay Comedies*** *series.*

"When Chaplin left Sennett to set up shop at Essanay studios, he removed himself from one kind of atmosphere and moved toward the artistic isolation that enabled him to create more personal and in some cases more 'serious' films. This was a transitional period, with more time to think about each new film and polish his screen character. The Essanay shorts are still rough-edged, but they represent a giant stride from the crudity of his Keystone comedies."

—Leonard Maltin, *The Great Movie Comedians.*

"The first few Essanays were moderately refined reworkings of ideas Chaplin had done at Keystone…While none of these is remarkable in a critical sense, each has its share of brilliant, telling moments…at Essanay, Chaplin allows Charlie to stop, observe, and think before reacting."

—James L. Neibaur, *Film Quarterly.*

"Some Chaplin fans look askance at [the Essanays], thinking they're not as fun and full of motion as the free-wheeling Keystone films he made before, or as developed and artistic as the Mutual shorts soon to come. These were almost like expensive home movies, where all the production money went into Chaplin's bank account, leaving little to be seen on the screen…[Nevertheless] the results are a testament to a comedic genius and the legend Chaplin continues to inspire."

—Michael Copner, *Cult Movies.*

"At Essanay Chaplin discovered who the little tramp figure was and how he related to the world of respectability and propriety that both surrounded and excluded him. To the tramp's pluck and toughness developed at Keystone, Chaplin added a greater sensitivity to those beings—usually personified by a woman, Edna Purviance—who deserved his sympathy. The tramp's enemies took on more specific form. No longer were they any human being that he could kick with his oversized shoe; they became representatives of antagonistic social and moral forces…He began to see that the tramp was doomed to fail at obtaining earthly rewards."

—Gerald Mast, *The Comic Mind.*

At Essanay, Chaplin was able to take more time to explore the comedic possibilities of a given situation. There were still traces of the raucous Keystone style, but increasing creative control yielded rewarding results. His screen persona began to mature, and the comic set-pieces were far more structured and fleshed-out than they had been in the past.

A major asset of the Essanays was the addition of Edna Purviance (1895-1958) to Chaplin's roster of supporting players. The lovely Purviance (rhymes with *appliance*) was no Keystone harridan—her natural beauty and poise lent a romantic ambiance to the proceedings that allowed Chaplin's character to exhibit hitherto unseen traces of warmth and humanity. Edna had no prior show business experience and though she never became a major dramatic actress, she had a charming screen presence and soon developed a great flair for comedy.

Purviance was Chaplin's finest leading lady. Unlike the Keystone females, she wasn't in competition with Chaplin for laughs and was more ideally suited to the tone of his later work. Edna and Charlie established an onscreen intimacy that no doubt reflected their offscreen romantic relationship at the time. Beginning with *A Night Out* (1915), Edna would appear in every Chaplin film—except *One A. M.* (Mutual, 1916)—until 1923.† Chaplin had difficulty finding a suitable replacement for her; many believe he never did.

During his yearlong stay (1915-16) at Essanay, Chaplin wrote and directed a total of 14 shorts. His first seven Essanays were completed and released within a three-month period. The others were released at a rate of one a month, as Chaplin began spending more time on the creation of each comedy. Around the time of *The Bank* (1915), Chaplin started shooting multiple takes. He also began "acting" on the side of the camera to set a mood for a scene. This marked the beginning of Chaplin's legendary obsessive work methods.

The last two Chaplin Essanays, *Burlesque on "Carmen"* and *Police* (both released in 1916), were re-edited without his approval. Essanay further milked the Chaplin cash cow by releasing *The Essanay Chaplin Revue of 1916*, which linked three shorts together to form an ersatz feature, and *Triple Trouble* (1918), a two-reeler that culled footage from earlier shorts and Chaplin's uncompleted feature *Life*, and mixed it with newer non-Chaplin material. (The Essanay Company had been irked by Keystone's Chaplin reissues competing with their product, and now their reissues were going head-to-head with Chaplin's First National releases.)

Though not in the same league as the brilliant comedies that would follow, the Chaplin Essanays reveal a gifted filmmaker growing by leaps and bounds. The Charlie Chaplin of *The Gold Rush*, *The Circus*, *City Lights*, and *Modern Times* would not have existed without these humble yet often quite entertaining intermediary endeavors.

†Edna Purviance starred in *A Woman of Paris* (1923), written and directed by Chaplin (who appears fleetingly as a porter). It was and is a fine film, but its box office failure foiled this attempt to launch a career for Purviance as a dramatic actress. She later had unbilled extra roles in Chaplin's *Monsieur Verdoux* (1947) and *Limelight* (1952).

THE CHAPLIN ESSANAYS

Unless noted, all were produced by Jess Robbins for the Essanay Film Manufacturing Company, and originally distributed to theaters through the exchanges of the General Film Company.

One reel of film (35mm) was approximately 1,000 feet in length, with a running time of 10 to 14 minutes, depending on the projection speed.

The entries for *Home-movie editions* refer to retitled (and usually abridged) versions issued to the home-movie market.

36. *His New Job*
(Two Reels; Released February 1, 1915)
British title: **Charlie's New Job**
Cast: Charlie Chaplin (*studio stagehand*), Ben Turpin (*assistant property man*), Charlotte Mineau (*leading lady*), Leo White (*receptionist* and *film actor*), Gloria Swanson (*stenographer*), Agnes Ayres (*extra wearing black lace*).
Credits: Written and directed by Charlie Chaplin.
Plot: At the Lockstone movie studio (a playful reference to "Keystone"), Charlie gets a job as a stagehand and creates havoc during the filming of a costume picture. When the lead actor storms off the set, the director surprisingly recruits Charlie as his replacement. Not so surprisingly, Charlie wrecks the entire production.
Source of print screened: **Chaplin's Essanay Comedies Vol. 1** (Kino On Video)
Comments: Though **His New Job** was Chaplin's first Essanay, it's really a Keystone comedy at heart. Despite the effort Chaplin makes to set up the admittedly loose premise, the film devolves into a mere succession of gags—many of them cruel and sadistic in the Keystone tradition—and grinds to a halt when the allotted time runs out, arriving at no genuine conclusion.

Marking the first time Chaplin received on-screen billing ("Featuring Charlie Chaplin"), **His New Job** was filmed entirely at—make that *in*—Essanay's facilities in Chicago, the base of the company's operation. The winter climate prevented any outdoor shooting, and Chaplin logically chose to confine the action to the studio setting. In this controlled environment, Chaplin begins to make tentative stabs at developing his own style, both visually and technically, although the primitive and claustrophobic working conditions at the Chicago studio didn't lend itself to anyone's artistic growth.

For *His New Job*, Charlie was paired with Ben Turpin, one of Essanay's established comedy stars, but it's not a full-fledged partnership. Chaplin's adversarial relationship with the subordinate Turpin is identical to the one he shared with Chester Conklin in the Keystone comedies, right down to such heavy-handed gags as running a saw blade across Turpin's rear end.

Charlie's attempts to act in Lockstone's costume melodrama provide *His New Job* with its funniest moments. Looking positively ludicrous in an oversized Cossack uniform, Charlie bends his sword, making it difficult to return it to its sheath, and knocks over a free-standing prop pillar; when he stoops to kiss the leading lady's hem, he accidentally rips her skirt. For this sequence, Chaplin employed a moving camera, a device rarely used in American films of the period.

Gloria Swanson (1899-1983) appears as the stenographer in the opening scenes of *His New Job*. At this point in her career, she was an anonymous bit player; in less than 10 years, she would become one of the most popular stars in Hollywood. Swanson performed expert imitations of Chaplin in *Manhandled* (1924) and *Sunset Boulevard* (1950), and narrated the Chaplin documentary *The Eternal Tramp* (1970).

This was the first and last Essanay that Chaplin made in Chicago. He hated the city's cold climate and returned to California after completing the film.

His New Job is one of the lesser Chaplin Essanays, representing the comedian embarking on a journey rather than arriving at a destination. Fans will want to check it out for historical reasons, but those who just want to settle back and enjoy a funny movie are advised to look elsewhere.

Other Views and Reviews: "It is absolutely necessary to laugh at Chaplin in ten-ninths of his antics in this disaster-attended search for a new job—the small point in which is evidenced the only irony in the picture."—*Chicago Tribune* (1915).

"Chaplin is still the incorrigible Keystone Charlie, cheerfully causing chaos by his insouciant incompetence."—David Robinson, *Chaplin: His Life and Art* (1985).

"The humor in *His New Job* is slightly forced, being presented more methodically than its immediate predecessors at Keystone, but not yet replacing speed with anything superior."—Glen Mitchell, *The Chaplin Encyclopedia* (1997).

"This short is hilariously funny."—anton-6, *The Internet Movie Database* (2001).

37. *A Night Out*
(Two Reels; Released February 15, 1915)

Reissue titles: **Charlie's Night Out, His Night Out**
Home-movie editions: **Charlie's Night Out, Charley Butts In, Charlie's Drunken Daze, Charlie at the Restaurant, Champagne Charlie**
Cast: Charlie Chaplin (*Charlie*), Ben Turpin (*his drinking pal*), Bud Jamison (*the headwaiter*), Edna Purviance (*the headwaiter's wife*), Leo White (*Frenchman* and *hotel receptionist*), Fred Goodwins (*hotel receptionist*).
Credits: Written and directed by Charlie Chaplin. Photographed by Harry Ensign.
Plot: Out on the town, Charlie and Ben are drunk and very disorderly. At a restaurant, the boys have a run-in the headwaiter. Later, Charlie returns to his hotel room and gets caught in a compromising situation with the woman across the hall—she just happens to be the headwaiter's wife!
Source of print screened: **Chaplin's Essanay Comedies Vol. 1** (Kino On Video)
Comments: Chaplin still hasn't divorced himself from his Keystone ancestry. The first half of *A Night Out* borrows heavily from **The Rounders**, while the second half is merely a reworking of **Mabel's Strange Predicament**. It's all very roughhouse in nature, although under Chaplin's direction it's smoother in execution. In fact, it's arguably the best-paced Chaplin film to date.

Chaplin was paired with Essanay contract comedian Ben Turpin, and the two make a surprisingly effective team in *A Night Out*. Turpin was never as subtle as Chaplin, but he knew how to throw himself into the spirit of things and deliver a gag for maximum effect. Throughout the first reel, Charlie and Ben play the drunk routine to the hilt, with lots of rigorous physical comedy. Judging by their precise interaction, you would think they had been partners for years. As they stagger their way into a restaurant or through a hallway in search of their hotel room, the two performers are completely in sync with each other.

Ben Turpin (1874-1940), whose crossed eyes were his trademark, had appeared in **His New Job**, Chaplin's first Essanay. *A Night Out* is their second and final pairing; Turpin played a minor supporting role in **The Champion** (1915), but had no interaction with Chaplin in the film, and Turpin's scenes in **Burlesque on "Carmen"** (1916) were added after Chaplin had completed the picture.

Turpin did not get along with Chaplin, complaining that Charlie's directorial methods were too exacting. Turpin would go on to star in his own series of successful comedies for Mack Sennett. He would later tell an interviewer, "I have since proved that I could work without him. I am now a star...and my films make lots of money." By the time talking pictures revolutionized the industry, Turpin was quite wealthy and made only occasional screen appearances.

Turpin died on July 1, 1940. Chaplin did not attend the funeral, but he did send a seven-foot spray of red roses in memory of his former teammate.

Edna Purviance made her film debut in *A Night Out*. She works well with Charlie, though there's no real indication at this early stage that she would become his finest leading lady.

A Night Out also marked the first time William "Bud" Jamison (1894-1944) worked with Chaplin. Here, Jamison wears thick painted-on eyebrows and a bushy mustache, giving him an uncanny resemblance to Eric Campbell, who co-starred in Chaplin's later Mutual comedies. Jamison, who also appeared in the majority of the Chaplin Essanays, would have an extensive career in short comedies, co-starring with Charley Chase, Buster Keaton, Harold Lloyd, Andy Clyde, Bing Crosby, W. C. Fields, Edgar Kennedy, and Clark & McCullough. Jamison is best remembered for his supporting roles in many Three Stooges two-reelers, including *Woman Haters* (1934), *Uncivil Warriors* (1935), *Disorder in the Court* (1936), *A Pain in the Pullman* (1936), *Whoops, I'm an Indian!* (1936), *Dizzy Doctors* (1937), *Termites of 1938* (1938), *Tassels in the Air* (1938), *A Ducking They Did Go* (1939), *Phony Express* (1943), and *Crash Goes the Hash* (1944). He was also seen in numerous feature films, among them: *The Chaser* (1928), *Moby Dick* (1930), *Blondie* (1938), *Topper Takes a Trip* (1939), *Li'l Abner* (1940), *Holiday Inn* (1942), and *Hello Frisco, Hello* (1943).

A Night Out was filmed at the Essanay Studio in Niles (a suburb of San Francisco), where Chaplin would make his next several releases.

Other Views and Reviews: "The film gives Chaplin full elbow-room for many extraordinary antics and touches of humorous detail, and the fun romps along at top speed…Turpin makes an excellent partner, and takes many a stunning knockout blow with paralytic indifference."—*The Cinema* (1915).

"Despite his pronounced dislike of Chaplin, [Turpin] worked well with the star and their interaction in *A Night Out* suggested the closest Chaplin ever came to having a true screen partner."—James Robert Parish and William T. Leonard, *The Funsters* (1979).

"Chaplin and Ben Turpin form a beautiful double act, sharing a solemn, unselfconscious, childlike air of mischief."—David Robinson, *Chaplin: His Life and Art* (1985).

"Chaplin employs 'fantasy' for the first time in the Essanays…In *A Night Out*, as the Tramp is pulled along the sidewalk by Ben Turpin, he believes that he is floating among water flowers on a river."—Jeffrey Vance, *"The Beginning of His Art" from Kino's Chaplin's Essanay Comedies* series (1999).

"Viewers interested in Chaplin's early work (i.e., the rough stuff, with lots of drunken foolery and butt-kicking) may well enjoy this film. I confess I enjoyed it, the way I might get a kick out of watching Championship Wrestling for 20 minutes or so. If it's Chaplin the Artiste you want, try the later features, but if you're in the mood for rude and unrefined slapstick, *A Night Out* should fit the bill nicely."—wmorrow59, *The Internet Movie Database* (2004).

38. *The Champion*
(Two Reels; Released March 11, 1915)
British title: **Champion Charlie**
Reissue title: **Charlie the Champion**
Home-movie editions: **Sparring Partner, Lucky Horseshoe, Lucky Day, His Lucky Day, The Boxer, Charlie the Boxer, Knock Out†, Gymnastics, Charlie the Champ, In the Ring, Charlie in the Ring, Battling Charlie, Charlie in Training**
Cast: Charlie Chaplin (*a would-be pugilist*), Edna Purviance (*the trainer's daughter*), Bud Jamison (*Bob Uppercut††*), Leo White (*crooked gambler*), Fred Goodwins (*Spike Dugan*), Ben Turpin (*ringside vendor*), Lloyd Bacon (*sparring partner*), Billy Armstrong (*sparring partner*), G. M. "Broncho Billy" Anderson (*fight spectator*), Spike the bulldog.
Credits: Written and directed by Charlie Chaplin. Photographed by Harry Ensign.
Plot: Charlie and his pet bulldog are walking past the training quarters for boxer Spike Dugan when Charlie notices a sign reading "SPARRING PARTNERS WANTED WHO CAN TAKE A PUNCH." Charlie gets a tryout, but increases the odds in his favor by putting a horseshoe in his glove. When he knocks Dugan unconscious, Charlie gets a bout with another boxer, Bob Uppercut. A crooked gambler tries to get Charlie to throw the fight, to no avail. In the ring, Uppercut gets the best of Charlie, until his bulldog rushes in and brings up the rear—Uppercut's rear!
Source of print screened: **Chaplin's Essanay Comedies Vol. 1** (Kino On Video)
Comments: After a couple of carbon copy Keystones, Chaplin begins to develop his own comedic style in *The Champion*. For the first time, a Chaplin film has a distinctly "Chaplinesque" opening: the Tramp shares his only meal, a hot dog, with his pet bulldog. But the bulldog waits until Charlie has taken a bite first, after which the hungry hound nibbles away. This charming set-piece immediately establishes Charlie as a sympathetic figure and reveals his close relationship

with his four-legged associate. (This key scene is missing from most DVD copies of the film. Fortunately, it has been restored in the Kino Video edition.)

The Champion reworks the plot of Fatty Arbuckle's *The Knockout* (Keystone, 1914), in which Chaplin turned in a brief appearance as a referee. This time it's Charlie's turn to play the would-be pugilist. The scenes at the training camp provide him with plenty of opportunity for physical comedy. After concealing a horseshoe in his glove, he becomes an unbeatable cock-of-the-walk, literally chasing Spike Dugan out of town. Hailed as a real contender, Charlie trains for an upcoming bout in his own unique manner, gulping down swigs of beer between the rigors of weightlifting.

In the climactic boxing match, Charlie is clearly outclassed by his mammoth opponent. Without the advantage of the lucky horseshoe, Charlie nimbly runs, skips, and staggers around the ring, managing to get in a few licks when he's not on the receiving end of his adversary's punches (and a few self-inflicted blows as well). This is a fast-paced, funny, and cleverly choreographed sequence that showcases Chaplin's graceful acrobatic skills. Here the fight is played strictly for laughs; for the brilliant boxing match in *City Lights* (1931), Chaplin would add a sense of dramatic tension to the hilarious antics.

As the trainer's daughter, Edna Purviance is onscreen briefly, having little to do but stand around and look attractive. (She has even less to do in most circulating copies of *The Champion*, which are missing the final romantic clinch between her and Charlie.) Leo White has one of his showier supporting roles as crooked gambler who tries to get Charlie to throw the big bout; Charlie refuses to take a dive, though he grabs the money anyway. Ben Turpin, who was paired with Chaplin in *His New Job* and *A Night Out*, appears as a ringside vendor during the boxing match; this time, Turpin has no interaction with Charlie, perhaps to the relief of both. Sadly, Spike the dog, Chaplin's *true* co-star in this film, was struck and killed by a car only a few weeks after production was completed.

While *The Champion* promises more than it delivers, it's a consistently entertaining piece that should satisfy Chaplin fans and dog lovers alike.

Trivia note: There were several imitators who capitalized on Chaplin's popularity, most notably Billy West, a talented mimic. However, one of the oddest was Minerva Courtney, who appeared in *Miss Minerva Courtney in Her Impersonation of Charlie Chaplin* (1915), a scene-for-scene copy of *The Champion*, minus the boxing sequence. Those who have seen the film report that Miss Courtney's attempts to replicate Chaplin's artistry are, in a word, putrid.

Other Views and Reviews: "Without doubt the funniest burlesque prize fight ever shown upon the screen."—*New York Dramatic Mirror* (1915).

"The *pièce de résistance* is the championship bout that ends the film. Running for six minutes, it is balletic in composition, with Charlie devising a series of exquisite choreographic variations."—David Robinson, *Chaplin: His Life and Art* (1985).

"The relationship of the Tramp and his dog would be fully developed three years later in **A Dog's Life** (1918), and Chaplin's brilliant choreography in the ring anticipates the boxing match in **City Lights** (1931)."—Jeffrey Vance, *Chaplin: Genius of the Cinema* (2003).

"This is where Chaplin's career as a great film comedian really begins...The film boasts lots of surefire gags, colorful supporting players, and an especially vigorous and winning performance from the leading player himself."—wmorrow59, *The Internet Movie Database* (2004).

†Not to be confused with **The Knockout** (Keystone, 1914).

††Many sources list Bud Jamison's character as "Young Hippo," but in the print we viewed he was identified as "Bob Uppercut."

39. *In the Park*
(One Reel; Released March 18, 1915)
British title: **Charlie in the Park**
Reissue titles: **Charlie in the Spring, Charlie on a Spree**
Home-movie edition: **Charlie in the Park**
Cast: Charlie Chaplin (*Charlie*), Edna Purviance (*nursemaid*), Bud Jamison (*nursemaid's boyfriend*), Leo White (*Frenchman*), Margie Reiger (*Frenchman's girlfriend*), Lloyd Bacon (*pickpocket*), Paddy McGuire (*tramp*), Ernest Van Pelt (*cop*), Fred Goodwins (*hot dog vendor*).
Credits: Written and directed by Charlie Chaplin. Photographed by Harry Ensign.
Plot: During a stroll in the park, Charlie has encounters with a nursemaid, a Frenchman, a hot dog vendor, and the law. A pickpocket and a stolen purse add to the confusion.
Source of print screened: **Chaplin's Essanay Comedies Vol. 1** (Kino On Video)
Comments: When Chaplin wound up spending more time than expected making **The Champion**, he was forced to turn out the next picture quickly in order to get back on schedule. **In the Park**, the resulting "rush job," is a well-executed version of a Keystone "park" comedy—**Twenty Minutes of Love** in particular—although it's still one of his least memorable Essanays.

The Keystone influence is apparent: Charlie uses Bud Jamison's open mouth for an ashtray, there's a fair amount of brick tossing (why are bricks *always* within arm's reach?), and the whole thing stops dead in its tracks at the finish. (You can tell this film was hastily made just by the fact that Bud Jamison's false mustache keeps changing size and density.) And yet the Chaplin influence is also evident: even though the actors play directly to the camera, their gestures are not as grandiose as they would have been in a Keystone production. By this time, Edna Purviance was becoming more relaxed onscreen; her best performances, however, were still to come.

Lloyd Bacon (1890-1955), who plays the pickpocket Charlie gets the better of, later became a prolific film director whose credits include *The Singing Fool* (1928), *Moby Dick* (1930), *42 nd Street* (1933), *Footlight Parade* (1933), *Gold Diggers of 1937* (1937), *Marked Woman* (1937), *A Slight Case of Murder* (1938), *The Oklahoma Kid* (1939), *Brother Orchid* (1940), *Knute Rockne—All-American* (1940), *Larceny, Inc.* (1942), *The Sullivans* (a.k.a. *The Fighting Sullivans*, 1944), *It Happens Every Spring* (1949), *The Good Humor Man* (1950), and *The French Line* (1954).

Filmed on location in San Francisco and Niles, California, *In the Park* represents a technical advance over Chaplin's previous Keystone efforts that involved a similar theme, although it's still a throwaway item within the context of his overall movie career.

Note: Chaplin's *Caught in the Rain* (Keystone, 1914) was reissued to the home-movie market by Official Films under the title *In the Park*. Most budget-priced DVD collections have confused the reissue for this Essanay effort, which is available from Kino On Video.

Other Views and Reviews: "The one and only Charlie is seen to the best advantage in this riotous farce which is as wildly funny as it is absurd. Unlike many comedians, Chaplin is always amusing. There seem to be no grey patches in his work. It is all one long scarlet scream."—*Bioscope* (1915).

"The Tramp here is at his least ingratiating. He is not only a pickpocket, but a cad as well...He even makes awful grimaces behind Edna's back."—David Robinson, *Chaplin: His Life and Art* (1985).

"A 'park' comedy in the Keystone mold, *In the Park* is better constructed and more incident-filled than its predecessors."—Glenn Mitchell, *The Chaplin Encyclopedia* (1997).

40. *A Jitney Elopement*
(Two Reels; Released April 1, 1915)

British title: **Charlie's Elopement**
Reissue title: **Married in Haste**
Home-movie editions: **The Tin Lizzy**, **Jitney**, **Charlie's Fiancée**, **Charlie the Playboy**
Cast: Charlie Chaplin (*Charlie, alias Count de Ha Ha*), Edna Purviance (*Edna*), Leo White (*Count Chloride de Lime*), Fred Goodwins (*Edna's father*), Lloyd Bacon† (*young servant* and *cop*), Paddy McGuire (*old servant* and *cop*), Bud Jamison (*cop with baton*), Carl Stockdale (*cop*).
Credits: Written and directed by Charlie Chaplin. Photographed by Harry Ensign.
Plot: Charlie is in love with Edna, but her father wants her to marry a wealthy Count. Charlie poses as Count de Ha Ha and the masquerade succeeds—until the genuine article, Count Chloride de Lime, shows up. Later, Charlie takes off with Edna in the Count's car, with the Count, Edna's father, and the police in hot pursuit.
Source of print screened: **Chaplin's Essanay Comedies Vol. 1** (Kino On Video)
Comments: For those of you under the age of 100, "jitney" was a slang term for automobile (other terms, like "flivver" and "tin lizzie," also popped up in films of the era).

A Jitney Elopement is basically modified Keystone antics, complete with a "park" comedy midsection (brick tossing, anyone?) and a car chase finale right out of the Keystone Kops. Yet Chaplin takes the broader aspects of the humor and makes them funnier by adding subtle little touches, as when he discreetly tries to gaze at a nude statuette (a bit he expanded in **City Lights**).

This time out, the Tramp is a bit nattier than usual: his coat and hat show no signs of excessive wear, and he's even wearing gloves. But he's still the same Tramp at heart, which allows Chaplin to explore the hypocrisy of perceived social status. Charlie's boorish behavior is tolerated as long as Edna's father believes he's royalty. So when Charlie is offered one cigar and helps himself to the entire box, his actions are dismissed with a shrug. The minute he's exposed as a *no-a-count*, however, he's socially unacceptable and is promptly shown the door. (Chaplin had used the masquerading-as-a-count motif in the Keystones **Caught in a Cabaret** and **Her Friend the Bandit**, and would repeat it in the Mutual comedies **The Count**, **The Rink**, and **The Adventurer**.)

Women are finally becoming full-fledged characters in Chaplin films—as opposed to the one-dimensional harpies that populate the Keystones—and nowhere is this more evident than in Edna Purviance's performance. No longer just mere window dressing, Edna's character is allowed to be, by turns, winsome, forlorn, amused, and petulant. Even romantic longing is conveyed via a charming Romeo-and-Juliet-type balcony scene between Edna and Charlie.

To many observers, Chaplin's cinematic style isn't as impressive as Buster Keaton's or Harold Lloyd's. Yet the car chase climax in *A Jitney Elopement* utilizes ambitious editing techniques (interweaving long shots, medium shots, and close-ups), impressive traveling shots, and well-executed stunt work.

While it can't be ranked among the very best Chaplin Essanays, *A Jitney Elopement* has enough good qualities to make it recommended viewing.

Other Views and Reviews: "It demonstrates the extraordinary ability of Mr. Chaplin to manufacture [two reels] of lively, knockabout comedy on a plot which is practically threadbare. He is admittedly a wonderful bag of tricks."—*The Cinema* (1915).

"Nowhere is the evidence of Chaplin's growing cinematic maturity more evident than in the subtle evolution of the Tramp's treatment of women in the Essanay comedies…The romantic longing at the beginning of *A Jitney Elopement* evokes this transformation."—Jeffrey Vance, *"The Beginning of His Art" from Kino's* **Chaplin's Essanay Comedies** *series* (1999).

"Chaplin goes beyond mere nuances or refinement of Keystone situations to present an original film that is far more substantial than his earlier work. Nearly all the humor in the film is quite delicate."—James L. Neibaur, *Film Quarterly* (2000).

"Once the real Count Chloride shows up, Charlie and Edna take flight in a 'jitney'…and the film slides into mindless action with no real laughs."—Alan Vanneman, *Bright Lights Film Journal* (2004).

†Misidentified in some prints as "Edna's father."

41. *The Tramp*
(Two Reels; Released April 11, 1915)
British title: **Charlie the Tramp**
British reissue title: **Just a Vagabond Lover**
Home-movie editions: **The Hobo, Charlie the Hobo, Charlie on the Farm, The Hired Hand, Damsel in Distress, Scrambled Eggs, Charlie on the Road, Charlie Gets a Job, Charlie Helps Out, Charlie's Hot Seat, Charlie's Broken Heart, Honest Charlie**
Cast: Charlie Chaplin (*tramp*), Edna Purviance (*farmer's daughter*), Fred Goodwins (*farmer*), Paddy McGuire (*farmhand*), Lloyd Bacon (*the girl's fiancé* and *second thief*), Leo White (*first thief*), Bud Jamison (*third thief*), Billy Armstrong (*minister*).

Credits: Written and directed by Charlie Chaplin. Photographed by Harry Ensign.

Plot: A tramp is walking down a country road. He gets a job on a farm after he saves the farmer's daughter from a group of hoboes. He isn't adept at any of the chores, but he does thwart the hoboes' attempt to rob the farmhouse, during which he gets shot in the leg. As the farmer's daughter nurses him back to health, he begins to interpret her attentiveness as love—until her sweetheart arrives. Realizing she could never have genuine feelings for him, he leaves her a good-bye note. Dejected but resilient, he hits the road once again.

Source of print screened: **Chaplin's Essanay Comedies Vol. 2** (Kino On Video)

Comments: The most acclaimed of all the Chaplin Essanays, **The Tramp** is considered to be Chaplin's first masterpiece. Its classic status stems from the beautifully rendered, emotional finale, which represents *the* major turning point in Chaplin's movie career. His character now has a heart; the beloved Little Tramp was truly born here. The rest of the film, however, is pretty rough around the edges, filled with crude and vulgar gags that make many of the passages seem like regressions to his earliest Keystones.

The film's opening sequence announces a stronger interpretation of the character. As Gerald Mast notes in *The Comic Mind* (University of Chicago Press, 1973):

> **The Tramp** *begins with a great gag as well as an important piece of psychological and social definition. (That combination of laugh plus implication is the essence of the mature Chaplin.) Charlie, the tramp, walks along a dusty rural road. A large automobile roars past, knocking him down and splattering him with dust. Charlie not only must walk rather than ride, but must suffer the carelessness and contempt of those who can afford an automobile. But he picks himself up, whisks himself off, and continues on his journey—dirtied but undaunted.*

Charlie is still the scrappy punk of his Keystone days, only now he performs his first genuine moral act, as he rescues Edna from a gang of thieving hoboes. And later, when the hoboes plot to rob the farmer, Charlie uses his "bad" image to his advantage by pretending to cooperate with them.

The humor is standard knockabout material, with plenty of swift kicks to the rear and heavy mallets to the noggin. Put to work on the farm, Charlie trots out the time-honored gag of placing a bucket under the cow's udder then pumping its tail in an effort to produce milk. Charlie immediately establishes a combative relationship with the farmhand; this is a throwback to Charlie the Tormentor of the Keystone days, as he repeatedly jabs the poor fellow with a pitchfork.

Moments like these are completely at odds with the film's tender conclusion; Chaplin would later learn how to better integrate comedy and pathos, rather than having the comedy come to an uneasy halt when the pathos is introduced, as when Charlie gets shot in the leg during the attempted robbery.

Chaplin saves the best for last, in the justifiably celebrated finale. Clueless to Charlie's true feelings, Edna introduces him to her beau. Slowly dying on the inside, Charlie politely excuses himself and goes into the kitchen to be alone. He looks himself over as if to say "Who am I kidding?," realizing that Edna could never go for such a shabby, inelegant figure. Grabbing a piece of paper, he sits down and writes her a note as best he can: *"i thout your kindness was love but it aint cause I seen him, XXX—Good-bye."* Spotting Edna's hat, he picks it up and gently kisses it (Chaplin effectively plays this with his back to the camera). Gathering his cane and handkerchief sack, Charlie pauses to wipe his tears on a window shade. He bids an unsuspecting Edna farewell; by the time she reads the note, he's already headed down the road. It doesn't take long for his defeated shuffle to turn into a jaunty stride, as he valiantly shakes off his heartache and sets out on his next adventure.

Despite the fact that there's been insufficient build-up to it, the entire sequence is positively heart-wrenching, and Chaplin performs it with stunning sincerity. (It should be noted that these scenes would not have the same emotional impact if Charlie didn't have someone as sweetly convincing as Edna to play against.)

At the risk of over-interpreting things, we noticed that the "iris" fade out is shaped like an inverted heart. Perhaps a symbol of Charlie's broken heart? Or perhaps we're just grasping at straws. At any rate, **The Tramp** establishes the motif of Charlie wandering into the lives of certain people then, at the end, wandering off alone, a theme that recurs in **Police** (1916), **The Adventurer** (1917), **The Idle Class** (1921), **The Pilgrim** (1923), and **The Circus** (1928).

Other Views and Reviews: "Chaplin's art, as all his multitudinous followers know, has no bad patches...When you go to see a Chaplin comedy you know that you will get your full measure of merriment down to the very last foot. And [**The Tramp**] is as good as any of them."—*Bioscope* (1915).

"We most often think of Charlie as the one who loses, as the one whose hopes must go down in defeat. Charlie first showed us this side of his nature, and his destiny, in **The Tramp**...This was the best picture he had made since he entered the movies."—Gerald D. McDonald, Michael Conway and Mark Ricci, *The Films of Charlie Chaplin* (1965).

"From [this] film on, the Chaplin film and the Charlie tramp acquired a clear individuality. Even his lighter, spoofy, purely funny films would have a greater richness and texture."—Gerald Mast, *The Comic Mind* (1973).

"The film is much more nearly a curio, a puzzle, a mysterious misstep than it is a declaration of style. It is, in fact, a failure: it solves none of its own problems of tone, answers none of the questions it raises...*The Tramp* took a step toward hinting that Charlie had a heart and could be hurt; but the hint was forced into a film that wasn't built to house it."—Walter Kerr, *The Silent Clowns* (1975).

"This remarkable film shows a staggering leap forward in its sense of structure, narrative skill, use of location, and emotional range. Charlie is now clearly defined as a tramp."—David Robinson, *Chaplin: His Life and Art* (1985).

42. By the Sea

(One Reel; Released April 29, 1915)

British title: **Charlie by the Sea**

Reissue title: **Charlie's Day Out**

Cast: Charlie Chaplin (*Charlie*), Bud Jamison (*husband*), Edna Purviance (*wife*), Billy Armstrong (*beachgoer*), Margie Reiger (*beachgoer's wife*), Harry "Snub" Pollard (*ice cream vendor*), Paddy McGuire (*cop*).

Credits: Written and directed by Charlie Chaplin. Photographed by Harry Ensign.

Plot: At the beach, Charlie flirts with two women, who are annoyed by his advances—and so are their husbands.

Source of print screened: **Chaplin's Essanay Comedies Vol. 2** (Kino On Video)

Comments: The first Chaplin Essanay produced in southern California (shot in a single day on location at Crystal Pier in Venice), **By the Sea** was made during an interim period when Chaplin was in the process of moving from Essanay's Niles facilities to the old Majestic studios in Los Angeles. This lesser, off-the-cuff Essanay effort is essentially a Keystone "park" comedy with sand instead of shrubbery, and comes across like a technically proficient version of someone's seaside home movies. Yet, for many Chaplin fans, the natural setting will be a big part of the film's charm. (Watch for the reflection of gathered spectators in a café window, and the lone sun-worshipper who goes running into the surf behind Chaplin and Armstrong, oblivious to the comedians' antics.)

In a role that Chester Conklin would have played had this been made at Keystone, Billy Armstrong (1891-1924) is cast as Chaplin's on-again, off-again pal/aggressor. (Armstrong was also a veteran of English music halls and appeared in several of the Essanays.) In a pantomime bit that serves as a forerunner to the flea circus routine in **Limelight** (1952), Charlie picks fleas off of Armstrong's scalp, then watches them leap from one hand to the other.

Other Views and Reviews: "More irresistible absurdities by the inimitable Charles…[his] humor needs neither description nor recommendation."—*Bioscope* (1915).

"A series of slapstick and situation variations skillfully managed within the restrictions of only nine camera set-ups."—David Robinson, *Chaplin: His Life and Art* (1985).

"An exercise in aimless violence."—Alan Vanneman, *Bright Lights Film Journal* (2004).

"Well done and well acted. Not as technical as other Chaplin shorts but funny as hell."—raskimon, *The Internet Movie Database* (2004).

43. *His Regeneration*

(One Reel; Released May 7, 1915)

Cast: G. M. "Broncho Billy" Anderson (*the regenerate burglar*), Marguerite Clayton (*society woman*), Lee Willard (*burglar's accomplice*), Hazel Applegate (*maid*), Charlie Chaplin (*tramp*), Belle Mitchell (*saloon girl*), Lloyd Bacon (*saloon girl's companion*), Robert McKenzie (*waiter*), Bill Cato (*first cop*), Darr Wittenmeyer (*second cop*), Victor Potel (*pawn shop clerk*), Harry "Snub" Pollard (*bit*).

Credits: Directed by G. M. Anderson, "slightly assisted by Charles Chaplin." Produced by G. M. Anderson. Written by Charlie Chaplin. Photography by Rollie H. (Roland) Totheroh.

Plot: During a skirmish at a dance hall, a woman comes to the aid of a down-and-out stranger. Later, the stranger and an accomplice break into the home of a society woman. When he discovers it's the same woman who helped him earlier, he changes his mind about the robbery, and gets into a fight with his partner, who is shot and killed. The woman allows the burglar to escape, and he vows never to return to a life of crime.

Source of print screened: **Chaplin's Essanay Comedies Vol. 2** (Kino On Video)

Comments: Gilbert M. Anderson (1880-1971), who co-founded Essanay, was a popular silent film star years before Chaplin became involved in the industry. Anderson was primarily known for his cowboy adventures; moviegoers knew him better as "Broncho Billy." **His Regeneration** is an undistinguished drama, no better or worse than dozens of others cranked out during this period. The most notable aspect of the picture is that it served as the inspiration for **Police** (1916), Chaplin's last bona fide Essanay production.

Chaplin's participation in the opening dance hall sequence amounts to a glorified cameo. After an unsuccessful attempt at flirting with a young lady, the Tramp interacts with the musicians, then gets shoved around by a crowd of dancing couples. (The latter bit anticipates scenes in **Modern Times** and **The Gold Rush**. It's also similar to the way the new arrivals are corralled in **The Immigrant**.)

Roland H. "Rollie" Totheroh (1890-1967), who would become Chaplin's cameraman during the Mutual years, photographed **His Regeneration**. Totheroh's association with Chaplin continued for decades, as cameraman, film conservator, and archivist.

G. M. Anderson played a fight spectator in **The Champion**, Chaplin's third Essanay film. Charlie returns the favor in **His Regeneration**. He makes an amusing contribution, but there's hardly anything here that could be called great comedy....or drama.

Other Views and Reviews: "Even in the short time at his disposal [Chaplin] assists the tale to make a very lively commencement, which is as novel in a production of this kind as it is pleasant."—*Bioscope* (1915).

"The guest appearance is forgettable, as is the rest of the movie that the appearance is in."—Mark Pollock, *Amazon.com* (2002).

"This works all right, although it could have probably been better...the story itself has a worthwhile plot, but would have been even more effective in more skilled hands. Someone like D. W. Griffith could have made it easier for the audience to overlook the crucial coincidences in the plot, and could have evoked more emotion in the climactic scenes."—Snow Leopard, *The Internet Movie Database* (2003).

44. *Work*

(Two Reels; Released June 21, 1915)

British title: **Charlie at Work**

Reissue titles: **The Paper Hanger**, **Only a Working Man**

Home-movie editions: **Charlie the Decorator**, **The Plumber**, **Fast Worker**, **Crazy Decorators**

Cast: Charlie Chaplin (*assistant painter-paperhanger*), Edna Purviance (*maid*), Charles Insley (*Izzy A. Wake, Charlie's boss*), Billy Armstrong (*home owner*), Marta Golden (*wife*), Leo White (*wife's secret lover*), Paddy McGuire (*workman*).

Credits: Written and directed by Charlie Chaplin. Photographed by Harry Ensign. Assistant director: Ernest Van Pelt.

Plot: Charlie and his boss are hired to redecorate a house. Once there, Charlie makes a considerable mess of things and shows more interest in flirting with the maid than he does completing the assignment. In the meantime, the home-owner's wife is having an affair with another man, who appears at an inopportune moment. As tempers flare between Charlie, his boss, and the entire household, a faulty kitchen stove explodes, covering everyone in a pile of rubble.

Source of print screened: **Chaplin's Essanay Comedies Vol. 2** (Kino On Video)

Comments: Chaplin's first seven Essanay comedies were released within a three-month period. Beginning with **Work**, Chaplin spent more time on the creation of his movies. And, for the most part, the greater care would show.

Although it's an uneven mixture of slapstick and marital farce, **Work** is one of Chaplin's best Essanay efforts. Here, he's no longer the defiant Charlie of **Mabel's Busy Day** or **The Property Man**. Pulling a broken-down wagon—loaded with the boss and all their supplies—Charlie is clearly a proletariat underdog. Critics who gripe that Chaplin's cinematic technique was static and old-fashioned are advised to check out these opening scenes. By simply tilting the camera to one side, Charlie appears to be struggling to pull the wagon (which resembles an oversized rickshaw) up an impossibly steep hill. It's a simple yet inventive *cinematic* touch that adds immeasurably to the humor.

Charlie and his boss finally arrive at the home they've been hired to redecorate. (The interior scenes were filmed at the Bradbury Mansion, which Essanay was using for various productions.) In time-honored comedy tradition, neither of them have any aptitude for their chosen profession. Their scruffy appearances aren't terribly reassuring either, as the lady of the house hurriedly locks her silverware in a safe. In retaliation, Charlie and his boss gather together *their* valuables as they cast suspicious glances back at the haughty woman.

The first half of **Work** contains some nice comic bits. Charlie takes off his coat and places it on top of a heavy safe. He then tries to slide the safe away from the wall, but can't budge it. Pausing briefly to assess the situation, he removes the coat from the top of the safe and finds that the safe now glides easily across the floor. Later, Charlie tries to ingratiate himself with Edna, the maid. He sits down beside her and relates a sad story. She becomes engrossed in his tale and all is fine until Charlie ruins the mood by covering her hand in dirt. This is a peculiarly subtle passage; though we have no idea exactly what Charlie is saying to Edna, Chaplin conveys a serious tone through his pantomime (at one point, however, he winks at the camera, making the legitimacy of his story highly suspect). The scene comes out of left field and eventually goes nowhere, but it does give an indication of Chaplin's growing dramatic ambition.

The rest of the film is obvious slapstick, with a variety of gags involving ladders, wooden planks, buckets of whitewash, wallpaper, and wallpaper paste. All of it is somewhat reminiscent of Chaplin's earlier ***Dough and Dynamite*** (Keystone, 1914), with the gooey paste taking the place of the gooey baking dough. (Perhaps Chaplin had ***Work*** in mind when he devised a comic paperhanging routine for ***A King in New York*** [1957], his last starring vehicle.)

For all the energy expended by the enthusiastic cast, ***Work*** begins to run out of steam during its second half. Nevertheless, as Gerald Mast asserts in *The Comic Mind*, Reel Two is not without merit:

> *The second section of the film—Charlie's botch of the paper-hanging—contains one gem of a bit that is pure Chaplin. In the rich lady's house Charlie notices a plaster statuette of a woman. He tips his hat to her. What else do you do to a lady? He eyes her; she is "artistically" bare. So he takes a lampshade and delicately hangs it over her bottom half. Charlie stares at this now proper plaster lady. Then he pushes the lampshade, and we suddenly see it turn into a hula skirt; the plaster figurine, as if by magic, dances the hula (better yet, the "hootchy kootchy"). Then Charlie's curiosity gets the best of him; he lifts the lampshade-skirt, which he himself added, to peek at the lady-figurine's forbidden parts. In this action Chaplin endows an inanimate object with life; he magically raises the dead and converts the corpse into the most wayward of women; and he confers sex appeal on the sexless. There is magic in this metamorphosis, indeed.*

This "hootchy kootchy" sequence is quite funny, though reviewers of the era found this and other comedic bits "dirty" and "disgusting." Can you imagine the apoplexy these critics would have suffered had they lived long enough to see an ***American Pie*** movie?

The basic problem with the second half is that it shifts the focus onto the marital farce and away from Charlie. As the irate husband chases his wife's lover around the house, Charlie is merely a bystander who gets caught in the middle of the chaos. (By this time, it was unusual for a Chaplin comedy to conclude with turmoil he didn't instigate.)

The final mêlée and the exploding stove gag that ends the picture with a literal bang seem awfully contrived, and are not worthy of a film filled with more than its share of clever moments.

Other Views and Reviews: "The humor is designed to rise in a long crescendo of screams to a climax of roars. Positively, the thing is irresistible."—*Bioscope* (1915).

"[***Work***] is the usual Chaplin work of late—mussy, messy and dirty. Chaplin has found the public will stand for his picture comedy of the worst kind, and he is giving them the worst kind, although as an excellent pantomimist with a reserve of decent comedy, Chaplin must have decided the time to put his other brand upon the screen is when his present style of 'humor' shall have ceased to be in demand."—*Variety* (1915).

"One of the best Essanays...It resembles the Keystone films in its mix of basic slapstick and marital farce, but is altogether better organized."—Glenn Mitchell, *The Chaplin Encyclopedia* (1997).

"**Work** is especially significant in that it contains perhaps the broadest slapstick of all the Essanay productions, yet still is far more refined in its presentation than anything Chaplin had done at Keystone."—James L. Neibaur, *Film Quarterly* (2000).

"His most political statement yet...The film is so ridiculous that you wonder how on earth it came together to fit so well."—Mark Pollock, *Amazon.com* (2002).

45. *A Woman*
(Two Reels; Released July 12, 1915)
British title: **Charlie the Perfect Lady**
Reissue titles: **The Perfect Lady**, **Charlie and the Perfect Lady**
Home-movie editions: **Charlie and the Perfect Lady**, **The Flirt**†, **Mademoiselle Charlie**
Cast: Charlie Chaplin (*Charlie*), Edna Purviance (*daughter*), Charles Insley (*father*), Marta Golden (*mother*), Margie Reiger (*flirt*), Billy Armstrong (*father's friend* and *cop*), Leo White (*Frenchman*), Jess Robbins (*soda vendor*).
Credits: Written and directed by Charlie Chaplin. Photographed by Harry Ensign. Assistant director: Ernest Van Pelt.
Plot: During a stroll through the park, Charlie gets into altercations with two men. Later, at Edna's house, he learns that one of the men is Edna's father. While trying to flee, Charlie disguises himself as a woman; the father and his friend become smitten with the charming young lady, unaware of "her" true identity.
Source of print screened: **Chaplin's Essanay Comedies Vol. 2** (Kino On Video)
Comments: Chaplin's third and final film involving female impersonation (after *A Busy Day* and *The Masquerader*), *A Woman* is a curious throwback to the Keystone days. An expanded "park" comedy with the usual quota of neck-wringing and ass-kicking, Charlie reverts to his Keystone wiseguy persona, while the other male characters are typical Keystone husbands who can't resist the urge to flirt with every woman they meet. Even the females behave like Keystone gals, as

Edna and her mother laugh uproariously at Charlie's atrocious table manners (he uses a long knife to scoop up donuts and gargles with tea).

The funniest sequence reworks and improves upon the basic premise of *The Masquerader*, as Charlie disguises himself as a woman in order to fool Edna's father. After removing Edna's clothes from a mannequin (coyly treating the dummy as if it were an actual living being), Charlie dons the wardrobe (using a pincushion for a bosom), shaves off his mustache, and proceeds to charm the father and his randy companion. With his slight stature and soft features, Chaplin makes a convincing dame, performing some very amusing pantomime as he outrageously flirts with both men.

This, however, is the only memorable passage in the film. *A Woman* will entertain most Chaplin fans, though they will have to admit the comedian has done much better work...like *Work*.

A Woman was the first Chaplin Essanay to be filmed at Essanay's new facilities at the former Majestic Studios (in addition to location shooting at Echo Park). Chaplin had reportedly found Essanay's studio in Niles (a suburb of San Francisco) to be inadequate and the "backwoods atmosphere" depressing. Except for scenes requiring location filming, the remainder of the Chaplin Essanays were shot at Majestic. Essanay even dug an embankment around the studio to prevent rival companies from luring away their star attraction!

Other Views and Reviews: "Chaplin needs a scenario writer, or if he doesn't Essanay does. In comedy pictures as much fun may be secured through a situation, with the humor starting at the suggestion of that situation, as by the actual comedy work involved in it. That is what is missing in the Essanay Chaplin film, the situation. Chaplin needs a scenario writer very, very badly."—*Variety* (1915). "This picture is a refutation of the belief held by many that Charles Chaplin can only do the kind of comedy that he has more or less created, for he opens up a new field of humor for him and one that should be as successful as the peculiar style that has gained him his immense popularity."—*New York Dramatic Mirror* (1915).
"A most charming, lilting thing."—Christopher Mulrooney, *The Internet Movie Database* (2001).
"*A Woman* is only important for trivial reasons, because Chaplin makes his last appearance in drag, with astonishing results."—Mark Pollock, *Amazon.com* (2002).
"An irresistible drag tour de force that leaves us wishing Charlie had used the bit more often."—Alan Vanneman, *Bright Lights Film Journal* (2004).

†Not to be confused with **Charlie the Flirt**, a home movie edition of **A Night in the Show** (Essanay, 1915).

46. *The Bank*
(Two Reels; Released August 9, 1915)
British title: **Charlie at the Bank**
Reissue titles: **In the Bank, Charlie in the Bank**
Home-movie editions: **Charlie at the Bank, Charlie Detective, Charlie the Cleaner, In the Bank**
Cast: Charlie Chaplin (*Charlie the bank janitor*), Edna Purviance (*Edna the secretary*), Billy Armstrong (*another janitor*), Charles Insley (*bank president*), Carl Stockdale (*Charles*), Lawrence A. Bowes (*salesman*), Leo White (*customer representative*), Paddy McGuire (*cashier*).
Credits: Written and directed by Charlie Chaplin. Photographed by Harry Ensign. Assistant director: Ernest Van Pelt.
Plot: Charlie is a janitor at a bank, where his antics hardly endear him to the employees or the customers. Edna, the secretary, buys a gift for a cashier whose name is Charles. Charlie sees the present and mistakenly thinks it's intended for him. He leaves flowers and a note on her desk; when she tosses them in the wastebasket, he is devastated. Later, he thwarts a bank robbery and wins the love of a now-grateful Edna. Just as it looks like a happy ending, Charlie awakens from his slumber—alas, his heroic actions were only a dream and Edna is still with Charles.
Source of print screened: **Chaplin's Essanay Comedies Vol. 2** (Kino On Video)
Comments: **The Bank** is one of the top Essanay Chaplins, and seems even better coming after the clever but uneven **Work** and the uninspired **A Woman**. Critics of the era noted that **The Bank** revealed a cleaner, more polished style to Chaplin's filmmaking technique and choice of comedy content.

A reworking of **The New Janitor** (Keystone, 1914), the film opens with one of the best gags in the series. Entering the bank, a confident Charlie strides purposefully through the lobby, down a flight of stairs, and approaches a huge bank vault. After carefully dialing the combination, he swings open the vault door, steps inside and...emerges with a bucket and mop. He may only be the janitor, but he treats his profession with great seriousness.

A wet mop in Charlie's hands means that someone will inevitably be on the receiving end of it. And sure enough, he finds endless ways of hitting people in the face with the soggy weapon. He even places it in an inverted top hat, mistaking the headgear for his bucket.

Later, the bank president hands Charlie a letter to mail. On his way to the mail slot, Charlie meets a customer and reacts as though the fellow doesn't look well. After taking the man's pulse, Charlie asks him to stick out his tongue. Concerned, the man complies, and Charlie uses the tongue to moisten a stamp, which he affixes to the letter. The mail slot is too narrow to accommodate the letter, so Charlie rips it into three pieces then slides each piece in. On his way back, Charlie again runs into the man, who still has his tongue struck out. Charlie courteously pushes it back into his mouth.

The gag sequences alone would make *The Bank* one of the funniest Essanays. What gives the film its true merit, however, is the manner in which Chaplin incorporates pathos. Here, Charlie is not a hero in the conventional sense, but audience sympathy is clearly with him. So when he leaves flowers and a note on Edna's desk, then watches her reaction from an adjoining room, we're rooting for him. (Sensitive about his own feelings, Charlie becomes a romantic voyeur, as he does with the blind girl in *City Lights*.) When Edna shows utter disdain for his present, he's devastated and so are we. Chaplin's performance in this scene is outstanding, and he uses close-ups to heighten the emotional impact.

This sequence, which foreshadows Chaplin's more mature efforts, works better than the conclusion of *The Tramp* because Chaplin has taken more time to build up to it. And, unlike his character in *The Tramp*, Charlie won't be able to shrug this one off so easily; the poor guy will still run into this couple during his duties at the bank. (Most available copies of *The Bank* end with Charlie waking from his dream. The Kino Video version is the only one we viewed that has a final shot of Edna with Charles, further emphasizing the futility of Charlie's desires.)

The Bank marks Chaplin's earliest use of the flower metaphor—flowers as surrogates for women he longs to possess—that would later turn up in *City Lights* (the blind flower girl) and *Monsieur Verdoux* (the serial killer who sends flowers to his potential victims).

Very funny and very moving, *The Bank* is a superior entry that compares favorably with Chaplin's later Mutual comedies, which are considered the highwater mark of his short film output.

Other Views and Reviews: "It's the most legitimate comedy film Chaplin has played in many a long day, perhaps since he's been in pictures. While there were no boisterous guffaws from upstairs that his slapstick would have pulled, the use of cleaner material brought more enjoyment to the entire house, also left a better impression."—*Variety* (1915).

"It is not as uproariously funny as some of the other Chaplin films, but, from one point of view, this is something in its favor. Its fun is frequently that of a smile, rather than the loud laugh, and the smile is often touched with a fleeting sympathy."—*The New York Times* (reviewing a 1919 revival).

"One of the series' best…The optimistic dreamer of Chaplin's mature work is more obvious here than in any of the other Essanay comedies…its central character combines inelegance with panache, underlined by the hopelessness of a would-be gentleman who is doomed never to rise above his humble station."—Glenn Mitchell, *The Chaplin Encyclopedia* (1997).

"*The Bank* is more than a little unsettling because Edna doesn't seem very sympathetic. She's entirely taken up with her middle-class boyfriend and doesn't seem to notice how poor Charlie is suffering."—Alan Vanneman, *Bright Lights Film Journal* (2004).

47. *Shanghaied*

(Two Reels; Released October 4, 1915)

Reissue title: **Charlie Shanghaied**

Home-movie editions: **The Sailor, Charlie the Sailor, Charlie on the Ocean, Charlie Goes to Sea, Charlie the Cook†, Sea Water Chief, In the Soup, Bad Soup, Charlie the Recruiter, Charlie the Invincible**

Cast: Charlie Chaplin (*Charlie*), Edna Purviance (*ship owner's daughter*), Wesley Ruggles (*ship owner*), Lawrence A. Bowes (*captain*), John Rand (*cook*), Bud Jamison (*second mate*), Billy Armstrong (*first shanghaied sailor*), Paddy McGuire (*second shanghaied sailor*), Leo White (*third shanghaied sailor*), Fred Goodwins (*cabin boy*), Lee Hill (*sailor wearing rain hat*).

Credits: Written and directed by Charlie Chaplin. Photographed by Harry Ensign. Assistant director: Ernest Van Pelt.

Plot: Charlie and Edna are in love, but her father, a ship owner, doesn't approve of him. Charlie helps the ship's mate to shanghai a crew, only to get shanghaied himself. Edna stows away aboard the boat; she and Charlie thwart a scheme (engineered by her father) to have the vessel blown up for the insurance money.

Source of print screened: **Chaplin's Essanay Comedies Vol. 3** (Kino On Video)

Comments: Though not up to the standards of *The Bank*, *Shanghaied* is one of the funnier Essanay entries, an exercise in pure slapstick. Like a seasoned stage performer who trots out his crowd-pleasing specialty routines, Chaplin presents a series of comic vignettes strung together by a thin storyline.

In *Shanghaied*, Chaplin takes an archetypal Keystone premise and tailors it to suit his own comedic approach. In the opening scenes, when Edna's father forbids Charlie from seeing his daughter, Chaplin handles the break-up as mock melodramatics, parodying parallel moments in legitimate dramas. (This time Charlie loses the girl at the beginning of the picture and gets her back again at the conclusion.)

The ship's mate enlists Charlie's aid in shanghaiing a crew; as the mate distracts each victim, Charlie renders them unconscious with a mallet. Here the use of the mallet actually serves a specific plot purpose as opposed to the indiscriminate way it was employed in the Keystones. The scheme backfires on Charlie when he gets clobbered on the head and becomes a member of the crew himself. (This routine was later repeated in Laurel & Hardy's *The Live Ghost* [1934].)

The shipboard scenes comprise the bulk of the film, and it's during these passages that Chaplin's physical comedy kicks into high gear. On board, Charlie trades his Tramp costume for a sailor's uniform; the change of apparel hardly transforms him into an expert seaman, as he buries the captain and crew while trying to unload cargo, washes dishes in the captain's soup, and becomes violently seasick while trying to consume a meal with other crew members. The latter sequence recalls his gastronomic encounters with soup-slurper Mack Swain in *His Trysting Place* (Keystone, 1914) and onion-devouring Albert Austin in *Behind the Screen* (Mutual, 1916).

Out on the ocean, the ship sails into rough waters; to convey this visually, interior sets were mounted on an apparatus that allowed them to be rocked back and forth while the camera remained stationary. (Chaplin would reuse this device for the teetering cabin climax in *The Gold Rush* [1925].) For the exteriors on the deck, the opposite tactic was used: the camera rocked back and forth as Charlie skittered around to give the illusion of turbulence. (Keen observers will notice that the ocean remains stationary.) By this time, Chaplin's editing technique was becoming more purposeful, using close-ups and fast cuts to heighten the action and punctuate the gags.

Much of the humor has an off-the-cuff feel to it. At one point, Charlie begins dancing a spirited version of the sailor's "hornpipe," twirling a hambone like a majorette's baton. Another example of Chaplin's dexterity is displayed when he's carrying a tray of dishes, slips and falls and does a somersault without dropping anything. (He did this with a tray of bread in *Dough and Dynamite*, one of his Keystones.) This impressive stunt was also performed by Buster Keaton in *College* (1927) and Bert Wheeler in *Half Shot at Sunrise* (1930), predating Chaplin's own attempts to carry a tray loaded with food across a crowded dance floor in *Modern Times* (1936) and avoid spilling a cup of tea in *Monsieur Verdoux* (1947).

All circulating copies of **Shanghaied** share the same flaws; evidently patched together from multiple source prints, several scenes are marred by heavy scratches and blemishes. It won't spoil your overall enjoyment, but it may be a bit puzzling for some viewers to watch a nice clean image suddenly switch to a tattered-looking one, then back again.

Shanghaied doesn't represent an artistic milestone in Chaplin's career. It's just a fast-paced, rowdy comedy that should please fans as well as casual viewers.
Other Views and Reviews: "As usual, Mr. Chaplin is funny with a funniness which transcends his dirt and his vulgarity."—Julian Johnson, *Photoplay* (1915).
"The picture is actually funny in the sense it would cause anyone to laugh without offending. That's odd for a 'Chaplin,' and through it **Shanghaied** is doubly amusing."—*Variety* (1915).
"Among the better-constructed of Chaplin's Essanay comedies."—Glenn Mitchell, *The Chaplin Encyclopedia* (1997).
"[A] comedy gem."—Jeffrey Vance, *Chaplin: Genius of the Cinema* (2003).
†Not to be confused with **The Cook**, a reissue title for **Dough and Dynamite** (Keystone, 1914).

48. *A Night in the Show*
(Two Reels; Released November 20, 1915)
British title: **Charlie at the Show**
Reissue title: **Night at the Show**
Home-movie editions: **A Night at the Show, A Night at the Burlesque House, Charlie at the Show, Charlie at the Theater, Charlie at the Music Hall, If Looks Could Kill, Charlie the Flirt†, Charlie's Fat Lady, Stage Struck, Stagestruck, Pies and Hose-Pipes, The Fire Eater, One in the Eye, Overture for Beginners, The Snake Charmer**
Cast: Charlie Chaplin (*Mr. Pest* and *Mr. Rowdy*), Edna Purviance (*pretty woman in the stalls*), Charlotte Mineau (*older woman in the stalls*), Bud Jamison (*Dash the singer*), May White (*La Belle Wienerwurst* and *fat lady in foyer*), Leo White (*assistant to La Belle Wienerwurst, audience member,* and *black patron in gallery*), John Rand (*orchestra conductor, audience member,* and *woman with baby*), Paddy McGuire (*theater attendant* and *musician*), James T. Kelly (*musician*), Dee Lampton (*fat boy*), Wesley Ruggles (*man with monocle*), Phyllis Allen (*audience member*), Fred Goodwins (*audience member*), Charles Insley (*audience member*), Carrie Clark Ward (*audience member*).
Credits: Written and directed by Charlie Chaplin. Photographed by Harry Ensign. Assistant director: Ernest Van Pelt.

Plot: The intoxicated Mr. Pest attends a variety show and creates disruptions for the acts, the audience, and the orchestra. Meanwhile, up in the gallery, the drunken Mr. Rowdy is also causing trouble.

Source of print screened: ***Chaplin's Essanay Comedies Vol. 3*** (Kino On Video)

Comments: One of Chaplin's better Essanays, *A Night in the Show* is the most atypical entry in the series. While the film may disappoint viewers expecting the exploits of the Little Tramp, it's a valuable document of Chaplin's background in the English music hall.

Based on the stage sketch "Mumming Birds" (also known as "A Night in the English Music Hall") that Chaplin performed during his pre-movie years with the Fred Karno Company, *A Night in the Show* presents Chaplin in dual roles: Mr. Pest, a well-dressed inebriate, and Mr. Rowdy, a sloppily-attired, equally intoxicated lowlife. In live theater performances Chaplin was limited to essaying the Pest role, but motion pictures enabled him to be in two places at once.

This plotless, gag-driven effort revolves around the simple idea of two drunks disrupting a variety show. As Mr. Pest, Chaplin is elegantly dressed in evening clothes, with his usually bushy hair neatly slicked back. In an alcoholic haze, Mr. Pest creates pandemonium all over the main auditorium. Approaching the orchestra pit, he lights his cigarette by striking a match on the tuba player's head, then tosses the match and his gloves into the open mouth of the instrument. Among other acts of impropriety, he flirts with another man's wife, sits on a gentleman's top hat, removes the plumage from a woman's headdress when it blocks his view, strikes a match on a snake charmer's bare foot, and pelts a singer with a gooey pie. If the Tramp had created this much commotion, he would have been promptly ejected from the theater—that is, if he even made it past the foyer. But because of Mr. Pest's refined appearance, most audience members are willing to tolerate his annoying antics. Here, Chaplin had touches upon the hypocrisy of perceived social status, as he had in *Jitney Elopement*, and as he would in post-Essanay efforts like *The Count* and *The Adventurer*.

Given far less screen time, Mr. Rowdy is a less successful characterization. He doesn't do much except spill drinks on patrons, throw food at the stage acts, and then finally drench the entire theater with a fire hose.†† Wearing a large mustache that obscures his facial features, most viewers probably won't even recognize Chaplin in this role.

Edna Purviance is seriously underused here, and that's a major drawback. Her brief scene as a woman who flirts with Charlie until her husband appears is amusing, but ultimately goes nowhere. That's a shame because the by-play between

Charlie and Edna seems quite natural, no doubt a reflection of their offscreen relationship.

Despite the unevenness of the film's construction, the role of Mr. Pest affords Chaplin plenty of opportunities to indulge his pantomimic skills. The gags themselves are pretty obvious, but Charlie's facial expressions and body gestures make the slight material seem far funnier than it actually is. The fast pace also helps, as does the editing, which is especially ambitious, with lots of effective crosscutting.

A Night in the Show marks the first time Chaplin played dual roles, which he repeated in *The Idle Class* (1921) and *The Great Dictator* (1940). He would again portray elegant inebriates in *One A. M.* (1916) and the aforementioned *The Idle Class*. And he would pay a melancholy return visit to the music hall in *Limelight* (1952).

Other Views and Reviews: "Chaplin loses the rails again by reason of no story. And still he is funny. When they showed me this mussy, and at times decidedly unpleasant visual narrative I punctuated it with ribald shouts. I couldn't help roaring. Oh, for a Chaplin author!"—Julian Johnson, *Photoplay* (1915).

"Charlie Chaplin, farce pantomimist without equal, is as funny as ever in *A Night in the Show*…It goes back to the custard-pie days and the simple comedy of smash-and-smear-up everything and everybody, but Chaplin is in it with his inimitable pantomime, and this gives it a quality not possessed by other farces of its age."—*The New York Times* (reviewing a 1919 reissue).

"Amid the progression in his work characterizing the Essanay series, Chaplin took a deliberate step back by filming the stage sketch in which he became famous, 'Mumming Birds.' Though perhaps an easy option in its day, the film provides a service in preserving Chaplin's performance."—Glenn Mitchell, *The Chaplin Encyclopedia* (1997).

"The most complete cinematic adaptation of any of Chaplin's old music hall sketches."—James L. Neibaur, *Film Quarterly* (2000).

"*A Night in the Show* is definitely not one of the best or most memorable of Chaplin's early films, but the quality is there and it is, as they all are, a cinematic curiosity piece in that it was made by one of the greatest filmmakers in the history of the medium."—Michael DeZubiria, *The Internet Movie Database* (2002).

†Not to be confused with *The Flirt*, a home-movie edition of *A Woman* (Essanay, 1915).

††Chaplin used the fire hose gag as early as *The Property Man* (Keystone, 1914) and would repeat it as late as *A King in New York* (1957).

49. *Burlesque on "Carmen"*

Also known as *Carmen* and *Charlie Chaplin's Burlesque on Carmen*
Reissue titles: *A Burlesque on Carmen, Charlie and Carmen*
Home-movie editions: *A Burlesque on Carmen, Charlie and Carmen, Charlie and the Toreador, Charlie and the Dancer, Charlie and the Smugglers, Charlie Fights a Duel*
(Originally scheduled for release on December 18, 1915 as *Carmen* in Two Reels; Released by Essanay on April 10, 1916 as *Burlesque on "Carmen"*, an expanded four-reel version; Reissued as *A Burlesque on Carmen* by the Quality Amusement Corporation in 1928 in a revised three-reel edition.)
Cast: Charlie Chaplin (*Darn Hosiery*), Edna Purviance (*Carmen*), Leo White (*Morales, Captain of the Guard*), John Rand (*Escamillo the toreador*), Jack Henderson (*Lilas Pastia*), May White (*Frasquita*), Bud Jamison (*soldier of the guard*). The expanded version also contains footage with Ben Turpin (*Le Remendado*) and Wesley Ruggles (*vagabond*).
Credits: Written and directed by Charlie Chaplin. From the novel "Carmen" by Prosper Mérimée, and the opera by Georges Bizet. Photographed by Harry Ensign. Assistant director: Ernest Van Pelt. Production designer: Albert Couder. (The four-reel version was reportedly directed and assembled by Leo White.)
Plot: The setting is old Seville. Darn Hosiery, a dashing and heroic soldier, is sent to apprehend a band of smugglers. Instead, he falls under the spell of an exotic gypsy named Carmen. Darn Hosiery's obsession with her leads him to kill Captain Morales, his superior officer. Carmen leaves Darn Hosiery to marry Escamillo, a toreador. The disgraced soldier tracks her down, draws a knife and stabs her. Then he uses the knife to take his own life. But wait—this is a Charlie Chaplin comedy! Darn Hosiery and Carmen revive, and he shows her that the weapon is only a "stage" knife with a retractable blade. Smiles, fade out.
Sources of prints screened: Two-reel version: *Chaplin's Essanay Comedies Vol. 3* (Kino On Video); Three-reel version: *Chaplin: The Legend Lives On* (Madacy Home Video).
Comments: When asked which is the best and which is the worst of Chaplin's Essanays, our answer to both is the same: *Burlesque on "Carmen."* Our reason for this is simple: there are *two* versions of the film—Chaplin's original cut and a longer edition that was expanded by Essanay without Chaplin's consent. Naturally, Chaplin's version is superior. What's surprising, however, is just how wretched the expansion is, considering that it contains most of the footage found in the shorter edition.

The original two-reel version of **Carmen** isn't as well known as its bloated counterpart, which is a shame because it's quite a revelation. This was Chaplin's most ambitious production to date and every element of it is first-rate: the costumes, the sets, the photography, the editing, and the lead performances by Chaplin and Edna Purviance. As the dashing soldier Darn Hosiery, Charlie may be attired in a fancy uniform but he's still the Tramp at heart, only with a sword in place of his cane and a plumed helmet instead of his traditional derby (although he does wear one briefly in a later scene). As Carmen, Edna is given an opportunity to flex her dramatic muscles. This is not the usual damsel-in-distress or faithful-girlfriend role she portrayed in previous Chaplins; in keeping with the novel and the opera, Carmen is a hedonistic vixen who toys with the heart of every man who crosses her path. It's not an easy role for anyone to play, let alone a relative newcomer, but under Chaplin's direction, Edna is up to the challenge. (Purviance would get a opportunity to play a full-fledged dramatic lead in **A Woman of Paris** [1923], which Chaplin wrote and directed but did not star in.)

Carmen has far more story structure than any previous Chaplin picture, with a smooth balance of gags and straight dramatics. Though it helps if you already know the basic plotline, it won't hinder your enjoyment of the film if you don't. There are subtler touches to the humor, and even the rowdier moments—such as Charlie's jubilant tabletop dance—are much more polished and choreographed than the frenzied Keystone approach. One of the highlights is the duel between Darn Hosiery and his superior, Captain Morales (Leo White). As the two men clash swords and struggle, their battle takes on the qualities of a pool game, an apache dance, an acrobatic act, and a wrestling match. (This sequence also employs a nicely executed tracking shot.) At one point during the fight, Charlie manhandles his opponent like a chiropractor, predating his own bout with a determined masseur in **The Cure** (Mutual, 1917).

Chaplin's deft handling of the dramatic scenes is impressive, and his use of close-ups and facial expressions to convey the non-comedic passages is particularly striking. There are moments when Carmen's duplicity and Darn Hosiery's despair are presented with great conviction, such as the genuine remorse on Darn Hosiery's face after he strangles Morales and later stabs Carmen. Though Chaplin would refine his talent for blending tragedy and comedy in later films, he is amazingly successful at achieving this goal at this stage in his movie career. (Charlie had once contemplated writing, directing, and starring in a dramatic film about Napoleon, and **Carmen**, his first period piece, gives us a tantalizing glimpse of what could have been.)

Chaplin had prepared his two-reel cut of *Carmen* late in 1915, but Essanay waited until the following year, after Chaplin left the studio, to release an expanded four-reel version retitled *Burlesque on "Carmen."* In an effort to offer the film to exhibitors as a special release (and, in the process, justify higher rental fees), Essanay added a superfluous subplot involving Ben Turpin as a gypsy named Le Remendado who has romantic designs on the hefty Frasquita (played by May White, who was also in Chaplin's original cut). By using identical settings, the Turpin scenes match the Chaplin footage quite well, from a technical standpoint. Content-wise, however, the insertion of Turpin's heavy-handed clowning completely ruins the rhythm and delicacy of Chaplin's original.

Reportedly, Essanay's mutilated version sickened Chaplin so much that it sent him to bed for two days. Essanay defended its revision of the picture, making the ludicrous claim that this was the first time Chaplin edited one of his films (he had actually been doing this since he first arrived at the studio), resulting in a finished product "not acceptable to us." Chaplin wound up suing Essanay for damages, but he eventually lost the case. (This was no doubt the primary reason why Chaplin remained bitter about his Essanay period for the rest of his life.) It was a hard lesson learned, and to prevent this from happening again, Chaplin stipulated in all of his future contracts that his films could not be altered without his approval.

There doesn't seem to be any copies of the four-reel *Carmen* currently in circulation on the home video market—none that we're aware of, at any rate. A three-reel version reissued by Quality Amusement Corporation in 1928 is commonly available from a number of budget-priced DVD distributors, and from this we can see just how badly Essanay mangled the original. There are so many new Turpin scenes that Charlie doesn't even make his entrance until nearly seven minutes have elapsed. And once the Chaplin-sanctioned footage gets underway, the pacing is destroyed by the continuous insertion of unrelated material. To add insult to injury, this fuzzy-quality reissue is a recut of the Essanay revision which further butchers the original by adding an over-explanatory "Foreword" by one "Duke Bakrak" (that seems to go on for a reel by itself) and rewritten title cards that change Chaplin's character name of "Darn Hosiery" to "Don José." (As bad as the three-reel version is, our minds boggle at the thought that there's an *additional* reel to this thing floating around somewhere.)

Fortunately, Kino Video offers archivist David Shepard's reconstruction of Chaplin's original two-reel cut† as part of their *Chaplin's Essanay Comedies* series, and it's this version that we highly recommend. Curiously, the Kino edition excludes Chaplin scenes that appear in the three-reel edition: Captain Morales nearly chokes the life out of Darn Hosiery as Carmen cheers from the sidelines; and Darn Hosiery strangles Morales, then tries to stab him with his sword, only to have the blade curl up like a New Year's Eve party favor. These may have been outtakes that Chaplin initially rejected; he may have felt that the curling sword bit was too similar to the final gag involving the "stage" knife. However, one particular close-up of a wild-eyed Carmen gleefully watching the two men fighting over her is unfortunately missing from Kino's restoration. Not only is it a choice piece of acting by Edna Purviance, it serves to exemplify the basic ruthlessness of her character.

Burlesque on "Carmen" spoofed two 1915 film productions of *Carmen*: the first was directed by Cecil B. DeMille (*The Greatest Show on Earth*, *The Ten Commandments*) and featured Metropolitan Opera star Geraldine Farrar as Carmen and Wallace Reid as Don José; the other was directed by Raoul Walsh (*White Heat*, *The Roaring Twenties*) and starred Theda Bara. Ironically, Chaplin's satire inspired two parodies featuring child actors: *Chip's Carmen* and *A Great Imitation of Charlie Chaplin's Burlesque on Carmen* (1916).

While many historians cite *Police* (1916) as Chaplin's best Essanay, we bestow that honor on Chaplin's original two-reel cut of *Burlesque on "Carmen,"* an entertaining and inventive effort that is even better than some of his later films for Mutual and First National. So be sure to check out the Kino edition, because the expanded version is, to paraphrase Comic Book Guy on *The Simpsons*, the "Worst Essanay Ever!"

Other Views and Reviews: "Charlie Chaplin's burlesque on 'Carmen' [was] given a private showing for review…It is in four reels and, on the whole, was voted unsatisfactory by the majority of exhibitors who attended. The consensus of opinion is that it is a very much padded picture."—*Variety* (1916).

"[The expanded *Carmen*] is a tedious botch of a film…restoring material that Chaplin had abandoned and adding a gruelingly unfunny Ben Turpin subplot in the hope that audiences wouldn't notice that Chaplin's and Turpin's paths never cross…I am sorry to say that I have never at any time seen [Turpin] do anything that made me laugh."—Walter Kerr, *The Silent Clowns* (1975).

"Primarily, Chaplin was a satirist. So his *Burlesque on Carmen* [the two-reel version] is one of his most genuinely funny films…[it] will have you laughing out loud and gasping for air."—Brandon Summers, *The Internet Movie Database* (2001).

"[The two-reel version is] among my favorite Chaplin films…classic comedy at its finest."—Warren H. Jones, *Amazon.com* (2001).

"The short is entertaining in part because it gives Edna her one 'bad girl' role and she has a lot of fun tossing her head and snapping her fingers and making poor Charlie her sex slave."—Alan Vanneman, *Bright Lights Film Journal* (2004).

†Shepard based his reconstruction on court documents from Chaplin's lawsuit against Essanay, as well as the Geraldine Farrar version of **Carmen**.

50. *Police*

(Two Reels; Released March 27, 1916)

Reissue titles: **Charlie in the Police, Housebreaker**

Home-movie editions: **Charlie and the Thief, Charlie the Burglar, Freed from Jail, The Hero**†

Cast: Charlie Chaplin (*Charlie, Convict 999*), Edna Purviance (*lady of the house*), Wesley Ruggles (*burglar* and *phony preacher*), Leo White (*flophouse proprietor, fruit peddler,* and *cop*), James T. Kelly (*drunk with pockets picked* and *flophouse customer*), Bud Jamison (*prissy flophouse customer*), Harry "Snub" Pollard (*gum-chewing flophouse customer*), Paddy McGuire (*tramp*), John Rand (*cop*), Fred Goodwins (*cop*), Billy Armstrong (*cop*).

Credits: Written and directed by Charlie Chaplin. Photographed by Harry Ensign. Assistant director: Ernest Van Pelt.

Plot: Newly released from prison, Charlie encounters a preacher who turns out to be a con artist. After getting kicked out of a flophouse, Charlie runs into his old cellmate, who convinces Charlie to help him commit a burglary. During the break-in, they're discovered by Edna, the lady of the house, who begs them not to go upstairs because her mother is seriously ill. Edna prepares a meal and tries to get them to reform. Realizing the error of his ways, Charlie has a change of heart and winds up foiling his partner's plans. When the police arrive, Edna identifies Charlie as her husband, preventing his arrest. Charlie departs, vowing that he'll go straight.

Source of print screened: **Chaplin's Essanay Comedies Vol. 3** (Kino On Video)

Comments: A number of fans and historians consider **Police** to be the finest and most mature of Chaplin's Essanay efforts. Typical of this praise is Walter Kerr's assertion in *The Silent Clowns* (Alfred A. Knopf, 1975) that **Police** is "Chaplin's last and best Essanay and a considerable advance over his final Keystone, **His Prehistoric Past** [released December 7, 1914]." Kerr goes on to comment:

> *I cannot pretend to know when Chaplin discovered for himself what was true, all-embracing, ultimate, and indivisible comic character was. I only know when I [saw] it for the first time—fleetingly, but with the force of a thunderbolt…With*

*no transition at all, Charlie becomes Edna's husband. Affable, outgoing, utterly
at home, digging his hands into his pockets and flexing his knees as though he were
master of his own domain and ready to get out the humidor, he is all bourgeois
bonhomie, the host par excellence, eager to show his guests about and have them
back soon again. No one has ever been more completely the man of the house. The
impression lasts for only a moment or two, but, for me, its implications are
immense. It is entirely clear that Charlie could have been this man at any time he
chose to adopt the role...No barrier stands between his talents and the assumption
of a role in which they might be exercised. He is no natural tramp.*

Police is definitely one of Chaplin's best Essanay entries, offering some memorable comic bits laced with social commentary. Personally though, of all the Essanays, we prefer Chaplin's two-reel version of **Burlesque on "Carmen,"** which we feel is better crafted, funnier, and more accomplished in its blend of comedy and drama.

A comedic remake of **His Regeneration** (1915), an Essanay drama with a guest appearance by Chaplin, **Police** begins with Charlie getting released from prison. Immediately, he is targeted by a phony preacher, whose "let me help you to go straight" spiel reduces Charlie to tears, enabling the preacher to pick his pocket. It proves to be a rude awakening for Charlie; when he later encounters a legitimate preacher with genuinely honorable intentions, an enraged Charlie furiously chases the poor fellow away.

A penniless Charlie attempts to spend the night at a flophouse. As each customer pays his way in, Charlie notices that the proprietor takes pity on an emaciated man, evidently suffering from consumption, and lets him in for free. Unable to pay, Charlie begins coughing, then sucks in his cheeks in a effort to give himself a sickly, undernourished appearance. The proprietor sees through his charade, and boots Charlie out. Though some might find this scene to be in highly questionable taste, Chaplin's pantomimic skills make it exceedingly funny, revealing that he was becoming more adept at walking the fine line between comedy and tragedy.

Charlie is reunited with his old cellmate, who gets Charlie involved with his burglary plans. As they break in and ransack her house, Edna telephones the police, who insist on finishing their tea before responding to the call. Edna confronts the pair, gives them a meal, and offers to help them "go straight"—something Charlie has heard before, but never with such sincerity. (However, remembering his encounter with the phony preacher, Charlie checks his pocket to make sure nothing is missing.) As usual, Chaplin and Purviance work exceedingly well together, with Edna making the most of her relatively limited screen time.

(Trivia note: The "interior" scenes were shot on open-air sets to take advantage of natural daylight; as a result, a breeze causes the tablecloth on the kitchen table to make billowing movements.)

The film's climactic showdown between Charlie and his erstwhile partner-in-crime is more like one you'd find in a Keystone comedy, complete with Keystone Kop-like figures arriving on the scene. It's a little too frenzied in light of the subtle humor and straight drama that preceded it, although it does provide a set-up for the moment where Edna identifies Charlie as her husband in order to prevent his arrest. Chaplin is no less than brilliant in this scene, which is one of the highlights of his entire Essanay output.

Police is the first Chaplin comedy to seriously deal with the power of redemption, and how one kind act is all it takes to change a person's life. Charlie, surrounded by corruption and momentarily seduced by it, finally finds someone who believes in him. Even though he walks away alone at the conclusion††, he's more secure because his faith in humanity has been restored. As a result, his future seems brighter than ever before. Walking down the road, Charlie has his arms extended Christ-like, signifying his spiritual "cleansing." And, for once, the road doesn't stretch into infinity; instead, there's a mansion in the distance, as if it were an attainable Shangri-La. (The faith-in-humanity and one-kind-act themes would recur in *City Lights*, *Modern Times*, *The Great Dictator*, *Monsieur Verdoux*, and *Limelight*.)

Throughout the film, Chaplin reveals a firm grasp of the cinematic language. The photography is impressive and Chaplin uses irises, close-ups, and panning shots to heighten the impact of scenes both comically and dramatically. Especially worthy of praise is the pre-housebreaking scene that shows the shadowy silhouettes of the two ex-cons as they approach Edna's house. (Charlie even works in his familiar "hat bounce," described in the entry for *The Masquerader* [Keystone, 1914].)

Wesley Ruggles (1889-1972), who performs double duty in *Police*, also appeared in the Chaplin Essanays *The Bank*, *Shanghaied*, *A Night in the Show*, and *Burlesque on "Carmen."* The younger brother of actor Charles Ruggles (*Trouble in Paradise*, *Love Me Tonight*, *Murders in the Zoo*), Wesley later became a director; his credits include *Cimarron* (1931; winner of the Best Picture Oscar that year), *No Man of Her Own* (1932), *The Monkey's Paw* (1933), *College Humor* (1933), *I'm No Angel* (1933), *Too Many Husbands* (1940), *See*

Here, Private Hargrove (1944), and *London Town* (a.k.a. *My Heart Goes Crazy*, 1946).

A reconstructed version of *Police* is the centerpiece of *The Chaplin Puzzle*, available on DVD as part of Brentwood Home Video's *Charlie Chaplin: 57 Classics* collection. This documentary posits Chaplin had completed the film as a three-reeler and that Essanay whittled it down to two reels prior to release. To back up this claim, the *Chaplin Puzzle* producers note that the flophouse sequence (originally intended for *Life*, Chaplin's abandoned feature film project, and eventually utilized for *Triple Trouble*) constituted a good portion of the excised reel. They also cite that reinstated scenes showing Charlie and Edna working together as kitchen hands (also shot for *Life* and included in *Triple Trouble*) were likewise intended for *Police*, and that these introductory passages are key to explaining how "they seem to know each other already" during the later burglary sequence. Without these scenes, it is contended, the apparently pre-established Charlie-Edna relationship is "bewildering."

While *The Chaplin Puzzle* presents a good argument, we're not convinced of its validity. Although it shares the same sets and some of the same actors, the flophouse sequence in *Police* varies significantly from the one that turns up in *Triple Trouble*. As Glenn Mitchell observes in *The Chaplin Encyclopedia*:

> Comparison with the flophouse scene in *Triple Trouble* poses the question of how it could fit into *Police*: in *Police* Charlie, penniless, feigns illness to obtain a bed but is thrown out; in *Triple Trouble* he has enough money to afford a cigar, and enters the establishment unchallenged.

The extended flophouse sequence in *Triple Trouble* was more likely an alternate cut that Chaplin jettisoned. In the revised *Police*, Chaplin goes to the flophouse *twice*, which makes for a rather unwieldy narrative. (For more about *Life*, see the entry for *Triple Trouble*.)

As for the "bewildering" Charlie-Edna relationship, the reinstated kitchen scenes really don't make any sense within the context of *Police*'s plotline and their inclusion raises several questions. Why would Edna be working as a servant when she already has a home just as good if not better than the one her employer owns? If she's only a servant, where did Edna get all the nice furnishings and fancy items in *her* home? Did she steal them between her duties at the other place? Or is she a well-to-do eccentric who enjoys scrubbing other people's floors?

When Edna discovers the pair burglarizing her home, Charlie stares at her intently. In the reconstructed version of *Police*, a title card is added to reinforce the idea of their prior acquaintance (*"He remembers the girl from the kitchen"*). Again, we're not buying it. Charlie isn't staring at Edna out of recognition, he's staring because the sight of a pretty woman smites him—and romance means more to Charlie than any material possessions. And if they *were* co-workers, why doesn't Edna immediately recognize Charlie? (If you worked with someone who looked like Charlie Chaplin, wouldn't *you* recognize him?) Trying to interpret this scene otherwise seems to be, in our opinion, merely wishful thinking.

Police was Chaplin's last official Essanay film (i.e., the last one he personally supervised) and represents a quantum leap from earlier Essanays like ***His New Job*** and ***A Night Out***. Chaplin's development as a filmmaker during his yearlong stint at Essanay was simply astonishing.

Other Views and Reviews: "Not so funny as [other Chaplins]...There was, seemingly, a tendency to strive for a more artistic ending, but in this instance it didn't quite hit the mark."—*Variety* (1916).

"Those who believe that Chaplin's abilities are limited to the mallet, the kick and the spinal curvature walk, should see this picture. They will be disillusioned. They will see a touch of heart interest just at the end of the subject, and they will see that Charlie's stock of pantomime includes pathos as well as fooling...The supporting cast is uniformly good, with Miss Purviance ranking easily next to the star."—*Motion Picture News* (1916).

"***Police***, the last of the Essanays, is perhaps the best. It certainly points the way most clearly toward later Chaplin films. The new ingredient of ***Police*** is a bitter, almost misanthropic irony; it is the first in a line of films that includes ***Easy Street***, ***Sunnyside***, ***The Pilgrim***, ***Modern Times***, and ***Monsieur Verdoux***...the wonder is that he can make such basically cynical, unpleasant material into something so funny and exciting."—Gerald Mast, *The Comic Mind* (1973).

"***Police*** is in many ways the most mature entry in the [Essanay] series. While there is still too much in the way of frenetic action and unbelievably silly policemen, Chaplin's comedy is increasingly whimsical...and contrasted with authentic drama."—Glenn Mitchell, *The Chaplin Encyclopedia* (1997).

"I just like Charlie Chaplin's work (period) so my opinion may speak in higher praise than the average. Regardless of what usually happens in a Chaplin film, I can always expect a beautiful ending—and guess what: this one has that kind of ending."—Carrie Deskins, *The Internet Movie Database* (2004).

†***The Hero*** is a composite of ***Police*** and ***The Adventurer*** (Mutual, 1917).

††The final shot of Charlie scurrying away when a cop reappears is intact in the Kino Video edition, but is missing from other copies of ***Police***.

51. *The Essanay-Chaplin Revue of 1916*
(Five Reels; Released September 23, 1916)
Alternate title: **The Chaplin Revue of 1916**
Cast: Charlie Chaplin (*Charlie*), Edna Purviance (*farmer's daughter* and *head-waiter's wife*), Fred Goodwins (*farmer* and *hotel receptionist*), Paddy McGuire (*farmhand*), Lloyd Bacon (*the girl's fiancé* and *second thief*), Leo White (*first thief, studio receptionist, film actor, Frenchman* and *hotel receptionist*), Bud Jamison (*third thief* and *headwaiter*), Billy Armstrong (*minister*), Ben Turpin (*assistant property man* and *Charlie's drinking pal*), Charlotte Mineau (*leading lady*), Gloria Swanson (*stenographer*), Agnes Ayres (*extra wearing black lace dress*). (In 1983, historian Rick de Croix reported that scenes were filmed with Graham Douglas impersonating Chaplin in order to link the footage together.)
Credits: Original footage written and directed by Charlie Chaplin. Photographed by Harry Ensign.
Source of print screened: Currently unavailable on DVD
Comments: The fact that Charlie's contract with them ended with **Police** didn't deter Essanay from continuing to ride the Chaplin gravy train. Essanay claimed this "revue" was based on three Chaplin films, which had been "worked over in such a way that they dovetail, forming a unified play." In actuality, Essanay merely strung together **The Tramp**, **His New Job**, and **A Night Out** in their entirety and attempted to weave a cohesive plot from three disconnected narratives. The results were unwieldy, to say the least. Opening with **The Tramp**, Charlie winds up working on a farm, becomes smitten with the farmer's daughter (Edna Purviance), then departs when he discovers she loves another. Then it's on **His New Job**, as Charlie applies for work at a movie studio. Finally, in **A Night Out**, he and his drinking companion Ben Turpin hit the town for an evening of fun. Diehard Chaplin fans may have been entertained by this cinematic recycling, despite Essanay's total disregard for Chaplin's original intent.

In a similar vein, the 12 classic short comedies Chaplin made for the Mutual Film Corporation were reissued in 1938 by Guaranteed Pictures in three feature-length anthologies: **Charlie Chaplin Carnival**, **Charlie Chaplin Cavalcade**, and **Charlie Chaplin Festival**. Each two-reeler had hyperactive music scores and sound effects that were added by the Van Beuren Corporation in 1932 (Van Beuren produced cartoons and scored these pictures like animated shorts). Films such as **Easy Street**, **The Rink**, **The Cure**, and **The Immigrant** were grouped four titles per anthology, with no attempt to make them conform to a single plotline. Thank goodness.

Other Views and Reviews: "The quality of the Essanay compilations were not as comparable to the Mutual compilations."—The Black Englishman, *The Internet Movie Database* (2002).

52. *Chase Me Charlie*

(Seven Reels; released 1917)

Distributed in England in 1917. Five-reel edition released in the United States by George Kleine System on April 8, 1918. Original source footage written and directed by Charlie Chaplin, and photographed by Harry Ensign.

Cast: Charlie Chaplin (*Charlie*), Edna Purviance (*Edna Sugar-Plum*), Ben Turpin (*movie studio stagehand*), Leo White (*Duke De Durti-Dog*), Billy Armstrong, G. M. "Broncho Billy" Anderson.

Credits: Compiled and titled by Langford Reed. Edited by H. G. Doncaster.

Reissue with sound: Produced and released independently by Edwin G. O'Brien in 1932. Narrated by Teddy Bergman (Alan Reed). Musical score by Elias Breeskin. Running time: 60 minutes. Reissued by Citation Films, Inc. (Alfred F. Schwalberg) in February, 1960.†

Plot: Charlie falls in love with Edna, a farmer's daughter (in scenes from *The Tramp*). Seeking permission from Edna's father to win her hand, Charlie does the unthinkable: he goes to work. The narrative follows his adventures as a bank guard (from *The Bank*), prizefighter (from *The Champion*), paperhanger (*Work*), stagehand and actor (*His New Job*). Finally he disguises himself (*A Woman*) to influence Edna's father.

Source of print screened: Currently unavailable on DVD

Comments: British director Langford Reed, usually concerned with dramatic productions, prepared this seven-reel compilation for European distribution. Advertised as "A Chaplin Jingle," it contained footage from the aforementioned Essanay titles as well as *A Night Out*, *Shanghaied*, *By the Sea*, and *In the Park*. Unlike *The Essanay-Chaplin Revue of 1916*, which basically strung three films together, *Chase Me Chase* mixed up the scenes in a crazy-quilt fashion, linking them with new subtitles. Essanay approved of Reed's work and modified it for American consumption; the company trimmed the feature to five reels and copyrighted it in March 1918. The film was released by Essanay's successor, George Kleine, eleven days later.

Chase Me Charlie was re-released as a 60-minute sound film in 1932, featuring a musical score by Elias Breeskin, concert violinist and former conductor of the Pittsburgh Symphony Orchestra. The film credited Breeskin "and his Famous Radio Orchestra." New York-based radio comedian Teddy Bergman made his motion-picture debut as the narrator. Bergman later became known as Alan Reed, the voice of "Fred Flintstone." When the sound version of **Chase Me Charlie** was reissued to theaters in 1960, the star was billed as he was in 1918: "Essanay's Charlie Chaplin."

Other Views and Reviews: "[The sound version] doesn't do the comic clown justice…much better showcases of his work available elsewhere."—*Blockbuster Video Guide to Movies and Videos* (1996).

"Inept attempt to string early Chaplin shorts into story line—[the] material used is often weak."—*Leonard Maltin's Classic Movie Guide* (2005).

†The promotional materials for this 1960 reissue bear a 1959 distribution date.

53. *Triple Trouble*

(Two Reels; Released August 11, 1918)
Produced by Essanay, released by V-L-S-E (Vitagraph, Lubin, Selig and Essanay)
Reissue title: **Charlie's Triple Trouble**
Home-movie editions: **Charlie's Triple Trouble, Charlie at the Night Shelter**
Cast: Charlie Chaplin (*cook's assistant*), Edna Purviance (*servant*), Leo White (*foreign count* and *flophouse proprietor*), Billy Armstrong (*cook* and *miser*), Wesley Ruggles (*hired assassin*), James T. Kelly (*drunken flophouse customer*), Bud Jamison (*burly flophouse customer*), Harry "Snub" Pollard (*flophouse customer*).
Credits: Written and directed by Leo White, using footage originally written and directed by Charlie Chaplin. Original source footage photographed by Harry Ensign.
Plot: Charlie gets a job as assistant cook at the home of Colonel A. Nutt, an inventor who has devised a wireless explosive. Agents of a foreign power, Pretzelstrasse, want to obtain the weapon for their own purposes, but Nutt refuses to deal with them. Representing the Pretzelstrassers, a count recruits an assassin to kill Nutt and steal the formula, unaware that a cop has overheard their plans and has arranged for a patrol to guard the colonel. After spending an eventful evening in a flophouse, Charlie runs into the assassin, who enlists his aid in breaking into the Nutt house. When the assassin enters, the police spring into action; during the ensuing mayhem, a stray bullet hits the invention. The resulting explosion blows up the Nutt house (and somehow manages to destroy the Pretzelstrass hideout as well), covering everyone—including Charlie—in debris.
Source of print screened: **Chaplin's Essanay Comedies Vol. 3** (Kino on Video)
Comments: In the late summer of 1915, Chaplin began working on **Life**, a feature-length film he envisioned as a seriocomic look at the struggle for survival among the downtrodden. However, Essanay was pressuring Chaplin to complete

a new comedy short every four weeks; eventually he was forced to abandon his time-consuming feature project. Some of the scenes shot for *Life* turned up in *Police*, but other footage went unused.

By 1918, Chaplin had signed with First National after having completed 12 short comedies for the Mutual Film Corporation. The Mutuals were a hit with audiences and critics alike, and with the release of *A Dog's Life*, his initial First National effort, Chaplin's popularity was at an all-time high. The success of these pictures didn't go unnoticed by the folks at Essanay. Not content to merely reissue the earlier films, Essanay devised a way to come up with a "new" Chaplin picture, despite the fact that he had left the company nearly three years earlier. Essanay president and co-founder George K. Spoor "explained" the delayed release in an August 1918 announcement to exhibitors:

> *If you bought a piece of real estate and foresaw that its value would quadruple if you held it a certain length of time, what would you do? Certainly you would hold it. That's just what we did with **Triple Trouble**. Essanay made this picture with Charlie Chaplin when he was at the zenith of his laugh-making powers. We knew there would come a time when it would be worth many times its weight in gold. We held this negative in our vaults for the most opportune time of release, which we believe is NOW. There has only been one new Chaplin film in several months. The public is eager for a NEW Chaplin comedy and will welcome **Triple Trouble** with open arms.*

So much for truth in advertising. *Triple Trouble*, prepared without Chaplin's knowledge or approval, combined leftover footage from the uncompleted *Life* with stock shots from *Police* and *Work*, plus new footage prepared by Essanay. We don't know exactly how many open arms greeted this incoherent mess, but it surely must have disappointed and confused an untold number of exhibitors and moviegoers.

We're not begrudging Essanay for cashing in on the Chaplin brand name; back in 1918, any studio that had access to unseen Chaplin footage would have been crazy not to exploit it. But to imply that *Triple Trouble* was a legitimate Chaplin creation is deception of the highest order.

The new, non-Chaplin scenes were written and directed by supporting actor Leo White (1882-1948). White co-starred in most of the Chaplin Essanays as well as three of the Chaplin Mutuals. White appeared in comedy shorts with Chaplin imitator Billy West, and was also seen in *The Lost World* (1925), *Ben-Hur* (1925), *Monkey Business* (1931), *The Devil's Brother* (1933), *The Thin Man* (1934), *A Night at the Opera* (1935), *Gold Diggers of 1935* (1935), *The*

Walking Dead (1936), ***Angels With Dirty Faces*** (1938), ***Yankee Doodle Dandy*** (1942), ***Casablanca*** (1942), ***Arsenic and Old Lace*** (1944), and ***The Fountainhead*** (1949). The last time White worked with Chaplin was in ***The Great Dictator*** (1940), cast as one of Adenoid Hynkel's barbers. (We wonder if the subject of ***Triple Trouble*** ever came up during a lunch break.)

The bona fide Chaplin footage in ***Triple Trouble*** provides an interesting glimpse at ***Life***, Chaplin's first attempt to create a feature-length comedy. In the opening household scenes, Charlie goes to empty a kitchen trash bin and unwittingly dumps a good portion of rubbish all over servant Edna Purviance and the freshly scrubbed floor. Charlie comforts Edna, then comes to her aid after she's physically abused by the cook. These scenes are relatively brief and were intended to set up the Charlie-Edna relationship. However, it ends abruptly and Edna disappears from the rest of the film. Evidently this is all the footage involving Edna that Chaplin shot, yet Essanay was determined to include it here, regardless of whether it made sense, probably to further the illusion of an "authentic" Chaplin comedy.

The flophouse sequence gives us a clearer picture of what Chaplin had in mind for ***Life***. The grimy, depressing, Dickensian ambiance is uncomfortably realistic; Chaplin no doubt drew upon painful memories of his own impoverished childhood for inspiration. There's a mean-spirited edge to the humor, which comes across even crueler in this bleak setting, yet Chaplin is able to make us laugh in spite of any guilty feelings we might be harboring. As soon as Charlie walks down the flophouse stairs—which in itself seems like a descent into Hell (think Maxim Gorki's *The Lower Depths*)—he lights his cigar by striking a match on a sleeping patron's bare foot, then gives the poor fellow a "hot foot" with the still-burning matchstick. After using another patron's bare foot as a combination hat rack/cane stand, Charlie notices an elderly drunk whose intoxicated singing is disturbing everyone's slumber. Charlie tries to silence him by flicking cigar ashes in his mouth, then kicking him, but to no avail. Eventually, Charlie resorts to smashing a bottle over the drunk's head to ensure his silence.

In the meantime, an assassin (Wesley Ruggles) runs into the flophouse and jumps into one of the unoccupied cots. As everyone tries to settle down to a good night's rest, a Faginesque miser (Billy Armstrong, who also played the cook in the earlier kitchen scenes) sneaks in to rob the sleeping patrons. Charlie observes him stealing from the others and decides to keep a eye on him by reversing his position on his cot; putting his shoes on his hands and covering himself with a blanket, Charlie watches as the miser spreads his ill-gotten gains across an empty cot. When the miser's back is turned, Charlie reaches forward, grabs the money, and slides back under his blanket. The enraged miser attempts to stab Charlie, who nimbly dodges the blade. The whole flophouse becomes involved in the mêlée; Charlie dashes out, managing to elude two cops along the way.

While this flophouse sequence would be surpassed by a similar, superior one in *The Kid* (First National, 1921), it does represent what is arguably the first full expression of Chaplin's artistic ambition.

The other Chaplin scenes in *Triple Trouble* consist of snippets culled from *Police* (1916), and the closing shot of Charlie sticking his head through an oven door from *Work* (1915) is also used for the final shot here.

Much of Leo White's new footage for *Triple Trouble* closely matches Chaplin's original shots. Still, White was no Chaplin, and his limited grasp of the filmmaking technique is evident whenever he attempts something ambitious. (An "explosion," with cops hurling through the air, has to be seen to be believed.) Either that or White was under enormous pressure by Essanay to churn out the footage as quickly as possible. White appears as the foreign count in the new scenes, and also appears fleetingly as the flophouse proprietor; obvious doubles for Wesley Ruggles and Billy Armstrong are used to bridge the Chaplin footage. (The identities of the actors playing Colonel Nutt, his daughter, their butler, the cops, and the Pretzelstrass agents are unknown.)

Although the editing is competent and occasionally clever, the new material is a tiresome retread of the undisciplined stuff Keystone was doing back in 1912. Leo White seems to have encouraged his actors to indulge in the worst sort of ham-fisted, arm-flailing histrionics. The sight of policemen (slavishly aping the Keystone Kops) running around willy-nilly is not funny in itself; even frenzied activity should build from some sort of comedic logic.

But logic is an element sorely missing from *Triple Trouble*. For instance, if Pretzelstrass (a punning reference to Germany; the film was made during World War I) is a foreign power, why would they entrust such an important mission to a back-alley thug? Why does the thug enlist Charlie's aid? Why does Charlie immediately go along with the scheme? Why are we even obsessing over this nonsense?

By the time *Triple Trouble* was released in August 1918, the market had been flooded by reissues of earlier Chaplins (retitled to give the false impression they were new) and "bogus Chaplins" that lifted segments from the Keystones and intercut new footage with other actors doubling for Charlie. Imitators Billy West and Billie Ritchie starred in Chaplinesque comedy shorts; West in particular looked like Chaplin and aped his mannerisms convincingly enough, though minus the emotional center Chaplin brought to his performances. Due to the proliferation of phony product, Chaplin began to "authenticate" his latest releases by having his signature appear on the opening title card, as it does in **Shoulder Arms** (First National, 1918). (Surprisingly, however, Chaplin lists **Triple Trouble** in the filmography of his 1964 autobiography.)

Triple Trouble has a certain archaeological value as an early example of creative film editing, juggling new and old footage. Movie producers resorted to this kind of patchwork for decades. Three Stooges fans, for example, can usually tell when a Stooge short of the 1950s includes footage from the 1940s. As late as 1982, after the death of Peter Sellers, writer-director Blake Edwards squeezed out another Inspector Clouseau comedy by utilizing leftover footage from the previous entries and filming new material to link it together. **Trail of the Pink Panther** is an erratic, cynical hack job that tries to pass itself off as a "tribute" but instead reveals a surprising amount of contempt for its target audience. Just like **Triple Trouble**. Nevertheless, we're recommending the picture (**Triple Trouble**, not **Trail of the Pink Panther**) to serious fans for its glimpse of what survives of Chaplin's first attempt to tackle a feature-length film.

Other Views and Reviews: "Charlie Chaplin's tricks in this offering will get the laughs, you needn't worry about that…The picture is free from vulgarity. The 'kicks' that used to be so common in the old days are absent except in one or two instances."—*Motion Picture News* (1918).

"Don't blame Chaplin for this film crime."—*Chicago Daily News* (1918).

"[An] atrocious patch quilt of ancient slapstick reels."—*The Moving Picture World* (1918).

"**Triple Trouble**, with its fancy splicing and fantastic doubling…has remarkable continuity and the parts fit together, almost miraculously."—Gerald D. McDonald, Michael Conway and Mark Ricci, *The Films of Charlie Chaplin* (1965).

"[**Triple Trouble**] is worthless, except for what it can tell us about the vein Chaplin was tempted to explore in imagining his own kind of feature [*Life*]…The few feet of rescued film seethe with inventive business he would not know how to use properly until later."—Walter Kerr, *The Silent Clowns* (1975).

"This is Chaplin's worst film. The story doesn't make any sense, it's crudely directed and IT ISN'T TERRIBLY FUNNY. I love Chaplin and I have seen almost more than 90% of his work but this is just bad."—Brandon Summers, *The Internet Movie Database* (2001).

AFTER ESSANAY

Late in 1915 Essanay made a $350,000 offer to Chaplin for another 12 two-reel comedies; negotiations ended when the studio refused to meet his demand for a $150,000 signing bonus. Time proved that Essanay could not withstand the loss of its most popular star attraction; the company was out of business by the 1920s. (However, the Chicago studio still bears the Essanay name; the soundstages there are used for the production of industrial films and music videos.)

In February 1916 Chaplin signed a one-year deal with the Mutual Film Corporation for a record $670,000 ($10,000 a week plus a $150,000 signing bonus) to make a dozen two-reelers. As a group, the Mutuals are still considered to be the finest and funniest short films Chaplin ever made. (For a listing of the Mutuals, see *Chaplin's Post-Essanay Films*)

After Mutual, Chaplin signed a million-dollar contract with First National, resulting in eight films released between 1918 and 1923; these included such major hits as *Shoulder Arms* (1918) and *The Kid* (1921; his first self-directed feature-length film).

In 1919 Chaplin, Douglas Fairbanks, Mary Pickford, and D. W. Griffith formed the United Artists Corporation, although Chaplin would still be under contract to First National for another four years. After leaving First National, Chaplin forsook the short comedy format altogether.

Chaplin only appeared fleetingly (and heavily disguised) in his first release for United Artists, *A Woman of Paris* (1923), a drama starring Edna Purviance. He returned to comedy and his familiar Tramp image for *The Gold Rush* (1925) and *The Circus* (1928).

Talking pictures were here to stay by 1931, but that didn't prevent Chaplin from releasing his silent comedy *City Lights* that year. It was hailed as Chaplin's masterpiece and was a huge box office success. Chaplin remained faithful to his screen persona with the release of the silent *Modern Times* (1936), which had a few brief dialogue passages (including a gibberish song performed by Charlie). Like *City Lights*, *Modern Times* was a box office smash.

Chaplin finally acknowledged the sound era with *The Great Dictator* (1940), playing two roles: a meek little Jewish barber and dictator Adenoid Hynkel, a caricature of Adolph Hitler. (Although the barber was often seen wearing the Tramp's trademark outfit, the last *authentic* portrayal of the Tramp had been in *Modern Times*.)

Chaplin dropped the Tramp characterization entirely for his roles in ***Monsieur Verdoux*** (1947), ***Limelight*** (1952), and ***A King in New York*** (1957)—although traces of the "Little Fellow" were still evident in his performances.

Chaplin made a cameo appearance in his final film, ***A Countess From Hong Kong*** (1967), a romantic comedy starring Sophia Loren and Marlon Brando. In his later years, he oversaw the theatrical reissues of the films he owned, arranging new musical score for them. He still planned on making one more film, ***The Freak***, before ill health forced him to abandon the project. Chaplin died on December 25, 1977 in Switzerland.

CHAPLIN'S POST-ESSANAY FILMS

*For the record, here is a listing of films written and directed by Chaplin after his Essanay period. This list does not include unreleased material (**How to Make Movies, Nice and Friendly, The Professor**) or "guest appearances" in films such as **The Nut** (United Artists, 1921), **Hollywood** (Paramount, 1923), and **Show People** (M-G-M, 1928).*

MUTUAL FILM CORPORATION
The Floorwalker (Two Reels; Released May 15, 1916)
The Fireman (Two Reels; Released June 12, 1916)
The Vagabond (Two Reels; Released July 10, 1916)
One A. M. (Two Reels; Released August 7, 1916)
The Count (Two Reels; Released September 4, 1916)
The Pawnshop (Two Reels; Released October 2, 1916)
Behind the Screen (Two Reels; Released November 13, 1916)
The Rink (Two Reels; Released December 4, 1916)
Easy Street (Two Reels; Released January 22, 1917)
The Cure (Two Reels; Released April 16, 1917)
The Immigrant (Two Reels; Released June 17, 1917)
The Adventurer (Two Reels; Released October 23, 1917)

FIRST NATIONAL PICTURES
A Dog's Life (Three Reels; Released April 14, 1918)
Shoulder Arms (Three Reels; Released October 20, 1918)
Sunnyside (Two Reels; Released June 15, 1919)
A Day's Pleasure (Two Reels; Released December 7, 1919)
The Kid (Six Reels; Released February 6, 1921)
The Idle Class (Two Reels; Released September 25, 1921)

Pay Day (Two Reels; Released April 2, 1922)
The Pilgrim (Four Reels; Released February 25, 1923)

LIBERTY LOAN COMMITTEE (U. S. GOVERNMENT)

The Bond (a.k.a. ***Charlie Chaplin in a Liberty Loan Appeal***; Half Reel; Released September 29, 1918): Chaplin wrote, directed, and starred in this humorous short film promoting the sale of Liberty Bonds during World War I.

UNITED ARTISTS CORPORATION

A Woman of Paris (Eight Reels; Released October 1, 1923): Chaplin wrote and directed but does not star in this dramatic film.
The Gold Rush (Nine Reels; Released August 16, 1925)
The Circus (Seven Reels; Released January 7, 1928)
City Lights (87 minutes; Released February 6, 1931)
Modern Times (85 minutes; Released February 5, 1936)
The Great Dictator (126 minutes; Released October 15, 1940)
Monsieur Verdoux (123 minutes; Released April 11, 1947)
Limelight (143 minutes; Released October 23, 1952)

ARCHWAY FILM DISTRIBUTORS/ATTICA FILM COMPANY

A King in New York (105 minutes; Released in the United Kingdom on September 12, 1957): This film remained unseen in the United States until December 1973.

UNIVERSAL PICTURES

A Countess From Hong Kong (108 minutes; Released January 5, 1967)

THE CHARLIE CHAPLIN
COMEDY THEATRE

During the early 1950s, the comedy shorts of Laurel & Hardy, Our Gang, and The Three Stooges† were broadcast on television, introducing these old favorites to a new generation of fans. Unfortunately, Charlie Chaplin did not enjoy a similar revival during this period. Some have surmised that Chaplin's films failed to find an audience because his expressive visual humor required a larger canvas than the boob tube could provide. This may have been true to an extent, but a bigger factor was the controversy surrounding Chaplin's perceived political beliefs. In 1950, WPIX-Channel 11, a New York station, withdrew its scheduled broadcasts of Chaplin shorts after receiving a letter from an East Coast branch (Hudson County, New Jersey) of the Catholic War Veterans which claimed that Chaplin had "definite Communist leanings," adding:

> It makes no difference if the pictures were made five, ten or twenty or more years ago. Entertainment for art's sake just does not exist when you talk about Communism.

It made no difference that these allegations against Chaplin were false. Running scared in an era of McCarthyism and blacklistings, WPIX program manager Warren Wade cancelled the Chaplin series after it had been on the air for only one week. Other local stations didn't dare add any Chaplin titles to their film libraries. In 1955, the trade publication *Variety* responded to the lack of Chaplin broadcasts by stating that markets should "distinguish between pre-political Chaplin and the later reputation, particularly since Chaplin received no money from TV sales of the shorts."

By the 1960s, the success of the syndicated series **Comedy Capers** and **Mischief Makers** (both featuring silent-era shorts revamped for kiddie viewers) proved there was a market, albeit a limited one, for silent comedies. In 1965 Vernon P. Becker produced a nationally syndicated half-hour series titled **The Charlie Chaplin Comedy Theatre**. Becker, who would later produce the Chaplin compilation *The Funniest Man in the World* (1967), made an earnest attempt to showcase the Keystone, Essanay and Mutual films—which were all, by this time, in the public domain.

The quality of the prints used for *The Charlie Chaplin Comedy Theatre* was generally good; some of the sound effects were cartoonish, but the music scoring, consisting of stock library themes orchestrated and recorded by Thomas J. Valentino, Inc., was admirably restrained if sometimes repetitive. The low-key narration by the uncredited Philip Tonken was tasteful and informative (offering cast and production data), though at times superfluous; for example, "Charlie loses his ice cream—down his pants." We can see what Charlie's doing, so we don't need a detailed explanation.

All of the films in the series were "step-printed," a process that stretches and slows down the visual action. Silent films are generally projected at 16 to 18 frames per second, but the rate of the early Keystones was as low as 12 frames. When these Chaplins were shown at the modern sound-film rate of 24 frames, the action could be literally twice as fast as originally intended. Perhaps Becker felt he was preserving the artistic integrity by adapting the silents to modern projection speed and making the films seem less frantic. In doing so, however, much of the action was *too* slow. Thus, in *The Rink* (Mutual, 1916) when Chaplin slips and slides on roller-skates, he seems to hang in mid-air for several seconds. The step-printing process also made these films *longer*, so footage had to be trimmed to accommodate a half-hour time slot. (So much for preserving artistic integrity.)

The series included such Essanay films as *The Tramp*, *A Jitney Elopement*, *Work*, *A Woman*, *A Night in the Show*, and *The Champion*, along with a two-part presentation of the Keystone feature *Tillie's Punctured Romance*. Shorter films, like Keystone's *The Fatal Mallet*, were combined to fill a half-hour segment.

During the 1970s, Chicago's WFLD-TV, Channel 32, came up with a Sunday afternoon lineup that was a comedy fan's dream: *It's Laurel and Hardy Time*, a two-hour block of features and shorts starring the celebrated duo, followed by *The Charlie Chaplin Comedy Theatre* and *The Abbott and Costello Show*. WSMW-TV, Channel 27 in Worcester, Massachusetts also broadcast Laurel & Hardy and Chaplin in a Saturday-evening block.

Copies of *The Charlie Chaplin Comedy Theatre* still circulate; the series' edition of *Work* is part of Madacy Home Video's *The Chaplin Collection Vol. 1* on DVD.

The Charlie Chaplin Comedy Theatre appealed to younger viewers who were unfamiliar with Chaplin's work. It can still serve as a satisfactory introduction for the uninitiated, so it's a shame that the program has disappeared from the airwaves. There's a new generation of potential Chaplin fans that ought to be exposed to his work, and this series could go a long way toward achieving that goal.

†Three Stooges shorts were broadcast as early as October 1949, when ABC-TV purchased the exclusive rights to 30 of the Curly-era Columbia two-reelers. Screen Gems, Columbia's television subsidiary, syndicated a package of 78 Stooge shorts in 1958; the films were so well-received that by the following year, all 190 Stooge Columbia shorts were made available to local markets.

REWORKED FOOTAGE

Footage from Chaplin's Keystone and Essanay work has turned up in countless documentaries, anthologies, and unauthorized releases, among them:

Mixed Up (1915)
A four-reel release composed of footage from Chaplin's Keystone comedies; Glenn Mitchell's *The Chaplin Encyclopedia* mentions that **Those Love Pangs**, **His New Job**, and **Laughing Gas** may possibly be among the titles that extracts were taken from.

The Fall of the Rummy-Nuffs (1917)
In 1917, Chaplin and his attorneys sought to prevent the distribution of "fake" Charlie Chaplin movies, which were cobbled together from the comedian's older films, using a double to bridge the footage. The feature-length **The Fall of the Rummy-Nuffs**, a parody of the dramatic production **The Fall of the Romanoffs** (1917) was one such fake Chaplin. Other bogus releases included the two-reelers **The Dishonor System** (satirizing 1916's **The Honor System**) and **One Law for Both**; **Charlie in a Harem**; and **Charlie Chaplin in "A Son of the Gods"** (based on 1916's **A Daughter of the Gods** starring Annette Kellermann). Chaplin not only had to contend with impersonators (Billy West, Billie Ritchie, Ray Hughes) who appropriated the Tramp character for their own comedies, he faced competition from *himself* in the form of these fraudulent releases.

The Perils of Patrick (1918)
A 30-episode serial fashioned from Chaplin's Keystone shorts; the title is a play on **The Perils of Pauline**, a popular movie serial starring Pearl White.

The Charlie Chaplin Revue (1918)
This Swedish compilation, running three reels in length, utilized footage from the Chaplin Essanays **His New Job**, **The Champion**, and **A Jitney Elopement**.

Comedy Cocktail (1930s)
A British two-reel short that contained footage from the Keystones *Laughing Gas* and *His Musical Career* and the Essanays *A Night in the Show* and *The Champion*.

La Grande Parade de Charlot (1948)
A French compilation utilizing footage from the Keystone *Making a Living* and the Essanays *His New Job*, *The Tramp*, *A Woman*, *Work*, *The Bank*, and *Shanghaied*, with commentary by Georges Sadoul.

Laughter Allowed (1950s)
A 45-minute compilation utilizing footage from the Keystones *Laughing Gas*, *The Masquerader*, and *Gentlemen of Nerve*, and the Essanays *The Champion*, *The Bank*, and *A Night in the Show*.

When Comedy Was King (1960)
This 81-minute compilation by producer Robert Youngson (*The Golden Age of Comedy*, *Laurel and Hardy's Laughing 20's*) has a segment titled "The Good Old Days at Keystone," which includes footage from *The Masquerader*, *His Trysting Place*, and *Gentlemen of Nerve*.

Merry Go Round (1962)
A European compilation that utilizes footage from the Essanays *The Champion*, *By the Sea*, *The Tramp* and *Triple Trouble*.

Chaplin's Art of Comedy (1966)
A 69-minute tribute written and compiled by Sam Sherman, relying on footage from the Chaplin Essanays *A Night in the Show*, *The Champion*, *A Woman* and *The Tramp*.

The Funniest Man in the World (1967)
A 90-minute compilation produced, written and directed by Vernon P. Becker (*The Charlie Chaplin Comedy Theatre*) and narrated by Douglas Fairbanks, Jr., utilizing footage from newsreels and Chaplin's Keystone, Essanay and Mutual comedies. Keystone footage includes scenes from *Making a Living*, *Kid Auto Races at Venice*, *Between Showers*, *Mabel at the Wheel*, *Caught in a Cabaret*, *The Masquerader*, *The Rounders*, *Dough and Dynamite*, *His Trysting Place*, *His Prehistoric Past*, and *Tillie's Punctured Romance*. Essanay footage

includes scenes from *His New Job*, *A Night Out*, *A Jitney Elopement*, *The Tramp*, *A Woman*, *A Night in the Show*, *Police*, and *Triple Trouble*.

Laughing Till It Hurt (1968)

Produced for and distributed exclusively by Wholesome Film Center, Inc. (Boston, Massachusetts). Unlike some Chaplin composites, this 70-minute feature is more biography than documentary, with most of the clips shown in chronological order and with no attempt to unite them into a story sequence. The excerpts are from the Keystones *Kid Auto Races at Venice*, *Between Showers*, *A Film Johnnie*, *Tango Tangles*, *Twenty Minutes of Love*, *Caught in the Rain*, *The Fatal Mallet*, *The Rounders*, *Dough and Dynamite*, and *Tillie's Punctured Romance*; the Essanays *His New Job*, *A Night Out*, *A Jitney Elopement*, *The Tramp*, *Work*, *The Bank*, and *A Night in the Show*; plus highlights from eight of Chaplin's Mutual comedies of 1916-17. *Laughing Till It Hurt* was produced by Norman R. Poretsky, written and directed by Nathan (Nat) Segaloff, and narrated by David MacAlary, with music composed and conducted by Peter Hazard. Nat Segaloff was only 19 years old when he made this film; he has since written and produced biographical studies for television (Darryl F. Zanuck, John Belushi, etc.), and is the author of the Everything series of "fun facts" books.

The Gentleman Tramp (1974)

Authorized by Chaplin, this 77-minute documentary contains footage from numerous Chaplin films, including the Keystone comedies *Kid Auto Races at Venice* and *The New Janitor*. Curiously, there is no footage to represent his Essanay period. (Perhaps Chaplin was still bitter about Essanay's handiwork regarding *Burlesque on Carmen* and *Triple Trouble*.) *The Gentleman Tramp* is narrated by Walter Matthau; Laurence Olivier reads passages from Chaplin's *My Autobiography*.

The Chaplin Puzzle (1992)
Part One: Chaplin Invents Himself (49 minutes)
Part Two: A Classic Restored (49 minutes)

This well-done two-part documentary—written by Joe Adamson; narrated by Burgess Meredith; produced, edited and directed by Don McGlynn—traces Chaplin's formative years at Keystone and Essanay, with some coverage of his Mutual period. Many of the Keystone excerpts are taken from better prints than the ones currently available to collectors. The centerpiece of Part Two is a three-reel reconstruction of *Police*.

Charlie Chaplin and Mack Sennett (2000)

A 26-minute documentary written and directed by Laurent Preyale, for French television.

Charlie: The Life and Art of Charles Chaplin (2003)

Produced, written and directed by Richard Schickel and narrated by Sydney Pollack, this 133-minute documentary traces Chaplin's life and career. Among the footage utilized are excerpts from the Keystones ***Kid Auto Races at Venice***, ***Between Showers***, ***Tango Tangles***, ***A Busy Day***, ***The Masquerader***, ***His New Profession***, ***The New Janitor***, ***Mabel's Married Life***, ***Those Love Pangs***, ***Dough and Dynamite***, ***The Rounders***, ***Getting Acquainted***, and ***Tillie's Punctured Romance***, and the Essanays ***His New Job***, ***A Night Out***, ***The Champion***, ***In the Park***, ***By the Sea***, ***The Tramp***, ***Work***, ***A Woman***, ***The Bank***, ***Shanghaied***, ***A Night in the Show***, and ***Triple Trouble***.

RETITLED CHAPLINS

Over the years, the early Chaplin films were chopped up, re-edited, reissued and redistributed countless times. The following are examples of Chaplin's Keystone and Essanay films that were retitled for theatrical reissues and home-movie editions. This list is by no means complete.

Retitled version	Original title
The Adventures of Tillie	Tillie's Punctured Romance
The Artist	The Face on the Bar Room Floor
At It Again	Caught in the Rain
At the Drugstore	Laughing Gas
Backstage Antics	The Property Man
Bad Soup	Shanghaied
The Baggage Man	The Property Man
Bakers Dozen	Dough and Dynamite
Barroom	The Face on the Bar Room Floor
Battling Charlie	The Champion
The Blundering Boob	The New Janitor
The Bonehead	His Favorite Pastime
The Boxer	The Champion
A Burlesque on Carmen	Burlesque on "Carmen"
Busted Hearts	Those Love Pangs
A Busted Johnny	Making a Living
Busy As Can Be	A Busy Day
Busy Little Dentist	Laughing Gas

Retitled version	Original title
Café Society	Caught in a Cabaret
Capturing the Robber	The New Janitor
The Caveman	His Prehistoric Past
Caveman Charlie	His Prehistoric Past
Champagne Charlie	A Night Out
Champion Charlie	The Champion
Charley Butts In	A Night Out
Charlie and Carmen	Burlesque on "Carmen"
Charlie and His Rival	Those Love Pangs
Charlie and Mabel at the Races	Gentlemen of Nerve
Charlie and the Dancer	Burlesque on "Carmen"
Charlie and the Mannequin	Mabel's Married Life
Charlie and the Perfect Lady	A Woman
Charlie and the Sausages	Mabel's Busy Day
Charlie and the Sleepwalker	Caught in the Rain
Charlie and the Smugglers	Burlesque on "Carmen"
Charlie and the Thief	Police
Charlie and the Toreador	Burlesque on "Carmen"
Charlie and the Umbrella	Between Showers
Charlie and Tillie's Elopement	Tillie's Punctured Romance
Charlie as a Piano Mover	His Musical Career
Charlie at the Bank	The Bank
Charlie at the Hotel	Mabel's Strange Predicament
Charlie at the Music Hall	A Night in the Show
Charlie at the Night Shelter	Triple Trouble
Charlie at the Races	Gentlemen of Nerve
Charlie at the Restaurant	A Night Out

Retitled version	Original title
Charlie at the Show	A Night in the Show
Charlie at the Studio	The Masquerader
Charlie at the Theater	A Night in the Show
Charlie at Work	Work
Charlie By the Sea	By the Sea
Charlie Caught Out	Dough and Dynamite
Charlie Detective	The Bank
Charlie Ditches Tillie	Tillie's Punctured Romance
Charlie Fights a Duel	Burlesque on "Carmen"
Charlie Gets a Job	The Tramp
Charlie Goes Mad	The Face on the Bar Room Floor
Charlie Goes to Sea	Shanghaied
Charlie Helps Out	The Tramp
Charlie in the Bank	The Bank
Charlie in the Park	In the Park
Charlie in the Police	The Police
Charlie in the Ring	The Champion
Charlie in the Spring	In the Park
Charlie in Training	The Champion
Charlie is Thirsty	His Favorite Pastime
Charlie Loses His Girl	The Face on the Bar Room Floor
Charlie on a Spree	In the Park
Charlie on the Boards	The Property Man
Charlie on the Farm	The Tramp
Charlie on the Ocean	Shanghaied
Charlie on the Road	The Tramp
Charlie Shanghaied	Shanghaied

Retitled version	Original title
Charlie Sneaks In	Gentlemen of Nerve
Charlie's Big Romance	Tillie's Punctured Romance
Charlie's Broken Heart	The Tramp
Charlie's Day Out	By the Sea
Charlie's Drunken Daze	A Night Out
Charlie's Elopement	A Jitney Elopement
Charlie's Fat Lady	A Night in the Show
Charlie's Fiancée	A Jitney Elopement
Charlie's Hot Seat	The Tramp
Charlie's Hot Spot	Dough and Dynamite
Charlie's New Job	His New Job
Charlie's Night Out	A Night Out
Charlie's Reckless Fling	His Favorite Pastime
Charlie's Recreation	Recreation
Charlie's Triple Trouble	Triple Trouble
Charlie the Actor	A Film Johnnie
Charlie the Bonehead	His Favorite Pastime
Charlie the Boxer	The Champion
Charlie the Burglar	Police
Charlie the Champ	The Champion
Charlie the Champion	The Champion
Charlie the Cleaner	Bank
Charlie the Cook	Shanghaied
Charlie the Decorator	Work
Charlie the Flirt	A Night in the Show
Charlie the Fortune Hunter	Tillie's Punctured Romance
Charlie the Hobo	The Tramp

Retitled version	Original title
Charlie the Invincible	Shanghaied
Charlie the Janitor	The New Janitor
Charlie the Nurse Maid	His New Profession
Charlie the Perfect Lady	A Woman
Charlie the Playboy	A Jitney Elopement
Charlie the Recruiter	Shanghaied
Charlie the Sailor	Shanghaied
Charlie the Toreador	Burlesque on "Carmen"
Charlie the Tramp	The Tramp
Charlie the Waiter	Caught in a Cabaret
The Children's Automobile Race	Kid Auto Races at Venice
The City Slicker	Tillie's Punctured Romance
The Cook	Dough and Dynamite
Cops and Watches	Twenty Minutes of Love
Counted Out	The Knockout
Crazy Decorators	Work
The Custodian	The New Janitor
Damsel in Distress	The Tramp
Day's End	Caught in the Rain
The Dentist	Laughing Gas
Doing His Best	Making a Living
The Doughnut Designers	Dough and Dynamite
Down and Out	Laughing Gas
A Dream	His Prehistoric Past
Exchange Is No Robbery	Getting Acquainted
Face on the Barroom Floor	The Face on the Bar Room Floor
A Fair Exchange	Getting Acquainted

Retitled version	Original title
Faking with Society	Caught in a Cabaret
Family Home	His Trysting Place
The Family House	His Trysting Place
Fast Worker	Work
The Fatal Lantern	The Star Boarder
The Female	The Masquerader
A Female Impersonator	The Masquerader
The Female Impersonator	The Masquerader
Filling a Prescription	Laughing Gas
Filling the Prescription	Laughing Gas
A Film by Johnny	A Film Johnnie
Film Johnny	A Film Johnnie
The Fire Eater	A Night in the Show
The Flirt	A Woman
The Flirts	Between Showers
For the Love of Tillie	Tillie's Punctured Romance
Freed from Jail	Police
Fun Is Fun	Recreation
A Gentleman with Nerve	Gentlemen of Nerve
Gentleman with Nerves	Gentlemen of Nerve
Getting His Goat	The Property Man
Going Down	The Rounders
The Good-for-Nothing	His New Profession
Greenwich Village	The Rounders
Gymnastics	The Champion
The Ham Actor	The Face on the Bar Room Floor
The Ham Artist	The Face on the Bar Room Floor

Retitled version	Original title
Happy Dreams	His Prehistoric Past
The Hash-House Hero	Star Boarder
Hello Everybody	Getting Acquainted
He Loved Her So	Twenty Minutes of Love
Helping Himself	His New Profession
The Henpecked Spouse	His Trysting Place
The Hero[1]	Police
The Hired Hand	The Tramp
His Daredevil Queen	Mabel at the Wheel
His Lucky Day	The Champion
His Night Out	A Night Out
His Recreation[2]	Recreation
His Trysting Places	His Trysting Place
Hit Him Again	The Fatal Mallet
Hits of the Past	The Property Man
The Hobo	The Tramp
Honest Charlie	The Tramp
Hoola-Hoola Dance	His Prehistoric Past
Hot Dog Charlie	Mabel's Busy Day
Hot Dogs	Mabel's Busy Day
The Hotel Mix-Up	Mabel's Strange Predicament
A Hot Finish	Mabel at the Wheel
Housebreaker	Police
The Hula-Hula Dance	His Prehistoric Past
I Am King	His Prehistoric Past
If Looks Could Kill	A Night in the Show
In Love with His Landlady	The Star Boarder

Retitled version	Original title
In the Bank	The Bank
In the Park[3]	Caught in the Rain
In the Ring	The Champion
In the Soup	Shanghaied
In Training	The Knockout
In Wrong	Between Showers
The Jazz Waiter	Caught in a Cabaret
Jitney	A Jitney Elopement
Just a Vagabond Lover	The Tramp
The Kid Auto Race	Kid Auto Races at Venice
Kid Auto Races at Venice, Cal.	Kid Auto Races at Venice
Kid's Auto Race	Kid Auto Races at Venice
King Charlie	His Prehistoric Past
Knock Out	The Champion
The Ladies' Man	His Trysting Place
Lady Charlie	A Busy Day
Laffin' Gas	Laughing Gas
Laffing Gas	Laughing Gas
The Landlady's Pet	The Star Boarder
Lord Helpus	Cruel, Cruel Love
Love and Lunch	Mabel's Busy Day
The Love-Fiend	Twenty Minutes of Love
Love Pains	Those Love Pangs
Love Pangs	Those Love Pangs
Love Riot	Tillie's Punctured Romance
The Love Thief	The Rounders
Lucky Day	The Champion

Retitled version	Original title
Lucky Horseshoe	The Champion
Mabel's Flirtation	Her Friend the Bandit
Mademoiselle Charlie	A Woman
Marie's Millions	Tillie's Punctured Romance
Married for Money	Tillie's Punctured Romance
Married in Haste	A Jitney Elopement
The Militant Suffragette	A Busy Day
The Million Dollar Job	A Film Johnnie
The Movie Nut	A Film Johnnie
Musical Tramp	His Musical Career
The Music Hall	Tango Tangles
A Night at the Burlesque House	A Night in the Show
A Night at the Show	A Night in the Show
The New Cook	Dough and Dynamite
The New Janitor[4]	The Masquerader
The New Porter	The New Janitor
Oh, What a Night	The Rounders
Oh, You Girls	Those Love Pangs
One in the Eye	A Night in the Show
Only a Working Man	Work
Overture for Beginners	A Night in the Show
Papa Charlie	His Trysting Place
The Paper Hanger	Work
The Perfect Lady	A Woman
The Perfumed Lady	The Masquerader
The Pest	Kid Auto Races at Venice
The Piano Movers	His Musical Career

Retitled version	Original title
The Picnic	The Masquerader
Pies and Hose-Pipes	The Property Man
The Pile Driver	The Fatal Mallet
The Plumber	Work
The Porter	The New Janitor
Prime Minister Charlie	Caught in a Cabaret
Props	The Property Man
The Pugilist	The Knockout
Pulling Teeth	Laughing Gas
Putting One Over	The Masquerader
A Rainy Day	Between Showers
The Reckless Fling	His Favorite Pastime
Revelry	The Rounders
The Rival Mashers	Those Love Pangs
The Rival Suitors	The Fatal Mallet
Roaming Romeo	Between Showers
The Roustabout	The Property Man
The Sailor	Shanghaied
Scrambled Eggs	The Tramp
Sea Water Chief	Shanghaied
Sleepless Night	Caught in the Rain
Some Nerve	Gentlemen of Nerve
The Snake Charmer	A Night in the Show
Sparring Partner	The Champion
Spring Fever	Recreation
The Squarehead	Mabel's Married Life
Stage Struck	A Night in the Show

Retitled version	Original title
Stagestruck	A Night in the Show
Stolen Umbrella	Between Showers
Take My Picture	Making a Living
Tango Tangle	Tango Tangles
Their New Home	Tillie's Punctured Romance
A Thief Catcher	Her Friend the Bandit
Thunder and Lightning	Between Showers
Tillie's Big Romance	Tillie's Punctured Romance
Tillie's Flirtation	Tillie's Punctured Romance
Tillie's Love Affair	Tillie's Punctured Romance
Tilly's Love Affair	Tillie's Punctured Romance
The Tin Lizzy	A Jitney Elopement
Tip Tap Toe	The Rounders
Troubles	Making a Living
Tuning His Ivories	Laughing Gas
Two of a Kind	The Rounders
Two-Timing Charlie	Tillie's Punctured Romance
Vamping Venus	The Property Man
Very Much Married	His Trysting Place
Vodvil Days	The Property Man
The Waiter	Caught in a Cabaret
When You're Married	Mabel's Married Life
Who Got Stung?	Caught in the Rain
The Window Washer	The New Janitor

[1] *The Hero* is a composite of *Police* (Essanay, 1916) and *The Adventurer* (Mutual, 1917)

[2] *His Recreation* is a composite of *Recreation* (Keystone, 1914) and *Laughing Gas* (Keystone, 1914).

[3]Not to be confused with *In the Park* (Essanay, 1915)
[4]Not to be confused with *The New Janitor* (Keystone, 1914)

There are additional home-movie editions for which we can't determine the source film; we haven't seen them and other reference sources don't acknowledge them. These titles include *All Dressed Up*, *All Wet*, *Assistance Wanted*, *At the Banquet*, *Bad Company*, *Bad Pair*, *Balled Up*, *Bashful Lover*, *Big Fight*, *Charlie Drops a Clanger*, *Charlie Rings a Bell*, *Charlie Steps Out*, *The Day Begins*, *His Great Fight*, *His New Girl*, *Homeless*, *In Trouble*, *The Nutty Helper*, *Pipe Dreams*, *Strong Arm Charlie*, *Surprise Meetings*, *Under Arrest*, and *Wrong Room*. (Some of these were no doubt lifted from Chaplin's post-Essanay films.)

MORE RETITLED CHAPLINS

*While researching the retitled Chaplin Keystones and Essanays, we uncovered retitled versions of his later Mutual and First National films (plus one United Artists cut-down, **The Sourdough**), mostly for home-movie editions. We include them here for reference purposes.*

Retitled version	Original title
Almost a Gentleman	The Count
Always Kind Hearted	The Pawnshop
At the Sign of a Dollar	The Pawnshop
The Audition	Behind the Screen
The Awkward Squad	Shoulder Arms
Behind the Scenes	Behind the Screen
Blaze Away	The Fireman
Broke	The Immigrant
Bumpy Bed	One A. M.
Call the Cops	Easy Street
Cause For Alarm	The Fireman
Charlie and the Hound	A Dog's Life

Retitled version	Original title
Charlie at the Ball	The Count
Charlie at the Clinic	The Cure
Charlie at the Dance	A Dog's Life
Charlie at the Party	The Adventurer
Charlie Dines Out	The Count
Charlie Gets His Man	Easy Street
Charlie Goes to the Party	The Adventurer
Charlie in a Spin	The Cure
Charlie in the Army	Shoulder Arms
Charlie is Late for Work	Pay Day
Charlie Joins the Police	Easy Street
Charlie Leads the Band	The Vagabond
Charlie Limbers Up	The Cure
Charlie Misbehaves	The Count
Charlie on the Beat	Easy Street
Charlie on Vacation	The Cure
Charlie Pays the Bill	The Immigrant
Charlie, Public Enemy No. 1	The Adventurer
Charlie Repents	Easy Street
Charlie Skates Around	The Rink
Charlie Spills the Beans	The Immigrant
Charlie Stops for Lunch	Behind the Screen
Charlie's Good Deed	Easy Street
Charlie's Knockout Drop	Easy Street
Charlie's Ladder Larks	The Pawnshop
Charlie's Pawnshop	The Pawnshop
Charlie's Tail	A Dog's Life

Retitled version	Original title
Charlie Takes the Order	The Rink
Charlie the Bricklayer	Pay Day
Charlie the Busker	The Vagabond
Charlie the Constable	Easy Street
Charlie the Cop	Easy Street
Charlie the Fiddler	The Vagabond
Charlie the Head Waiter	The Rink
Charlie the Hero	The Fireman
Charlie the Immigrant	The Immigrant
Charlie the Impostor	The Adventurer
Charlie the Tailor	The Count
Charlie the Vagabond	The Vagabond
Charlie the Violinist	The Vagabond
Charlie to the Rescue	Easy Street
Cheers	The Cure
The Constable	Easy Street
Constable Charlie	Easy Street
The Convert	Easy Street
Convict at Large	The Adventurer
Convict 99	The Adventurer
The Cop	Easy Street
The Cops	Easy Street
The Crook	The Pawnshop
Diaper Days	Easy Street
Dining on a Dollar	The Immigrant
Drunken Charlie	One A. M.
Escaped Convict	The Adventurer

Retitled version	Original title
The Fiery Circle	The Fireman
Fire Alarm	The Fireman
First Come First Served	A Dog's Life
Freedom For Ever	The Adventurer
The Gallant Fireman	The Fireman
Gypsy Life	The Vagabond
Hello U.S.A.	The Immigrant
Hero Charlie	The Fireman
High and Low Finance	The Pawnshop
The Hobo	A Dog's Life
The Hollywood Stand-In	Behind the Screen
The Hot Dog	A Dog's Life
The House Guest	The Adventurer
In for the Swim	The Cure
In Hollywood	Behind the Screen
The Kidnapped Heiress	Easy Street
Kitchen Help	The Pawnshop
The Last Tram Home	Pay Day
Man Hunt	The Adventurer
Man's Best Friend	A Dog's Life
A Modern Columbus	The Immigrant
The Movie Breaker	Behind the Screen
Musical Bars	The Vagabond
The New World	The Immigrant
One Over the Eight	A Dog's Life
On Skates	The Rink
The Patient	The Cure

Retitled version	Original title
The Policeman	Easy Street
The Pride of Hollywood	Behind the Screen
The Refugee	The Immigrant
The Rescue	The Adventurer
Rolling Along	The Rink
Rolling Around	The Rink
The Scene Shifter	Behind the Screen
Shop	The Floorwalker
Skating	The Rink
Sleepless Night	One A. M.
Solo	One A. M.
The Sourdough	The Gold Rush
The Store	The Floorwalker
Tailor's Apprentice	The Count
Take Over Bid	The Pawnshop
Taking Steps	The Pawnshop
Thirsty Fiddler	The Vagabond
Uncle Charlie	The Pawnshop
Waiter!	The Rink
The Waiter	The Rink
The Waiting Game	The Rink
The Water Cure	The Cure

KEYSTONE AND ESSANAY
CHAPLINS ON DVD

Kino On Video

Specialists in "World Cinema," Kino offers three volumes of **Chaplin's Essanay Comedies**. These are easily the finest quality restorations (by archivist David Shepard) of these films available on DVD, and we highly recommend them. Address: 333 W. 39 St., New York, NY 10018. Phone: 800-562-3330. FAX: 212-714-0871. Website: www.kino.com

Delta Entertainment Corporation

Delta's 12-volume series **The Essential Charlie Chaplin Collection** includes most of the Essanay films and 26 of the 34 Keystone shorts. The quality of the Keystones is extremely variable, but in some instances, they're the only versions available to collectors at this time. These are more for the serious Chaplin student than the casual fan. Some of the shorts have jazz music scores—with occasional vocals! Even more bizarre is an alternate audio track marked "Film Projector Loop" which consists of nothing more than the sound of the whirring gears of a projector. Address: 2663 Sawtelle Blvd., Los Angeles, CA 90025. Website: www.deltaentertainment.com

Madacy Home Video

Madacy offers Chaplin DVDs with most of the same variable-quality Keystone and Essanays found on discs from other distributors; they're the same prints, with the same virtues and flaws, including music tracks with disruptive vocals. Some titles, however, are only found on the Madacy releases: **The Charlie Chaplin Collection, Vol. 1** contains **The Property Man** (under the French title **Charlot, Garcon de Théâtre**) and **Gentlemen of Nerve** (under the French title **Charlot et Mabel aux Courses**); the five-disc, 31-film collection **Chaplin: The Legend Lives On** contains **Mabel's Busy Day**, **His Trysting Place** (as **His Trysting Places**) and **His Prehistoric Past**. (In the **Legend Lives On** collection, **A Night** *in the Show* is listed as *A Night in the Snow*, and the "Chaplin Trivia Quiz" erroneously credits *The Tramp* as Chaplin's first film.) Address: P. O. Box 1445, St. Laurent, Quebec, Canada H4L 4Z1

Brentwood Home Video

Brentwood offers *Charlie Chaplin: 57 Classics*, a five double-sided disc collection that includes, among others, 28 Keystones and 12 Essanays. Overall, the quality is extremely variable, and the double-sided discs are misidentified: all Side As are really Side Bs, and vice versa. However, this collection does contain a good documentary, *The Chaplin Puzzle*, which includes a restored three-reel version of *Police*. Website: www.bcieclipse.com

Image Entertainment

Image's eclectic catalogue—which runs the gamut from foreign-language classics to micro-budgeted exploitation fare—includes a beautifully restored editions of *Tillie's Punctured Romance* and the Keystone short *Mabel's Married Life*. If you absolutely must have *Tillie's Punctured Romance* in your collection, then the Image disc is the one to get. Address: 9333 Oso Avenue, Chatsworth, CA 91311. Phone: 818-407-9100. Website: www.image-entertainment.com

Laughsmith Entertainment

Laughsmith offers *The Forgotten Films of Roscoe "Fatty" Arbuckle*, a four-disc DVD collection containing 32 beautifully restored films starring and/or directed by Arbuckle, including two discussed in this volume, *The Knockout* and *The Rounders*. This highly recommended set is a must for anyone with an interest in silent cinema—or cinema in general. Available from Mackinac Media at www.mackinacmedia.com

Platinum Disc Corporation

Platinum offers two *Charlie Chaplin* DVD sets: an eight-disc, 58-film collection that includes several Keystone and Essanay titles; and a two-disc, 14-film collection that includes the Keystones *Caught in a Cabaret*, *His Favorite Pastime*, and *The Knockout*, plus the Essanays *A Woman*, *The Tramp*, and *The Bank*. Qualitywise, these copies are on par with those found in other public domain releases. Address: P. O. Box 2798, La Crosse, WI 54602-2798.

Front Row Entertainment

You're more likely to find Front Row's cheaply-priced DVD titles in the discount racks at drug stores rather than standard home entertainment outlets. The quality is extremely hit-or-miss—usually the latter. Front Row's **Charlie Chaplin Double Feature: Tillie's Punctured Romance and A Burlesque on Carmen** features the shortened edition of **Romance** (without narration, mercifully) and the expanded (three-reel) version of the **Carmen**. Neither film is "typical" Chaplin, despite the "typical" portrait photo on the cover. Website: frontrowentertainment.com

Golden Hollywood Video

Golden Hollywood Video offers five volumes of "the Eternal Tramp's original Keystones," 24 titles in all. Volume One is called **Charlie Chaplin's First Keystone Shorts**; the rest are **Charlie Chaplin Keystone Shorts**. This outfit is the only source we're aware of that has **Mabel at the Wheel** on DVD (it's included on Volume 5); the remaining titles are also available elsewhere. We don't have any information on this company; there is no address or website listed on the packaging. They were completely unknown to us until these volumes began turning up on eBay.

SELECTED BIBLIOGRAPHY

Books

Asplund, Uno. *Chaplin's Films*. South Brunswick and New York: A. S. Barnes, 1976.

Brownlow, Kevin. *The Parade's Gone By...*New York: Alfred A. Knopf, 1968.

Chaplin, Charles. *My Autobiography*. London: The Bodley Head, 1964.

_____ *My Life in Pictures*. London: The Bodley Head, 1974.

Flom, Eric L. *Chaplin in the Sound Era: An Analysis of the Seven Talkies*. Jefferson, North Carolina: McFarland & Co., Inc., 1997.

Geduld, Harry M. *Chapliniana Vol. 1: The Keystone Films*. Bloomington and Indianapolis: University of Indiana Press, 1987.

Gifford, Denis. *Chaplin*. London: Macmillan, 1974.

Grossman, Gary. *Saturday Morning TV*. New York, Dell Publishing, 1981.

Huff, Theodore. *Charlie Chaplin*. New York: Henry Schuman, 1951.

Kamin, Dan. *Charlie Chaplin's One-Man Show*. Metuchen, New Jersey: Scarecrow Press, Inc., 1984.

Kerr, Walter. *The Silent Clowns*. New York: Alfred A. Knopf, 1975.

Lahue, Kalton C. *World of Laughter: The Motion Picture Comedy Short, 1910-1930*. Norman, Oklahoma: University of Oklahoma Press, 1966.

_____ and Terry Brewer. *Kops and Custards: The Legend of Keystone Films*. Norman, Oklahoma: University of Oklahoma Press, 1968.

Lorenz, Janet E. *Charles Chaplin: The Short Films* (from *Magill's Survey of Cinema: Silent Films*, edited by Frank N. Magill). Englewood Cliffs, New Jersey: Salem Press, 1982.

MacGillivray, Scott. *Laurel & Hardy: From the Forties Forward.* Lanham, Maryland: Vestal Press, Inc., 1998.

Maltin, Leonard. *The Great Movie Comedians.* New York: Harmony Books, 1978.

Mast, Gerald. *The Comic Mind: Comedy and the Movies.* Indianapolis, Indiana: The Bobs-Merrill Company, 1973.

McCabe, John. *Charlie Chaplin.* Garden City, New York: Doubleday & Co., Inc., 1978.

McDonald, Gerald D., Michael Conway and Mark Ricci. *The Films of Charlie Chaplin.* New York: Citadel Press, 1965.

Mitchell, Glenn. *The Chaplin Encyclopedia.* London: B. T. Batsford, 1997.

Parrish, James Robert, and William T. Leonard, with Gregory W. Mank and Charles Hoyt. *The Funsters.* New Rochelle, New York: Arlington House, 1979.

Quigly, Isabel. *Charlie Chaplin: Early Comedies.* London: Studio Vista, 1968.

Robinson, David. *Chaplin: His Life and Art.* New York: McGraw-Hill, 1985.

Vance, Jeffrey. *Chaplin: Genius of the Cinema.* New York: Harry N. Abrams, Inc., 2003.

Yallop, David. *The Day the Laughter Stopped: The True Story of Fatty Arbuckle.* (Filmography by Samuel A. Gill.) New York: St. Martin's Press, 1976.

Articles

Agee, James. "Comedy's Greatest Era." *Life* vol. 27, no. 10 (September 5, 1949).

Berglund, Bo. "The Day the Tramp Was Born." *Sight and Sound* 58, no. 2 (Spring 1989).

Copner, Michael. "Chaplin's Essanay Comedies." *Cult Movies* #31 (2000).

Everett, Eldon K. "A Great Imitation of Charlie Chaplin's Burlesque on Carmen." *Classic Film Collector* #45 (Winter 1974-75).

MacKnight, Dr. F. C. "Collecting Chaplin." *Classic Film Collector* (Fall 1974 to Fall 1978).

Neibaur, James L. "Chaplin at Essanay." *Film Quarterly* (Fall 2000).

Okuda, Ted. "New Titles for Old Films." *Classic Film Collector* (Spring 1974 to Fall 1976).

Sundt, Gerhardt, with Ted Okuda. "Re-titled Films." *Classic Film Collector* #56 (Fall 1977).

Vanneman, Alan. "Looking at Charlie: Keystone and Essanay Days." *Bright Lights Film Journal* #45 (August 2004).

FILM TITLE INDEX

The number after each title and year of release refers to the film entry number, not the page number.

NAME INDEX

The number after each name refers to the film entry number, not the page number.

Allen, Phyllis 20, 26, 29, 30, 32, 33, 35, 48
Anderson, Gilbert M. (G. M.) "Broncho Billy" *As actor:* 38, 43, 52; *as director:* 43; *as producer:* 43
Applegate, Hazel 43
Arbuckle, Roscoe "Fatty" Arbuckle 5, 6, 7, 17, 24, 25, 26
Arley, Cecile: *see* Arnold, Cecile
Armstrong, Billy 38, 41, 42, 45, 46, 47, 50, 51, 52, 53
Arnold, Cecile (Cecile Arley) 21, 22, 24, 25, 28, 29, 30, 31, 33, 34
Avery, Charles 17
Ayres, Agnes 36, 51

Bacon, Lloyd 38, 39, 40, 41, 43, 44, 51
Barry, Viola: *see* Pearce, Peggy
Bennett, Billie 18, 35
Bennett, Charles 21, 22, 23, 29, 35
Bergman, Teddy (Alan Reed) 52
Bordeaux, Joe 10, 21, 30, 35
Bowes, Lawrence 46, 47
Breeskin, Elias 52

Cato, Bill 43
Cavender, Glen 6, 8, 12, 16, 18, 25, 27, 29, 30, 32, 33, 35
Chaplin, Charlie *As actor:* 1 thru 53; *as director:* 11, 12, 13, 16, 18 thru 34, 36 thru 53; *as writer:* 11, 12, 13, 16, 19 thru 34, 36 thru 52
Chaplin, Syd 34
Chase, Charley: *see* Parrott, Charles
Chene, Dixie 21, 26
Clayton, Marguerite 43
Clifton, Emma 4
Cline, Edward F. 26

ABOUT THE AUTHORS

TED OKUDA is the author of *The Columbia Comedy Shorts* and *The Monogram Checklist*, and co-author of *The Jerry Lewis Films* (with James L. Neibaur), *The Golden Age of Chicago Children's Television* (with Jack Mulqueen), and *The Soundies Distributing Corporation of America* (with Scott MacGillivray). He also contributed chapters to the books *Science Fiction America* and *Guilty Pleasures of the Horror Film*, and wrote the Foreword to Scott MacGillivray's *Castle Films: A Hobbyist's Guide*. His articles, interviews, and movie reviews have appeared in such publications as *Filmfax*, *Cult Movies*, *Classic Images*, *Classic Film Collector*, *Big Reel*, and *Movie Collector's World*. He has appeared on *Three Stooges Stooge-A-Palooza*, *Your Chicago Show*, *Chicago Tonight*, *The Today Show*, and *Channel 5 News*. Ted resides in Chicago, Illinois.

DAVID MASKA is a film collector/historian whose articles, interviews, and reviews have appeared in such publications as *Classic Images* and *Filmfax*. He has been a contributor to several media-oriented documentaries and has served as research consultant on pop culture books, including *The Golden Age of Chicago Children's Television*, *Stooge Mania*, and *Stooges Lost Episodes*. He has a Bachelors Degree in Communications from Columbia College; he was a news producer for radio station WBBM-FM (B-96), and was producer/host of a weekend jazz program for WDCB-FM as well as a weekend news/entertainment program for WCRX-FM. He has performed in local theatre productions, including the Berkshire Ballet Theatre's annual performance of *The Nutcracker*. David resides in Roselle, Illinois.

978-0-595-36598-2
0-595-36598-1